GW00469744

JERSEY: INDEPENDENT DEPENDENCY?

JERSEY:

Independent Dependency?

The Survival Strategies of a Microstate

Luke Le Rendu

ELSP

Published in 2004 by
ELSP
1 The Shambles
Bradford on Avon
Wiltshire   BA15 1JS

www.ex-librisbooks.co.uk

Design and typesetting by
Ex Libris Press

© 2004 Luke Le Rendu

ISBN 1 903341 89 2

Printed and bound by Cromwell Press, Trowbridge, Wilts

Contents

~ To Mum and Dad ~

Acknowledgements

I am indebted to my supervisor Mr Nevil Johnson, formerly Reader in the Comparative Study of Institutions, for his support and assistance in studying this rarely examined subject. Miss Gillian Peele, Dr Fiona Campbell, Mrs Debra Popham and Mrs Thea Backhouse all provided valued support to enable me to be a dyslexic scholar at Oxford.

I would like to thank the following for their help in my research, they were a constant source of advice and encouragement: Roy Le Hérissier, John Christensen, Richard Stoneman, Christian Swalander, Edward Warrington, Godfrey Pirotta and Andrew Le Sueur.

Many individuals in Jersey provided advice and assistance without which the study would not have been completed. I should like to thank in particular:

The States of Jersey Education Department for their generous grant; Geoffrey Coppock, the Greffier of the States, and the staff at the States Greffe, in particular Frank Hunt and everyone in the Registry section; Colin Powell, former Chief Adviser to the States and now Chair of the Financial Services Commission; and the staff at the Société Jersiaise library as well as the Policy and Resources Committee for permission to include the Summary of Recommendations of the Report of the Review Panel on the Machinery of Government as an appendix.

I should also like to express my gratitude to all of the interviewees in Jersey, Guernsey, the Isle of Man and the United Kingdom who gave of their time generously and were a vital source of information.

Finally, I would like to thank my family for their support and encouragement without which this thesis could not have been written.

Foreword

To readers used to placing states in clear categories, Jersey is particularly frustrating. It is a Crown Dependency with a strong sense of its distinctiveness. It has often behaved as if it were independent, and continues to do so. In particular, its internal government defies straightforward categorisation and appears to be a melange of various historical developments, none of which resulted in a clean break with the past. Rather, there is an almost unique admixture so that the Island's Government is presided over by a Speaker, the Bailiff, who is also the Chief Judge. The strongly entrenched municipalities, the Parishes, are presided over by Connetables who technically still head the Parish police force while sitting as politicians in the Island's Legislature, the States.

It might be thought that this uniqueness prevents Jersey from acting as a model or point of reference for other small jurisdictions. Not so.

While readers will be initially confused by the complex, multi-layered development of the Government and polity, Dr. Le Rendu focuses on how the external pressures which the Island is facing are impacting on its internal institutions and analyses how the Island is adjusting to such pressures. It is further a narrative of how an enterprising small jurisdiction is facing up to growing and potentially damaging international pressures brought about by globalisation and the ever increasing influence of bodies like the European Union.

Dr Roy Le Hérissier, Deputy of States of Jersey

Prologue

What follows was written to satisfy the requirements of a Doctorate of Philosophy in Political Science at Oxford University. Since completion, a number of people have kindly suggested that I publish the thesis as it would provide useful background material to the political debates going on in Jersey. In publishing it, I hope not only to provide information in an area where little published information exists, but also to broaden the debate on Jersey's relationships with its neighbours. No attempt has been made to publish a study of Jersey using political science since Dr. Roy Le Hérissier's book in 1974. Much of the material that has been written has reflected the legal perspective of those who wrote it. I believe political science offers an equally valid and useful perspective on Jersey's situation in the modern world. A political scientist, while utilising constitutional law, also assesses political, economic and sociological influences on how the island interacts with its neighbours. Sometimes focusing too much on constitutional law may obscure these equally important influences on Jersey's position in the world.

Politics is, by its nature, a dynamic subject as events happen every day. For practical reasons, a thesis must have a cut-off date. For this thesis, that date was November 1998. I have included an epilogue (Chapter 10), which gives some consideration of events up to 2001. Unfortunately, family and work commitments have not allowed me to update the book any further. As a result, certain recent events affecting the island are therefore not covered in this work.

As with all authors, the responsibility for any errors rests entirely with myself.

Luke Le Rendu
London
November 2003

Chapter 1 – Introduction

There exist in Europe a number of small communities with well-defined territories and independently functioning political and administrative structures.[1] This book will present a qualitative case study of the external policies of one of these communities in order to highlight the strategies that not only ensure its survival, but also bring considerable prosperity to it.

The subject of this study is the Bailiwick of Jersey. It is the largest of the Channel Islands with a population of 84,082.[2] It has an area of forty-five square miles and is situated ninety miles from the south coast of England, fourteen miles west of Normandy and thirty miles north of Brittany. Jersey is a separate Bailiwick from the rest of the Channel Islands which form the Bailiwick of Guernsey.[3]

This study concentrates on the last thirty years and ends in November 1998. It focuses on the survival strategies developed and the constraints applying to external policy, with particular reference to the effects of scale on policy and the strategies chosen to overcome these constraints. I will argue that these strategies are essential to the creation of Jersey's current prosperity and will also consider their effectiveness in countering threats to the island's prosperity and autonomy. As part of this, I shall assess the extent to which the insular authorities seek to actively manage their dependency relationship with the United Kingdom.

Jersey is a microstate with distinctive external policy processes and objectives. Its policy priorities are different from those of the United Kingdom which forces it to pursue its own separate external policy. The differences derive not only from Jersey's size, but also from its economic dependence on offshore finance. The island has sufficient autonomy to implement external policy and it is therefore possible to study Jersey as a separate political entity. External policy will, in this study, be defined as that related to events and circumstances beyond the island's coastline which affect the island's interests. This definition of external policy is necessary to allow a fruitful study of Jersey's unconventional external relations. Jersey's fundamental relationship is with the United Kingdom, its sovereign power, responsible for Jersey's foreign relations and defence. However, a convention of non-interference by the United Kingdom in fiscal and domestic affairs governs the relationship and, barring exceptional circumstances, this results in virtually unconstrained freedom for the island to make policy while maintaining a constitutional link with a larger state. The United Kingdom has also allowed Jersey to develop distinctive policies with other external parties, not least with regard to the European Union and the extension of international agreements to the island. This is a result of a well-established Home Office policy of allowing Jersey to determine its own external relations provided they do not conflict with the United Kingdom government's perception of Britain's national interest.

The adoption of the broad conception of external policy outlined above will facilitate analysis of the manoeuvrings of the insular authorities to manage their relationships with the United Kingdom and the European Union. I shall present the hypothesis that Jersey's relationship with the United Kingdom represents a pragmatic acceptance that dependency status is inevitable for a microstate. In Jersey's case I shall argue that this formalised dependency status offers a framework within which it can manage its dependent position in the world, and also that Jersey offers a model of a successful, non-colonial dependency. The book will, therefore, define the extent of Jersey's autonomy and illustrate how it differs from full sovereignty. It is hoped the outcome will be a case study of a form of autonomy short of full sovereignty which appears to offer a middle way between independence from, or absorption into, the United Kingdom.

The study illustrates some of the techniques used by Jersey as a small community in an unequal political and economic union to ensure both its survival and prosperity. Indeed, it illustrates how the management of a limited autonomy within such a relationship can still produce economic prosperity and *de facto* day to day independence. With the help of both comparative and historical analysis it is intended to provide an account of the policy-making process with special reference to external matters. An account will also be provided of the evolution of policy by Jersey's neighbours insofar as this has affected the island. In summary, a study of how Jersey interacts with its international environment will be offered. Qualitative analysis will predominate since Jersey lacks the resources to compile all of the statistics required for a much more quantitative treatment of the issues arising.

Jersey is dependent on its larger neighbours to create the geopolitical stability to ensure its stability and economic growth. Its essential vulnerability as a microstate was amply demonstrated in 1940 when the island was abandoned by the United Kingdom as impossible to defend if a hostile power held the neighbouring French coast. In order to prosper, Jersey relies on the geopolitical stability in Western Europe, especially as its two dominant industries, financial services and tourism, are very dependent on political stability and likely to relocate elsewhere should prolonged political instability develop in the region. This is an area over which Jersey has very little influence, indeed microstates in general are viewed as inherently vulnerable to global instability. Sheila Harden in "Small is Dangerous" refers to the propensity of a microstate to become "pawns in the game of international power politics."[4] Yet here again potential may exist for a microstate to manage its admittedly very weak position. An example of successful management is the negotiation of Protocol 3 when the United Kingdom sought accession to the European Economic Community.

The case study is constructed within the framework of managed dependency.

The notion of managed dependency is derived from Baldacchino[5], Hampton[6] and Warrington[7] and is predicated on the assertion that all the small states are in dependency relations of some kind with larger neighbours. Edward Warrington defines the concept as "they [micro-states] exploit their contact with the outside world and its agents to guarantee subsistence, to spread risks, to sustain remarkably affluent lifestyles, and to generate wealth."[8] The theory that independent small states and microstates manage their inevitable dependence on larger states to their advantage will be extended to Jersey. This concept, although evolved to apply to independent small states, can effectively be extended to Jersey with the added element that a formal dependency exists to be managed. I shall seek to illustrate that the formal nature of Jersey's constitutional link with the United Kingdom is to Jersey's advantage in positively managing dependency as it creates a structure within which the relationship can operate. The hypothesis will thus be developed that Jersey's economic prosperity and internal stability are predicated on successful management of a positive dependency relationship with the United Kingdom.

Scale and Statehood

To begin with, we need a definition of what constitutes small. Jersey's population, for comparative purposes, is similar to those of Dominica and Grenada and larger than Cape Verde Islands, Kiribati, Liechtenstein, Andorra, Marshall Islands, Monaco, Nauru, St Christopher and Nevis, San Marino, the Seychelles, Tuvalu, and the Vatican City State,[9] all of which are considered large enough to be recognised as sovereign states under international law. Scale has hitherto usually been defined predominantly by reference to population where microstates are taken to include all political communities exhibiting a high degree of autonomy with populations below 100,000. This would place Jersey within a body of literature on the theme of microstates and how they survive and prosper in the modern world.

Attempts to define what is small have also proved problematic, in part due to the fact that the term is relative to all characteristics of a state which, by definition, vary. Greenland, for example, has a small population of 55,117 (1993) but an area of 2,175,600 square kilometres; two thirds of the size of the United States of America[10]. The definitions of what is a small state or microstate as defined by population vary from Chenery and Taylor who cite 15 million as an upper limit[11] to Kohr whose optimum social size is 4,000 -5,000[12].

For the purpose of this work, I will reject both definitions. Chenery and Taylor's because it is too inclusive and would include significant European nations such as Belgium and Sweden. In their case, constraints of scale on policy represent a fundamentally different problem as their "smallness" is only in relation to the major powers. Jersey is dwarfed by its near neighbours in a way which is not paralleled by, for example, the relationship between the Netherlands and Germany. The Netherlands, due to its larger absolute size, can muster far more countervailing factors in disputes with larger powers than

Jersey. The large upper boundary suggested by Chenery and Taylor must therefore be rejected because, although some elements will be common to all asymmetrical power relationships, it is necessary for the purpose of this study to maintain a low absolute upper threshold for comparative size. This will allow the study to focus on the issues facing a state which is not only small in comparative, but also in absolute, terms.

Kohr's analysis of optimum social size serves to highlight a significant facet of microstates by concentrating on the high degree of personalisation in a microstate and the political significance acquired by an individual's primary group. In contrast to Chenery and Taylor, this definition is too exclusive as it identifies a group of communities which, although exceptionally small, face severe challenges due to their size.

The parameters which will be used in this book are those defined by a Commonwealth Consultative Group of one million for a small state, 200,000 for a mini-state and 100,000 for a microstate.[13] This definition is more satisfactory with regard to the proposed case study than the prevailing definition in literature of one million for a small, micro or mini state,[14] as it excludes a large of number of communities with populations significantly larger than Jersey. The division reflects a degree of clustering amongst the small states in Europe. Twelve sovereign or autonomous states have populations of less than 100,000, the microstates; three have populations between 200,000 and one million, the small states. Jersey is the largest of the microstates listed.[15]

The study of Jersey will assist in attempts to differentiate between those constraints imposed by scale and those imposed by poverty. It will also serve to illustrate the extent to which richer microstates can use their wealth to counter the constraints imposed by scale. This will differentiate the study from most literature which has tended to focus on scale as an impediment to development in developing countries. An example of this is Burton Benedict's seminal "Problems of Smaller Territories" with its themes of constraints of scale on the economic and social modernisation of small states.[16] This debate has tended to ignore the success and development of European small and microstates. The extent to which Jersey represents a suitable model for underdeveloped microstates has already been assessed in economic terms by Mark Hampton.[17] It is hoped that this book will add to the literature with an assessment on the political aspects of Jersey's evolution as a developed microstate. For this reason I have rejected the practice of defining small by gross national product.[18] This practice not only equates smallness with poverty, which is disproved by the large number of affluent microstates, but also masks the questions of whether, and if so how, Jersey with all the vulnerabilities of a microstate has been able to create a more successful and dynamic economy than its metropolitan power.

I will thus argue that population, perhaps paradoxically, is the determinant of size; this despite its apparent pliability when compared with gross domestic product and scale. Consequently, population is the comparative factor I will use to determine small and micro in this work as I believe it is the factor which defines the constraints on policy development in Jersey most effectively. This practice is consistent with the consensus of the majority of the literature. Nevertheless, it is recognised that gross domestic product and geographical size are also influential.

Having defined micro now it is necessary to define state. For the purposes of this book I will utilise the broad definition of state as being an entity with substantial autonomy over domestic and fiscal affairs operating outside the confines of a federal constitution. It is accepted that Jersey is not a state as recognised by international law. However, to cite Edward Dommen and Phillippe Heine [19] "It [the State] is a concept of rich and flexible signification." The United Nations in its own report on small states concludes that "It is doubtful that the Security Council or the General Assembly will ever embark on a discussion on the definition of state".[20] The traditional four criteria for a state as defined by Rosalyn Higgins are that the political entity should possess a permanent population, a defined territory, a government and the capacity to enter into relations with other states. Jersey has without doubt a permanent population.[21] Its territory is defined, partly due to geographical reasons and partly through judgements made by the International Court regarding the possession of disputed reefs around Jersey. The challenge to any assertion that Jersey is a state must therefore centre around the fact that the United Kingdom is responsible for Jersey's international relations and good government and therefore that the island lacks absolute sovereignty. However, legal sovereignty forms what may be seen as an artificial divide on the continuum between absolute independence of action for a political entity and absolute powerlessness. Both extremes of this spectrum can be argued to be ideals rather than realities. Thus sovereignty can be viewed in practical terms to be an area on a continuum and this study will concentrate on the area of this spectrum consisting both of those microstates and small states with internationally recognised sovereignty and those with extensive internal autonomy often amounting to practical sovereignty. The blurring of the boundary can be emphasised by Liechtenstein's internationally recognised sovereignty. Liechtenstein is considered a nation because it has the right to request the power responsible for its foreign affairs and currency, in this case Switzerland, in theory, to return responsibility in these matters to Liechtenstein. Jersey, on the other hand, has no such powers. This technical ability to renounce the dependency relationship amounts to the extent of the difference between autonomous and sovereign microstates in Europe. All microstates are in dependency relations of some kind with a larger neighbour. The only difference is that autonomous microstates have a formalised dependency relationship, whilst independent states do not.

The Effects of Scale

Politics in Jersey is profoundly affected by scale. Burton Benedict points out that a small society is characterised by a small social field which creates a distinct problem for all small societies in that a large number of economic, political, religious and kinship roles have to be performed by the same relatively small group of people and these roles often overlap. Benedict cites Gluckman's definition of this as "'multiplex' in that 'nearly every social relationship serves many interests'".[22] Following Benedict, these multiplex relationships create a tendency to what Weber termed as particularism in a small society. This stands in contrast to what Weber termed universalism which is deemed essential for a modern state to function. Particularism is characterised by Benedict as "functionally diffuse"[23] and therefore unable to sustain the neutrality necessary to maintain a modern economy, which is predicated on roles being functionally specific.

A brief description of Weber's ideas is necessary to discuss their applicability to Jersey as a microstate. Weber lists two of the characteristics of modern bureaucracies as "There is the principle of fixed and jurisdictional areas, which are generally ordered by rules"[24] and "The regular activities required for the purposes of bureaucratically governed structure are distributed in a fixed way as official duties."[25] Authority is strictly delineated by impersonal rules and carried out within a disciplined hierarchy to prevent abuse of power, employment is by merit and regular salaries are paid if the bureaucrat fulfils the job competently. Thus Weber's bureaucracies required impersonal, universalised, rule-led administrations which had careful divisions and definition of tasks, recruitment on merit and control exercised by a disciplined hierarchy. Microstate public administrations have attracted academic interest because their scale makes it more difficult to match the ideals described above. Their small scale means that they have had to adapt and create a different policy-making environment to that of larger states. Thus Jersey's size exercises a pervasive influence on the island's political culture and government. Exactly to what extent this manifests itself in the island's external policy development process and current political culture will be explored.

Particularism is a useful concept as it highlights the fact that many relationships in Jersey have characteristics which could potentially hinder interactions predicated on Weber's universalistic values described above.[26] There are many relationships between individuals known to each other and these contacts will be repeated on a regular basis, often over many years. Social relationships entered into for one reason are often intermingled with others. Consequently, it may be difficult to find a work environment which does not already include a friend or relative, or to socialise without meeting work colleagues. Thus a potential exists that actions, which in larger societies are emotionally neutral and conducted between anonymous individuals, are overlaid with positive or negative feelings built up over years of interaction. Such interaction can be difficult to escape in a small society where scale may determine that only one office or individual provides a particular service. The concept of particularism and related effects caused by Jersey's small size must not, however, be overstated. Half of the population is born outside the island and Jersey's key industries, finance and tourism, are global and concentrate on dealing with

18

outsiders. This all serves to dilute the effects of the multiplex social networks as does the strong ethos of universalism which has been absorbed in the local public service via the Whitehall model of civil service neutrality.

Burton Benedict correctly assesses that particularism not only has the potential to lead to more social cohesion, but also intense factionalism as issues rapidly become personalised through multiplex relationships.[27] Thus paradoxically small societies, although on the whole more cohesive than larger neighbours, have a tendency to be more bitterly divided than larger neighbours when they do fragment due to individuals interacting in a more complex way involving the possibility of social, professional and kinship interaction. This interaction can serve to reinforce both friendship and enmity. Both social cohesion and factionalism are reinforced by Jersey being an island and therefore more difficult to escape from in times of conflict. Scale makes government in Jersey more immediate and integral to life than in larger states. There are also no alternative political arenas to the States, so that being sidelined in the States often equals total political marginalisation. The interaction of the forces militating for social cohesion and those militating for factionalism hinders the creation of organised political parties or formal opposition within the States. This is due to the fact that opposition not only tends to be fragmented but also has to overcome the high levels of social cohesion which tends to bracket opposition to the political orthodoxy with disloyalty.

Scale creates disincentives to radical policy initiatives. The face to face contact which characterises both internal civil service relationships and civil service relationships with politicians not only places a premium upon interpersonal skills, but also creates a disincentive against proposing ideas which may alienate colleagues with whom an individual may have to work with for the rest of his or her career. In addition, as it cannot be assumed that all members of the administration will have amicable relations at all times, personal animosity may influence administrative actions in a way which the scale of larger civil services would dilute.

Robert Dahl and Edward Tufte in "Size and Democracy" present the argument that small democracies closely approximate 'Athenian' democratic ideals and therefore, on a theoretical level, have a number of potential advantages due to their scale.[28] Their very homogeneity in political terms is an advantage in that, although Jersey has quite a diverse demography, it lacks the scale to have regional separatist minorities. The relation between self-interest and the public good is more direct and visible, if only because each individual benefits directly from more of the services provided by government. Moreover, smaller democracies exhibit more social cohesion as their size makes it easier for their citizens "to internalize norms and values."[29] These universal norms can be exemplified by the near universal acceptance by the population that the finance industry is of benefit to the island and that, to ensure the industry's survival, political stability must be maintained. The social cohesion tends to produce a more homogenous political outlook which simplifies political accommodation in Jersey. The process is amplified by the ease of emigration afforded on the island which gives those who dislike the ascendant political orthodoxy the option to leave. This exclusive attitude has passed into local usage with the common use of the phrase "there is a mail boat in the morning" as a response, in particular to those not born locally, when the island is criticised. Social cohesion can thus be dangerous by excluding from power those who are talented but hold heterodox views. The defeat of Deputy Gary Matthews at the 1996 election can, in large part, be attributed to his criticism of the Limited Liability Partnership Law, much of which later was echoed in a States' Committee of Inquiry.[30] Matthews appears to have lost the election less for his views than for holding them at the time when they went against the political consensus. Social cohesion therefore, despite the political stability it brings, can operate to restrict effective opposition.

It is also necessary to examine the effects of scale on democratic society itself. Dahl and Tufte argue that small democracies are more effective democracies. Six characteristics of a small democracy are given to support this hypothesis:

> leaders in small democracies deal directly with the people;
> leaders observe popular feelings directly;
> leaders deal directly with the electorate rather than via sub-leaders;
> communications between leaders and citizens can be directly reciprocal;
> communications are direct rather than via the media;
> top leaders are not specialist politicians and also have roles outside politics.[31]

It is important to examine the implications of this model for policy making in Jersey. This analysis, even within these constraints, can be applied to Jersey because even if the island as a whole is too large to qualify, the powerful parishes which send twelve Constables to the island's Parliament are both small enough and do approximate to the Athenian model in that the parish is governed by an assembly of all ratepayers who may speak and vote. On a national scale the high number of States members to population, fifty three for a population of eighty-four thousand, means it is statistically likely that a member of the States is within an individual's primary group and thus Dahl and Tufte's theories should apply.

When applying the model I believe great care should be taken as Jersey is a modern, urbanised state which present problems for a hypothesis which argues that small scale creates simple democracies while large scale creates complex democracies. Politicians in Jersey are very accessible and direct communication is possible. Names and addresses of States' members are in the telephone book and the electorate does use these avenues to communicate with politicians. A political culture has therefore evolved of rapid popular access which allows the politicians to gauge the reaction of, at least, the assertive element of the electorate rapidly. However, political communication is not directly reciprocal outside the elite because politicians communicate with the public via the island's media.

Moreover, the availability of the answer phone means it can be used as a cheap and effective gatekeeper. Thus a model can be envisaged of politicians addressing the public via the media, an action characterised by Dahl and Tufte as that of a larger state, and the electorate responding individually to the relevant politician, a characteristic of a small democracy. The States operates as a representative assembly in a way analogous to most parliaments but direct democracy may be said to exist at parish level. However, it is necessary to caution against utopian views of more direct democracies such as exist in Jersey. All ratepayers may have the right to attend parish assemblies and govern the parish but very few do and low turn outs, both at parish and insular level, are characteristic of local politics. The island must thus be viewed as a hybrid of characteristics applicable to large and small systems as its wealth helps overcome some problems caused by its size.

Direct democracy is practised by the island's powerful parishes, however, participation is low. The author attended a parish assembly in the Parish of St Helier where about two hundred out of a population of 27,523 attended.[32] The gathering was not one of all those entitled to attend, that is ratepayers, but rather a gathering of the assertive and those with the time and inclination to become involved in politics. The low turnout limits the legitimacy of the assembly. Thus, Jersey's political culture offers those who wish to participate productive ways to do so, in a way analogous to Dahl and Tufte's analysis of small states, but this does not mean that individuals take these opportunities. Indeed, recent evidence shows that the majority of the population does not take the opportunity to participate in elections in Jersey.

Microstate civil services are faced with administrative task little different to that of larger nations. They may administer a more homogenous and physically smaller state, but many tasks to be undertaken remain essentially the same. Comparisons with local government, particularly English unitary authorities, are less productive as service provided have to match the requirements of a complex financial services based economy. Thus small cannot be equated to simple; microstates are expected to match large state standards of administration regardless of their internal constraints.

Therefore Jersey's democracy is both more pervasive and more responsive than that of a larger state. This can hinder efficient government as policy development and implementation are subject to continual democratic oversight at a level rare in larger states. The fragmentation at the heart of government, therefore, while hindering policy development and implementation, enhances democratic oversight over policy.

Research Issues

Small states and territories have thus far tended to be ignored in favour of a concentration on what are essentially the very large nations. This study will, hopefully, play a small part in redressing that balance. The study of the constraints and policy adaptation of the smaller states may prove to be just as productive an area of study as the study of larger states. These states have no option but to survive in dependent relationships and this raise useful issues for larger states entering interdependent relationships. Jersey has been in a form of economic union over which it has had little control for centuries.

This case study will provide a useful extension of the works already written on the island's constitution, economics and social history. It will also supply material for other comparative work on microstates. At present, such analysis is hindered by the fact that many of the case studies concentrate on either underdeveloped or sparsely populated archipelago microstates. By tending to concentrate on impoverished microstates, the literature has ignored the success of a number of small states and microstates, notably in Europe.[33] Studies of impoverished microstates alone cannot differentiate between the constraints on developments imposed by scale, and those imposed by poverty. In contrast, a study of Jersey can and may point to the conclusion that in fact Jersey represents a more appropriate model of development for underdeveloped small states. Thus this study of Jersey concentrates less on the constraints of scale which dominate writing in this area, but more on what strategies have been developed to enable Jersey to cope and prosper despite these constraints.

The volume of secondary literature on Jersey is more limited than would be the case with a larger state. Secondary sources exist on constitutional history,[34] economics[35] and social history[36] together with numerous works on the German occupation of the Channel Islands during the Second World War.[37] Articles on Jersey have appeared regularly in Commonwealth journals[38] and the Société Jersiaise Annual Bulletin as well as in the European University Working Paper Series.[39] Comparable literature exists on the other two Crown Dependencies.[40] No specific study, however, has been written on Jersey's external policies and relationships. A significant number of thematic studies, though, exist on microstates.[41] These, however, are largely studies of developing states in the Pacific and Caribbean regions. These states, though dissimilar in wealth and development, share many other resource, structural and scale problems with Jersey. They are, therefore, of some value as comparative sources, but must be used with care due to the fact that the microstates considered often face radically different economic and geopolitical problems to Jersey. The general literature on small states and microstates will be used to illuminate aspects of "the Jersey model" and this literature will also be used, where possible, to assist in the analysis of the effectiveness of the policy processes identified.

This study is largely based on primary source material. General comparative material can be obtained via the Commonwealth Secretariat and several universities have a special interest in microstates, examples being the University of the West Indies and the University of Malta. I have undertaken research trips to Guernsey and the Isle of Man to conduct interviews and gather material to enhance the comparative elements of this study. Moreover, I have completed structured interviews with senior officials, politicians and experts including the Bailiff and Lieutenant-Governor of Jersey, the Chief Minister and Deemster in the Isle of Man and the President of the Senior Committee in Guernsey.[42] Comparative material has been sought and interviews obtained with representatives of the Cayman Islands, the Falkland Islands, the Turks and Cacaos Islands and St Helena.

Extensive use has also been made of the variety of government publications produced by the States of Jersey. The Policy and Resources Committee publishes annual economic and statistical digests and reviews defining policy together with regular summaries of the latest position with regard to matters of local concern such as the European Union and what items of European legislation and International legislation have been adopted by the island. Local newspaper sources are important as they are often the only available record of events. Two prominent examples of this are the fact that no formal record of election results is kept and no written record of States debates exists; for both the only available source is the local newspaper. A major source of information on the island has been developed in the form of legal advice to various Royal Commissions relating to the islands. A series of detailed submissions of particular relevance was made to the Royal Commission on the Constitution in 1971,[43] principally from the States, the Home Office and a pressure group, the Jersey Constitutional Association. The negotiations prior to the United Kingdom's accession to the European Economic Community also provoked fierce academic debate and a series of articles was published to define and defend the decisions taken by the island at the time. The United Kingdom also invested considerable effort in justifying the agreement to the Crown Dependencies. These sources taken together are essential in clarifying in particular the United Kingdom's attitude to its relationship with Jersey. The legal debates which have surrounded the development of the constitution have produced a significant source of material for the analysis of different interpretations of the insular constitutions, particularly with regard to relations with the United Kingdom and the European Union.

I shall begin with a survey of the political institutions in Jersey together with the role of the Home Office appointed Crown Officers. The effects of the incremental and *ad hoc* nature of their development will be considered. The chapter will define the limits of the legislative powers of the States and highlight the effects on policy development of Jersey's fragmented executive, centred around the Committees of the States. This is necessary as it is by the exploitation of Jersey's distinct constitution and its autonomy from the United Kingdom that Jersey has been able to survive and prosper.

It will then be necessary to examine the basis of Jersey's external policy. This section begins to evaluate the island's constitution in comparison with the alternatives available, these being independence or the integration of Jersey into the United Kingdom.[44] The dilemmas presented to Jersey by international law are also highlighted. The adoption of international legal norms can provide an effective framework for protecting smaller communities against larger neighbours. However, the use by a microstate of international law is problematic as international law can not only be slow, expensive and notoriously difficult to enforce, but also entail the adoption of new domestic legislation or have periodic reporting requirements. This can impose a considerable burden on small administrations. In Jersey's case the anomalous status of the island under international law arising from its non-sovereign status creates further problems, particularly in relation to organisations such as the United Nations which refuse to recognise non-sovereign political entities. The international legal position presents an opportunity to study, not only the influence of external political and legal models on the island, but also the confused international response to the existence of Crown Dependencies and the implications this situation has for managed dependency in Jersey.

An understanding of Jersey's unusual economy will then be developed. This is essential in order to comprehend the evolution of external policy. Jersey's economy is dominated by the finance industry. In 1994 the financial services sector's estimated contribution to the island's gross domestic product was fifty four per cent with investment holding contributing a further fourteen per cent.[45] Therefore, much of government policy cannot be understood without reference to the influence and aims of the finance industry. The development and survival of the offshore finance centre in Jersey will be presented as an example of the island's survival strategies in action. The threats and challenges of the dominant industry in the island being global in nature will be considered in the light of the openness and vulnerability of small island economies. Whether the island can diversify away from finance is examined and an assessment of the extent to which Jersey's economic growth has been achieved through the active management of its autonomy and how far that autonomy attracted the business necessary for that growth to take place will be made.

The island's relationship with its metropolitan power, the United Kingdom, is pivotal and an analysis of it is essential to defining the operation and extent of the island's autonomy. Jersey's economic and political autonomy is predicated on successful management of the relationship with the United Kingdom. The reasons why the United Kingdom supports the current constitutional arrangements will be examined as well as the United Kingdom's aims in developing policy on issues affecting the relationship. It is also necessary to look at the relationship when it has been under pressure such as during the sacking in 1992 of the Deputy Bailiff by the Home Office. This will throw light on the United Kingdom's perception of the fundamental parameters of Jersey's autonomy.

Jersey's relationship with the European Union represents the most significant change in its dependency relationships this century. Jersey is not a full member of the European Union, but has to adopt the European legislation required not only by its associate status but also that required to maintain its close economic integration with the United Kingdom. At the time of the United Kingdom's accession to the European Economic Community, there was fierce local debate as to whether the island should seek membership. The negotiations surrounding the drafting of Protocol 3 will be assessed to ascertain whether the agreement was the result of a conscious policy of managed dependency or of good fortune. The relationship with the European Union will be compared with the more conventional relationship with the United Kingdom. A study of the interaction of the island's relationship with the United Kingdom and through it the European Union, will form part of an assessment of the long term viability of Jersey's association agreement with the European Union in the light of its continuing transformation. The United Kingdom government, due to its sovereignty over the island, is responsible for protecting Jersey's interest within the European Union. However, it is necessary to examine the extent to which the United Kingdom can prioritise Jersey's relationship with the European Union over its own interests, and whether alternative arrangements could be developed to allow Jersey a more direct and effective relationship with the European Union.

A study of Jersey's relationship with France is of interest because it allows an exploration of the reasons why France has become increasingly irrelevant to Jersey in political and economic terms. The relationship is dominated by minor disputes surrounding the definition of the sea boundary, and associated fishing rights, and the safety of a nuclear installation on the French coast adjacent to the island.

A selective comparison will be undertaken with the other Crown Dependencies: the Isle of Man and the Bailiwick of Guernsey. This will examine how far Jersey's case is replicated elsewhere. This will not be a full comparative case study since the fragmented sources and sites required for such a project are beyond the scope of this book. The Crown Dependencies have been selected for comparison because they share similar constitutional relationships, economies and populations. Such a comparison will also allow the identification of successful policies which have been adopted by all the Crown Dependencies to positively manage their dependency.

In conclusion, I hope to offer an account of the relationships which Jersey has developed with the United Kingdom, the European Union and France which will contribute to an overall evaluation of the parameters of Jersey's autonomy. An assessment will also be made of the extent to which Jersey's relations with the outside world promote successful managed dependency. The description of external policies will help both to define and to evaluate the success of survival strategies adopted by the insular authorities and how far Jersey's dependency on the United Kingdom is actively managed.

References

[1] Examples include Guernsey, Alderney, the Isle of Man, Andorra, Liechtenstein, Monaco, San Marino, the Vatican City, Gibraltar, Greenland and the Faeroes.

[2] 1991 Census, States Greffe, Jersey, 1992.

[3] The Bailiwick of Guernsey consists of the islands of Guernsey, Alderney, Sark, Herm, Jethou, Brechou and Lihou.

[4] Harden, S. ed., Small is Dangerous, Frances Pinter, London,1985, 1.

[5] Baldacchino, G., "Bursting the Bubble: The Pseudo-Development Strategies of Microstates" in Annales, 47, no 4-5, July - October 1992, 29- 51.

[6] Hampton, M. P., "Treasure Island or Fool's Gold: Can and Should Small Island Economies Copy Jersey?" in World Development, vol.22 no. 2, 237-250, hereafter, Treasure Island.

[7] Warrington, E., "Lilliput Revisited" in The Asian Journal of Public Administration, vol. 16 no.1, June 1994, 3-14.

[8] Warrington, E., "A Capacity for Policy Management: Re-Appraising the Context in Micro-States in Asian Journal, 114.

[9] Whitaker's Almanack 1995, J. Whitaker and Sons Ltd, London, 1994, hereafter, Whitaker's 1995.

[10] ibid.

[11] Chenery, H.B. & Taylor, L., "Development patterns: among countries and over time", Review of Economic Statistics, 1968, vol.1, no.4, 391- 416.

[12] Kohr, L. The Overdeveloped Nation, Christopher Davis, Swansea, 1977.

[13] Vulnerability: Small States in the Global Society, Commonwealth Secretariat, London, 1985, 9.

[14] Rapaport, J, Muteba, E & Therattil, E. Small States & Territories Status and Problems, Arno Press, New York, 1971, 30, hereafter, Small States.

[15] The Microstates and Small States of Europe, together with their respective populations, are: the Vatican 1,000; Aland 23,600; San Marino 24,399; Monoco 28,000; Gibraltar 28,848; Liechtenstein 29,868; Faroes 47,287; Greenland 55,117; Andorra 5,000; Guernsey (incl. Alderney and Sark) 61,759; Isle of Man 69,788; Jersey 84,0082; Azores 255,100; Iceland 264,922; Madeira 271,400; Malta 366,541; Luxembourg 395,200; Cyprus 725,000. Source: op. cit., Whitaker's Almanack 1995.

[16] Benedict., B., ed., Problems of Smaller Territories, Athlone Press, London, 1967, hereafter, Benedict.

[17] Hampton, M.P., The Offshore Interface Tax Havens in the Global Economy, Macmillan Press Ltd, London, 1996, hereafter, The Offshore Interface.

[18] Jalan, B., Problems in Small Economies, London, Croom Helm, 1982.

[19] Dommen, E. & Hein, P., ed., States, Microstates and Islands, Croom Helm, Dover, 1985, 1, hereafter, Dommen & Hein.

[20] op. cit., Small States, 127.

[21] Higgins, R., The Development of International Law through the Political Organs of the United Nations cited ibid., 126.

[22] ibid., 47.

[23] ibid., 48.

[24] Geri, H. H. & Wright Mills, C., From Max Weber: Essays in Sociology, Routledge & Kegan Paul Ltd., London, 1970, 196.

[25] ibid.

[26] op. cit., Benedict, 49.

[27] ibid.

[28] Dahl, R. & Tufte, E. R., Size and Democracy, Stanford University Press, Stanford, 1974, 5, hereafter, Dahl & Tufte.

[29] ibid., 13

[30] Limited Liability Partnerships (Jersey) Law 199: Committee of Inquiry - Report, States Greffe, Jersey, 1997 R.C. 23/97.

[31] op. cit., Dahl & Tufte, 13.

[32] The figure quoted represented the entire population of St. Helier as derived from the Report on the Census for 1996, Etat Civil Committee, Jersey, 1997, 26, hereafter, Census 1996. The meeting took place on 21 February 1995.

[33] Examples include not only Jersey, Guernsey and the Isle of Man, but also Andorra, Monaco and Liechtenstein.

[34] Bois, F de L., A Constitutional History of Jersey, States Greffe, Jersey, 1972; Heyting, W. J., The Constitutional Relationship between Jersey and the United Kingdom, Jersey Constitutional Association, Guernsey, 1977, hereafter, Heyting; and Le Hérissier, R., The Development of the Government of Jersey, 1771 -1972, States Greffe, Jersey, 1974, hereafter, Le Hérissier.

[35] op. cit., The Offshore Interface.

[36] Kelleher, J. D., The Triumph of the Country: The Rural Community in Nineteenth Century Jersey, John Appleby Publishing, Jersey, 1994, hereafter, Kelleher, and Syvret, M. & Stevens, J., Bailleine's History of Jersey, Phillimore, Chichester, 1981, hereafter Syvret & Stevens.

[37] For two contrasting views see Bunting, M., The Model Occupation: The Channel Islands under German Rule 1940 -1945, Harper Collins Publishing, 1995, & Cruickshank, C., The German Occupation of the Channel Islands, The Guernsey Press Co. Limited, Guernsey, 1975.

[38] Australian Journal of Public Administration, vol. 53, no.1, March 1994.

[39] Horner, S.A., "The Isle of Man and the Channel Islands - A study of their status under Constitutional, International and European Law" in European University Institute Working Paper No.98, European University Institute, Florence, 1984, hereafter, Horner 1984.

[40] Marr, L. J., A History of the Bailiwick of Guernsey, Phillimore, Chicester, 1982; Kermode, D.G., Devolution at Work: A Case Study of the Isle of Man, Saxon House, Farnborough, 1979; Kinvig, R.H., The Isle of Man: A Social Cultural and Political History, 3rd edition, Liverpool University Press, Liverpool, 1975; Solly, M., Government and Law in the Isle of Man, Parallel Books, Isle of Man, 1994.

[41] Examples of such works include Baker, R., ed., Public Administration in Small and Island States, Kumarian Press, West Hartford, 1992, hereafter, Public Administration; op. cit., Benedict; and op. cit., Dommen & Hein.

[42] Deemsters are the equivalent of High Court Judges in the Isle of Man.

[43] The Royal Commission on the Constitution, HMSO, Cmnd. 5460, HMSO, London, 1973, hereafter, Kilbrandon 1973.

[44] "Democracy in the Channel Islands", Nos Iles: A symposium on the Channel Islands, C. I. Study Group, Middlesex, 1944.

[45] States of Jersey, Statistical Review 1996, Finance and Economics Committee, Jersey, 1996, 44.

Chapter 2 - Internal Political Structures: The Foundations of Autonomy

Introduction

The constitution of the Bailiwick of Jersey has been described as "...unique and not capable of description by any of the usual categories of political science. It is full of anomalies, peculiarities and anachronisms, which even those who work the system find it hard to define precisely."[1] Unlike most of the other British dependencies it is medieval in origin, being founded upon a series of charters confirmed once the Crown lost its continental Norman possessions in 1204. Jersey's change in status from a backwater of the Duchy of Normandy to an isolated frontier province of the English King required the English Crown to grant it political and judicial autonomy in exchange for the loyalty of the island's elite.[2] Judicial autonomy was confirmed to the island in 1368 when an attempt to bring an action of trespass committed in Jersey to court in England was defeated. By this period the island had distinct and developing courts.[3] This court system was headed by the Royal Court, the supreme court in Jersey, consisting of the Bailiff and twelve Jurats.[4] This court began inviting the Parish Constables and Rectors to *ad hoc* meetings from at least 1497, thereby creating the body which became the legislative assembly, the States.

The development of the constitution cannot, however, be characterised as a smooth process. The power struggle between the Bailiffs and the Governors was essential to the evolution of the island's autonomy as the Bailiffs were able to successfully portray themselves as defenders of the islanders' ancient privileges.[5] The final resolution to the power struggle was decided in 1618 when a special Commission granted the Bailiff independence from the Governor.

The nearest document Jersey has to a constitution arose as a result of an economic crisis in 1770. In response the Privy Council dispatched Colonel Bentinck to the island. Bentinck took it upon himself to compile a list of laws operative at the time, since known as the Code of 1771. However, a comparison with a codified constitution is inappropriate as not only are significant laws on immigration and excise included, but also laws regulating such matters as the ownership of dogs. The comparison is further weakened as the list of laws is incomplete and the operative elements of the Norman Coutume are not included. The Coutume is the residual ancient Norman customary law which was preserved by Jersey's judicial autonomy. It formed the basis of Jersey's common law and its impact today is predominantly within local land law. Bentinck also initiated other reforms, the most significant of which removed the Royal Court's legislative powers, thereby making the States the only body empowered to initiate legislation on the island.

The Code of 1771 remained pivotal for two hundred years. The removal of the anti-usury provisions which imposed an interest rate ceiling of 5% per annum in the Code of 1771 was necessary in 1962 to allow the offshore finance industry to develop in Jersey. A further requirement for the finance industry to develop was the removal of the so called Bailiff's clause. This clause was inserted into the articles of incorporation of Jersey companies to prevent their holding assets which would be liable to United Kingdom Estate Duty. The clause had been the result of a joint Channel Island Treasury Conference in 1927. The conference was called as the result of Treasury concern about high net worth individuals taking up domicile in the islands to avoid death duties.[6] It was not, however, entirely internal changes in regulation that drove the creation of the offshore finance centre. Changes in tax management in the late 1950s and the 1960s were necessary to allow the development of legal ways to utilise an offshore finance centre. An example of such a development was the discovery that, as Jersey did not count as part of the United Kingdom, property held in Jersey was not liable to British Estate Duty.[7]

During the Second World War, the Channel Islands were occupied by German forces and this event precipitated the most significant constitutional reforms in the twentieth century when the war ended. The strains of administering an island under occupation proved too much for the moribund pre-war political settlement and government was carried out instead by an *ad hoc* Superior Council.[8] Moreover, the fact that the authorities were willing to administer the island during the occupation branded them as collaborators in the eyes of some elements of the population. The effect of a proportion of the population believing in these allegations discredited the old establishment and made both reform and election of a new generation of States members inevitable. It is against this background that the clamours for reform of the constitution must be seen. The situation was compounded by the fact that the United Kingdom emerged victorious from World War II with a confident, reforming socialist government while Jersey was economically devastated and politically divided.

The first major reform was the Franchise (Jersey) Law 1945 which extended the franchise to all persons over twenty-one in time for the 1945 deputies election. In the words of the Attorney General at the time, the reform of the franchise and the unprecedented series of reforms which were derived from a report of the Privy Council in 1947 saw the development of a fully democratic assembly.[9] The States created by these reforms is more or less unchanged today; the major subsequent alterations being the addition of a further deputy in 1974 and the reduction of the Senatorial term to six years in 1966. This period is, therefore, fundamental to an understanding of the operation of the modern States and marked the creation of something akin to a modern democratic legislature.

The end of the occupation also signalled a brief return to party politics.[10]

The catalyst for this revival of party competition on the island was the Jersey Democratic Movement. This had emerged during the occupation as an organisation opposed to the alleged collaborative activities of the Superior Council. Not surprisingly, it demanded radical constitutional and social reforms of the political system at the end of the war. Effective opposition to the Movement could not, however, come from the existing States members who were not only discredited in the eyes of much of the electorate, but were also part of what was viewed as an ossified political elite resistant to any form of change. Instead a new party, the Jersey Progressive Party, was launched on 31st October 1945. In his thesis, Roy Le Hérissier defines the position of the Progressive Party as "a compromise position between what it saw as the left-wing extremism of the Democratic Movement and the reactionary attitudes that had played such a predominant part in the pre-war Assembly".[11] Opponents viewed the Party as a front for the establishment designed to preserve its members in power by minimising, as far as possible, the demands for reform.[12] However, both the Progressive Party and the Democratic Movement accepted the need for reform, what they disputed was how far reaching these reforms should be. The result of the 1945 election was a victory for social conservatism. Thirteen Progressive Party candidates and one Movement candidate were elected. This apparently crushing defeat for the latter must be put into context. The Jersey Democratic Party's share of the votes was 34.25% and the Jersey Progressive Party's 27.12%. However, the Progressive Party formed alliances with independents in three-sided elections. The Progressive - Independent alliance thus ensured a combined vote of 63.13% and this, given the first past the post system used in deputies' elections, gave the Progressive Party a resounding victory. This emphasises the Progressive Party's dependence on the support of the independent candidates. The Progressive Party dissolved after successfully countering the perceived threat to the island posed by the Jersey Democratic Movement. The competition between the Jersey Democratic Movement and the Jersey Progressive Party represented the last occurrence of party politics in a form comparable to the operation of parties in the United Kingdom.

A committee of the Privy Council was appointed to "inquire into the proposed reforms in the constitution and procedures of the States of Jersey and of Guernsey, and into the proposed judicial reform, and advise thereon".[13] The Privy Councillors selected to produce the report were Viscount Samuel, Lord Ammon, Richard Butler, Sir John Beaumont and James Chuter Ede, the last being in the chair. The principal proposals put forward by the committee included increasing the number of deputies to twenty eight to replace the Rectors of the Parishes who, it was decided, should no longer sit ex-officio in the States. The Dean of Jersey would retain the right to speak in the States but not vote. Jurats, whilst continuing to sit in the Royal Court, should no longer sit in the States where they would be replaced by twelve elected States Jurats.[14] This represents a tentative move towards separation of powers as the jurats had roles in the legislature, executive and judiciary. In this way it mirrored the removal of the rectors from the States which created a clearer divide on the island between the secular and religious establishments. A formal retirement age for Jurats was instituted for the first time and set at seventy or, by permission of the Lieutenant Governor, seventy-five. Further, an electoral college was created for the selection of Jurats to replace the old system of popular election qualified by a very small property threshold. Moreover, the Committee recommended that the business of the States, the Royal Court and legislation should be in English not French, a proposal accepted as an inevitable but momentous consequence of social change in Jersey.[15]

The United Kingdom's desires to accede to the European Economic Community and to explore the possibility of devolution within the United Kingdom provoked a major crisis in the relationships between the island and its metropolitan power.[16] The island did not wish to be part of the European Economic Community and campaigned for special arrangements with the Community should the United Kingdom accede.[17] During the same period the United Kingdom government appointed the Royal Commission on the Constitution to examine proposals for devolution.[18] An examination of the constitutions of the Crown Dependencies was included in the remit of the Commission. This action was perceived as a threat to the island's autonomy and the insular authorities, together with local interest groups, presented substantial and detailed evidence to the Commission. Therefore, despite the Commission recommending no substantial changes to the island's constitution in its conclusions, the considerable evidence submitted and heard by it represents the most thorough examination of Jersey's constitution and external relationships since the immediate post war reforms.

The announcement, without prior consultation with the islands, by the Labour government of a review of the financial regulation in the Channel Islands and the Isle of Man in January 1998 precipitated another crisis in the relationship. The causes of the crisis mirror, in part, the dispute surrounding the Royal Commission on the Constitution twenty years earlier in that it has arisen at a time of internal constitutional reform within the United Kingdom. Any review of the offshore finance centre, no matter how positive its conclusions are about the industry, reduces investor confidence while it is underway, and thus investment into the island. Perhaps more seriously, the fact that the insular authorities were not consulted before the review was announced illustrates a lack of knowledge of, or respect for, the island's autonomy. A further potential threat to the island is that the new government has a radical reforming agenda with respect to constitutional reform. Such an agenda includes devolution, a British-Irish Council and a modernised partnership for the United Kingdom Overseas Territories. Devolution is a threat because as the number of small politically autonomous communities increases, their combined significance increases too and the United Kingdom government may be tempted to rationalise the anomalous political units, the most anomalous being the Crown Dependencies. Each of the preceding possibilities is potentially a threat to the

31

island's existing constitutional relationship with the United Kingdom.

The similarities between Jersey's constitution and that of its metropolitan power are striking. Both have Norman antecedents, are uncodified and have archaic elements. It is also possible to extend Bagehot's distinction between dignified and efficient parts of the constitution to Jersey. This distinction is best illustrated by the dignified façade of rule by Crown in Council and the efficient reality of control by a junior Home Office Minister. The operation of such a division with respect to Jersey is useful as it provides the façade of equality before the Crown while in reality allowing for the relatively low priority the affairs of the island have for the United Kingdom. Bagehot's distinction, therefore, highlights the dichotomy within Jersey's constitution of a medieval core and a democratic overlay. However, the façade remains an integral part of the relationship as it would be much harder to preserve the relationship if it were openly expressed as compliance with the demands of a junior Home Office Minister sitting in a Parliament they do not elect, than if it takes the form of loyalty to the Crown by the island.

The social cohesion and personal loyalties apparent in a small state help buttress the established system. Large scale constitutional change is rare and tends to be precipitated by outside events, such as the occupation in the key post-war reforms. The ability to appeal beyond the island's establishment to a higher authority, however theoretical, provides an escape valve for discontent which might otherwise become focused more directly on internal political structures. The relationship with the United Kingdom also provides a degree of separation of powers as judicial oversight is by the judicial committee of the Privy Council, legislative and executive oversight by the Crown in Council and the Home Office.

Contemporary Constitutional Structures and Institutions

Jersey's present formal constitutional position in relation to the United Kingdom is defined by the Interpretation Act 1978 Section 5, Schedule 1. It defines the British Islands as consisting of the United Kingdom, the Channel Islands and the Isle of Man, thereby confirming in statute law that Jersey is not part of the United Kingdom.[19] Jersey, Guernsey and the Isle of Man form the Crown Dependencies, which, although not sovereign, have considerable devolved legislative powers. The title emphasises that the Channel Islands predate England as a possession of the Crown. The island's links with the United Kingdom also predate the evolution of Parliament as a modern legislature. Jersey's status as a Crown Dependency confers a distinct identity in that it is a British dependency not by force, but by choice. This explains why islanders view Crown Dependency status as important and object strongly to any perception of their being a colony. Jersey's different status is highlighted from those of former British colonies, now defined as United Kingdom Overseas Territories, by the fact that Jersey's good government is overseen by the Home Office, not the Foreign and Commonwealth Office.

Lieutenant Governor

The post of Lieutenant Governor at first sight would seem essentially ceremonial. Whilst this partly reflects the truth it would be a mistake to assume the post is completely decorative. Its holder is the Crown's representative on the island. As the formal link between the island and the United Kingdom is expressed through the Crown, he is, therefore, the formal representative of the United Kingdom in the island. He possesses the right to veto any resolution of the States if the matter concerns the special interests of the Crown. This veto, though, has not been used in the twentieth century. He is also the Commander-in-Chief of all military units on the island; although as the only units stationed on the island consist of a territorial army unit, this role must be regarded as solely honorific. His powers are not as extensive as those of Governors in United Kingdom Overseas Territories or Manx Lieutenant Governors in the past; for example, the Lieutenant Governor does not sit on any body akin to an executive council and also lacks a general power of veto.

The Lieutenant Governor, in theory, acts as a conduit for messages to and from the Home Office, conveys local concerns to the Home Office, and briefs the Home Office on events in the island. If all this were to be true the Lieutenant Governor would be pivotal to the relationship and essential to the management of the relationship between Jersey and the United Kingdom. The value of this formal link can, however, be questioned. The Home Office, when considering whether the post of Lieutenant Governor should be abolished in 1957, noted that "Since the war, the position of the Lieutenant Governor as the Channel Of Communication between the Home Office and the Islands has become a complete fiction."[20] This view is supported by the fact that with modern technology, there is no reason to prevent communications from being directly with the Home Office. This is noted later in the same letter "we have developed close, and as you know, personal relations between officers of the Department and the Crown Officers in the States. You and I are constantly in touch with the Bailiff and with the Attorney-General and Solicitor-General in each Island."[21] The officials also note with reference to both Jersey and Guernsey that "on no occasion have we ever felt the need to go to or receive from either Lieutenant Governor impartial advice."[22] Thus the evidence available under the thirty year rule suggests that the United Kingdom does not value the post as an intermediary between itself and the insular authorities. Formal communication, however, is still transmitted via the Lieutenant Governor's office.

The Lieutenant Governor has responsibility for certain executive actions that the United Kingdom has been unwilling to devolve to the island, such as control of the Immigration and Nationality Department. This power is of particular relevance in an island suffering from population pressure. The United Kingdom, is however, unwilling to delegate that power to the island. The Immigration and Nationality Department is therefore paid for by the island and staffed by locally recruited staff, but under the authority of the Lieutenant Governor. The task is not undertaken by the Lieutenant Governor's office as it has no more than six employees. There is, however, no reason why this role could not be carried out by Home Office staff in the United Kingdom who are consulted on matters of importance in this area already.

The reason the post is still in existence exemplifies the need to maintain a dignified façade to the relationship. Thus the Lieutenant Governor attends a round of social gatherings in a way analogous to the programme of the Lord Lieutenant of an English county. The Home Office in 1958 abandoned the notion of reform when it became clear there was no support in the island for such an action. The post is funded by the insular authorities and thus is not a drain on the United Kingdom. Instead, it can be regarded as a reward posting available to the Ministry of Defence at no cost to that department since it is, by tradition, occupied by a retired senior military officer prior to retirement. Jersey was also wary of reform in case a backbench politician would be appointed.[23] Another option would be to add the duties of the Lieutenant Governor to those of the Bailiff, who already acts a Deputy Governor.[24] However, this would add another layer of powers and responsibilities to an office whose fused powers were already in dispute. Indeed, the Lieutenant Governor offers a position which could be used as a counter-weight to an overmighty Bailiff. The post was also viewed by the post-holder in 1958 as offering "impartiality of outlook uncoloured by local influence."[25]

Lieutenant Governors hold office for five year terms and, with the notable exception of Sir Michael Wilkes, usually have little or no detailed knowledge of the island when they arrive. This can be seen as an advantage to Jersey as it allows the insular authorities to brief a new Lieutenant Governor themselves. Inversely, it can be to the new Lieutenant Governor's advantage because, as his term is limited, he is less bound by the social disciplines of the island. However, this freedom is constrained by the fact that neither the insular authorities, nor the Home Office, would wish him to make political pronouncements without prior consultation with one or both parties.

The Lieutenant Governor's role, therefore, reflects an accommodation between the United Kingdom's preference for indirect control over the island and the desire by the insular authorities to maintain formal and visible structures to help the island manage its dependency on the United Kingdom. His powers may appear to be significant. However, it is difficult to assess the Lieutenant Governor's true influence given that his powers are only exercised in consultation with the Home Office and that significant secrecy surrounds the post. The post has, however, been preserved in order to accommodate the wishes of the insular authorities to preserve a personification of the head of state on the island, thus maintaining a significant dignified element in the relationship between the United Kingdom and the insular authorities.

Crown Officers

The holders of the posts of Bailiff, Deputy Bailiff, Attorney General and Solicitor General, referred to in Jersey and Guernsey as the Crown Officers, are unique in the Commonwealth as regards the fused nature of their powers as well as holding office at Her Majesty's pleasure. The Crown Officers are appointed by the Crown but form the core of Jersey's Court system and are the senior legal advisers to the insular authorities. In the position of Bailiff they represent the ultimate expression of the fusion of powers in Jersey and exemplify the archaic nature of much of Jersey's constitution. The Attorney General and Solicitor Generals not only appear in the Royal Court, but also act as advisers to the States and its Committees. They also perform certain executive functions, such as oversight over the activities of the honorary police, whilst giving advice to both the legislature and the executive committees. Therefore, at the heart of the government of Jersey, exist senior Crown-appointed officials whose fused powers predate the concept of separation of powers.

As Crown Officers hold their office at Her Majesty's pleasure, they can be dismissed for offences other than gross misconduct, and moreover, there is no domestic democratic veto on the use of this power. In 1992 the Deputy Bailiff was dismissed by the Crown in. The fact that an external power has so much influence over such an important area of government, even if the power is rarely invoked, distinctly limits Jersey's autonomy and can create tension in the relationship with Britain. The fact that the Bailiff is appointed by the Crown could be regarded as evidence that the United Kingdom has effective control of all the levers of power in Jersey through this appointee. However, the current procedure can be defended as an effective way to prevent politicisation of the appointment, which might occur if it were in the gift of the States.

The appointment of Crown Officers is a significant element in the dependency relationship. Although consultation is not required, it occurs as a result of the good relationship between the dependency and the metropolitan power. The appointment system, according to Sir Peter Crill, is largely the responsibility of the Bailiff or, in the case of the post of Bailiff itself, the retiring Bailiff who will consult a Consultative Panel chosen by the States. The Home Office then endorses their recommendation. The power demanded by the United Kingdom over Jersey is not the ability to appoint every Crown Officer, but to intervene if the procedures are seen as working in a way contrary to British interests.

As Crown appointees to key positions in the island's government, the uncertain nature of Crown Officer loyalties creates problems at times of tension in the relationship with the United Kingdom. In the Prison Board Case of 1894, the island's Attorney General, in his role as Crown Officer, prepared the evidence for the Crown, the Crown in this case being the United Kingdom authorities. This created a situation where Jersey had to mount a legal defence of its position without access to its own law officers. Crown Officers in such a position may not be best placed to give advice to the United Kingdom. Crown Officers are usually born in Jersey, have made a career at the local bar and have close kinship links to the island. Thus, they are normally treated as part of the Jersey establishment, rather than as officials of the United Kingdom and, should a conflict arise, their current status is not ideal for either the governments or individuals involved. Their status is, however, anomalous as they have loyalties to both Jersey and the United Kingdom. This fragmentation of loyalties may be viewed as archaic but does create a situation where it is possible for the Crown Officers to act as an interface between the desires of the metropolitan power and those of its dependency.

The Bailiff

The Bailiff is the island's senior judge and, as President of the States, its civic head. He acts as the first point of contact for formal communications from the Home Office and is regarded as the island's Chief Citizen or "Mr Jersey."[26] The medieval nature of the post is such that no formal qualifications are required for Bailiff or Deputy Bailiff, although the nature of the post dictates that it should be held by a lawyer. The Bailiff also acts as Deputy Governor by virtue of his office. The fact that the Bailiff has this role allows the United Kingdom to inform him of decisions while insisting that all other members of the insular authorities of which he is the senior official are not notified. A recent example has been the Government's decision in 1998 to institute a review of Jersey's financial services.

As President of the States, the Bailiff has the right to veto any resolutions of the States which he believes to be *ultra vires*. Article 22 States that:

> The Bailiff has power to enter his dissent to any resolution of the States susceptible of implementation if he is of the opinion that the States are not competent to pass the resolution and, where the Bailiff exercises the power aforesaid, the resolution shall immediately be transmitted to Her Majesty and, in the meantime and unless the consent of Her Majesty is obtained thereto, the resolution shall be of no effect.[27]

Further, the Bailiff possesses the casting vote which, by convention, must be cast for the *status quo*. The Bailiff's role as President, or Speaker, of the States, is therefore more extensive than that of Speaker of the Houses of Commons, not only by virtue of his veto, but also because he is routinely consulted on legislative matters.

The Bailiff's influence over the executive originates in his role as the first effective point of contact between the United Kingdom and the insular authorities. He also gives advice to committees or States members on issues deemed to have constitutional importance. The first role allows the Bailiff to operate as a co-ordinator of information and discussion between the island and its metropolitan power, hence making him a key figure in external policy development. The influence of this role was demonstrated in 1984 when the United Kingdom requested an annual contribution to its defence costs. The request was transmitted initially to the Bailiff and Sir Frank Ereaut responded by asking the Father of the House to form a Committee to examine the issue.[28] Thus, when the island was faced by a situation which was not catered for in the structures of the insular administration but involved matters of the constitution or the relationship with the United Kingdom, the co-ordination of the response became the responsibility of the Bailiff. The second role derives from the Bailiff's position as President of the Royal Court. A tradition of consulting the President of the Royal Court on matters of constitutional importance has allowed the Bailiff to adopt the mantle of guardian of the constitution. This involvement is likely to be particularly pronounced in external affairs as this is the area of executive activity which tends to throw up the highest proportion of constitutional issues. Bailiffs also use their positions in the executive to influence policy more directly. Sir Philip Bailhache has sought to promote an improvement in the island's relationship with France.

The Bailiff's influence, however, depends on whether he adopts a wide-ranging or a more minimalist interpretation of his multifaceted role within an uncodified constitution. The Bailiff during the occupation and the post-war reform period, Lord Coutanche, pushed his powers to their furthest extent in the twentieth century.[29] Le Hérissier argues that "Coutanche occupied a unique position of influence in the pre-war period, and, at times, acted as de facto Prime Minister."[30] He was an assertive and able man, acquiring whatever power he felt was necessary to govern the island through a period of great political instability. He chaired the Superior Council during the occupation, a body which in many ways mirrored the operation of a cabinet. He was also influential in engineering the post-war reforms and was known to summon Committee Presidents to his offices to discuss policy.[31] Sir Robert Le Masurier deliberately shied away from such an assertive role in the States and sought to concentrate on his work in the Royal Court. This created the space for the Committee Presidents to reassume the leadership role in the States. Thus, the Bailiff's role in the executive has to be regarded as significant, but ultimately it is fluid and dependent on his own interpretation of the role within the executive. The Bailiffs succeeding Le Masurier: Sir Frank Ereaut, Sir Peter Crill, and Sir Philip Bailhache have tended to seek a middle way between Coutanche's role as, at times, quasi-Prime Ministerial and Le Masurier's preference for minimising the Bailiff's legislative role and so moving nearer to evolution of a separation of powers.[32] The potential for a Bailiff to adopt a more prime ministerial line still exists in constitutional terms as the structures Coutanche used to develop such a dominant position as Bailiff still remain largely intact. It is unclear, however, whether popular opinion on the island would tolerate such an assertive Bailiff as Coutanche again.

The role of Bailiff in Jersey has been compared with that of Lord Chancellor in the United Kingdom in that the Lord Chancellor sits in the Cabinet, appoints the judiciary and Queen's Counsels and acts as a judge as well as Speaker in the House of Lords. The comparison is useful in that it highlights the origin of both offices deriving from pre-modern and uncodified constitutions, but the fundamental difference between them is that of potential power. The Bailiff, owing to his dual role of President of a unicameral Parliament and senior judge, has both a more powerful position and fewer other office-holders acting as checks on his power than the Lord Chancellor who must contend with the Government Leader and the Law Lords in the House of Lords.

Reform of the post of Bailiff to institute some form of separation of powers was rejected by both the Report of the Committee of the Privy Council on proposed reforms in the Channel Islands and the Royal Commission on the Constitution.[33] The reasons given on each occasion were that "It is an advantage in a small community, and in a legislative body very limited in numbers that this dissent [the Bailiff's veto] should be expressed, or intimation given that it may have to be expressed directly to the States."[34] This view is based on the assumption that Jersey lacks the wealth and expertise to have separate legal advisers for the legislature and judges. Although this may have once been true, it is doubtful whether it is the case today. A second assumption underlying the statement is that the existing workload is inadequate to sustain two posts. The appointment of a Deputy Bailiff in 1958 and the subsequent rapid expansion of legal activity associated with the development of the offshore finance centre proves that this assumption is flawed. In fact, 1958 must be regarded as a lost opportunity for reform where the option could have been taken of splitting the roles of speaker and chief justice. A similar reform has already occurred in the Isle of Man where the Deemsters no longer sit in the Legislative Council, but solely act as judges.

The current state of affairs where the Bailiff is both President of the Royal Court and the States might, however, create a situation where the Bailiff or the Deputy Bailiff would find himself ruling in the Royal Court on the legality of a law passed by a session of the States he presided over. It is only due to the fact that executive-judicial conflicts are rare, and consequently the fusion of powers seldom being highlighted, that this issue has not been more salient. This fusion of powers could be seen to compromise the Bailiff's position and independence, particularly considering his right to veto acts of the States which he believes to be *ultra vires*. In such a case an appeal to the European Court of Human Rights might result in a ruling that the lack of separation of powers is potentially unjust, thereby imposing reform from outside. A current action before the courts in Jersey where Advocate Sinel, for Mayo Associates and others, is suing the Finance and Economics Committee has focused on this issue.[35] In Guernsey one such ruling has already been made by the Commission.[36] The risk of external intervention in Jersey's affairs resulting from the situation described above is unnecessary, particularly as splitting the post would not, as argued by some, destroy the distinctiveness of Jersey's law. Indeed, a situation could be envisaged where the Bailiff shorn of his legislative and executive functions could act as a protector of Jersey's judicial autonomy against laws from a legislature which could potentially undermine it. The reform would also facilitate the development of judicial review under Jersey law, a move favoured by Sir Peter Crill, but one currently constrained by the Bailiff's role in the States.[37] The Bailiff's medieval fusion of powers, therefore, presents a potential difficulty for Jersey in managing its dependency. Moreover, the fusion of powers at the heart of the constitution exemplified by the Bailiff provides for fewer countervailing forces since, in a small state, fewer posts are available to act as a balance to those individuals in power.

The States

The Bailiff presides over a unicameral Parliament, the States, which consists of twenty nine constituency based Deputies elected every three years, twelve Senators, six elected every three years for six year terms on an island-wide basis, and twelve Constables who sit in the States by virtue of their role as head of one of the island's parishes together with the Dean of Jersey, the Attorney General and Solicitor General who all have the right to speak, but not vote, in the States. The Lieutenant Governor has the right to attend and must see the minutes of all meetings. The States is, therefore, divided into three estates: the Senators with an island wide basis, parish based Constables, and deputies often sitting in multimember population based constituencies.

The States consist of an executive embedded in a legislature. This combination gives States members power restrained only by the Royal Court, with which it shares some members, and by a metropolitan power uninterested in Jersey's domestic politics. Though rarely acknowledged in public, no attempt has been made to replicate even the limited separation of powers which exists between the Royal Court and the States with respect to the legislative and executive functions of the States.

Although there are infrequent and unsuccessful attempts to operate parties within the assembly, a long tradition of antipathy towards the idea of political parties exists in the States. This, therefore, makes a whole dimension of political analysis irrelevant to Jersey where policy making must be regarded as the outcome of the interaction of fifty three individuals who, although they may form *ad hoc* groupings over various issues for periods, essentially are independent and immune from any form of executive discipline designed to implement executive policies.

The States also reflects a more general fragmentation of the government as Jersey, despite its size, operates a quasi-federal constitution with considerable power vested in the twelve parishes. The elected leader of each parish, the Constable, sits in the States by virtue of his office and the Constables give the parishes a block vote of twelve of the fifty three States members. Elections for Constables occur every three years and are held when the previous term expires. This, together with the staggered election of Senators, means that Jersey has no event resembling a general election. The parishes also control the honorary police whose powers exceed those of the parallel professional States of Jersey police force; for example, only the senior honorary police, the Centeniers, have the power to charge an individual with a crime. Aside from the policing role, the parishes control the provision of welfare and the maintenance of many of the roads as well as fulfilling many of the functions of a United Kingdom local authority. The parishes are, therefore, a force to be reckoned with in Jersey politics. Only three of them can be regarded as urban and the traditions associated with the rights of the parishes are medieval.[38] Consequently, they tend to act as a force for rural conservatism and are often hostile to ideas which are viewed as emanating from outside the island.

The States has the authority to pass laws subject to their receiving the Royal Assent, which must not be considered automatic.[39] The United Kingdom may also extend Acts of Parliament to Jersey, but by convention it seeks prior approval from the States as far as this is possible. The United Kingdom does not legislate in areas of domestic or fiscal affairs as a convention of non-interference in these matters exists between Jersey and the United Kingdom. Thus, the insular authorities regard it as "unconstitutional for Parliament, otherwise than with the concurrence of the States, to impose taxation on the Islanders".[40] However, the division between domestic and external matters is becoming more complicated as the scope of responsibilities of such international organisations as the European Union expands. The extent of this convention has also been brought into question by the United Kingdom's instigation of a review into the island's financial regulation, despite the fact that this legislation has, by definition, received the Royal Assent.

The powers of the legislature reflect Jersey's intermediate position between complete statehood and absorption into the United Kingdom. Legislation may take the forms of any of the following: Acts of Parliament extended by Order in Council; Statutory Instruments extended by Order in Council; Acts of the States; Statutory Instruments; Triennial Regulations and Regulations promulgated by the States of Jersey arising from Acts of the States and Administrative Orders.

A constitutional convention has evolved that Parliament seeks the consent of the States before extending an Act of Parliament to the island. The force of this convention is limited by the fact that the United Kingdom, as Jersey's sovereign power, maintains the right to ensure the good government of the island. Further, the concept of the States of Jersey having an effective veto on the actions of Parliament, even if that action is to extend an Act of Parliament to the island without the island's consent, is problematic since this would seem to run counter to the doctrine of parliamentary supremacy. Heyting counters this difficulty by denying such supremacy on the grounds that Jersey's autonomy predates the claims of the British Parliament. He has also argued that Jersey's relationship has always been with the Crown, rather than with Parliament.[41] The formal position of the States of Jersey in its submission to the Royal Commission on the Constitution was that of acceptance of the "theoretical omni-competence of Parliament"[42] but it was felt that "in relation to the self-governing territories outside the United Kingdom, parliamentary sovereignty is to a very large extent a legal abstraction"[43] and that this abstraction was qualified further by constitutional conventions and binding usages. In contrast the United Kingdom upheld Parliament's ultimate sovereignty over the island. Before the Royal Commission the Home Office submitted that "so long as Her Majesty's

Government has responsibility for the good government of the Islands, it is essential for the United Kingdom to retain its residual power to legislate, if need be, on matters that are domestic to the islands."[44] The gap between the positions taken on parliamentary sovereignty by the States and the United Kingdom government is not as wide as appears on paper. As with the appointment of Crown Officers, at its core the Home Office's desire is to preserve an unrestricted right to intervene in insular affairs should the island act in such a way as to jeopardise the interest of the United Kingdom as defined by the Home Office. The Home Office, however, does not envisage imposing legislation except under these circumstances and no piece of United Kingdom legislation has been imposed on the island without its consent in the period under consideration.[45]

The insular authorities do, however, use Acts of Parliament extended by Order in Council; partly as a means of extending complex legislation beyond the resources of the island to draft and partly to implement legislation of limited local importance required to meet international obligations in an efficient way. Both parties view such legislation as a vital tool to ensure the standardised enforcement of certain measures usually derived from international agreements across all the possessions of the Crown. Further flexibility is allowed for in the extension of United Kingdom Acts of Parliament to the island by a form of words that has been developed by the Crown Dependencies in consultation with the Home Office to signify the elements of the legislation that are to be extended to the island. This form of words is, in part, an acknowledgement of the island's separate and distinctive legal system and includes provision for "such exceptions, modifications, and adaptations, if any, as may be specified in the Order."[46]

United Kingdom Acts of Parliament, therefore, represent to the States a form of legislation which, although not without its problems constitutionally, allows the States to guarantee absolute equivalence with the United Kingdom in areas where both parties desire this. Orders in Council can also be used to relieve pressure on the island's own legislative process by importing legislation from the United Kingdom when it is deemed appropriate. It must be noted, however, that this practice can be regarded as diluting insular autonomy as the laws extended are those of the United Kingdom rather than insular laws. The authorities in the Isle of Man feel this use of Orders in Council to be detrimental to their autonomy. [47] Whenever possible, they prefer to re-enact legislation extending to the Isle of Man by Order in Council as Manx Law. In contrast, the use of Orders of Council is viewed as a legitimate legislative vehicle for the States of Jersey to request. In terms of relations with the United Kingdom, the use of Orders in Council may be viewed as a way of managing a dependency as it ensures that the metropolitan power can have the legislation it feels is necessary to maintain its sovereignty in place as Acts of its Parliament. In terms of the attitude of the States of Jersey, it represents a pragmatic use of the greater law drafting capacity of its metropolitan power. Further, it is extremely doubtful whether a self-denying ordinance on the use of Order in Council by the Isle of Man would prevent the United Kingdom legislating in such a way, should it wish to assert its right to do so.

Acts of Parliament extended to the island have required formal registration in the Royal Court since 1805. The significance of this practice is a source of dispute. Heyting has argued that only the Crown, and not Parliament, has authority over Jersey. Registration of United Kingdom Orders in Council in the Royal Court is therefore necessary to enable them to come into force.[48] However, the submission of the States of Jersey (which in this case concurs with that of the United Kingdom) stated that "The legal operation of an Act of Parliament which applies to the Island in terms or by necessary implication is not dependent on registration and publication, the purpose of which is merely to give notice to the inhabitants, and such an Act has effect in the Island even though not registered."[49] The significance of the debate on registration is that if registration is necessary to give force to an Act, the Royal Court would gain an effective veto on the metropolitan power's ability to impose legislation on the island.

United Kingdom statutory instruments derived from Acts of Parliament, when extended to the island, substitute the authority of the relevant United Kingdom Minister for that of a Committee of the States or the States as a whole, as provided for in the relevant Order of Council. Registration in the Royal Court is normally required, but can be waived with the States' consent. The States of Jersey have the power to pass secondary legislation in the form of Regulations derived both from Orders in Council and Acts of the States. These regulations do not require the sanction of the Crown in Council.

The bulk of the primary legislation deriving from the States consists of Acts of the States which, when in force, are referred to as Laws. A proposal for an Act of the States is presented to the States by a States member or, more normally, a Committee of the States. Laws must be sanctioned by the Crown in Council and this can not be considered automatic as it was withheld from the Isle of Man over the Wireless Telegraphy (Isle of Man) Bill. The withholding of Royal Assent would be symptomatic of a considerable deterioration in Jersey's relationship with the United Kingdom. At present, neither side would allow a dispute to develop into such an open and politically destabilising crisis. The right to withhold consent mirrors the conventions about the use of Orders in Council. It is a reflection of Jersey's status as a dependency and exemplifies the effective legislative power of veto retained by the United Kingdom government.

Acts of the States are submitted to the United Kingdom as part of the drafting process. The Home Office will then forward them for comments to the relevant United Kingdom Ministry. This procedure illustrates the productive synergy available in a formalised dependency arrangement, which allows the Home Office to raise doubts informally about any areas of the legislation it is unhappy about at a comparatively early stage in the Act's drafting. Jersey, in the process, can choose to avoid a potentially damaging public confrontation with the Home Office by accepting informal advice while enjoying access to the expertise of a far larger government machine.

The States of Jersey also have the power to pass Triennial Regulations or Règlements. These regulations are passed by the States and do not require the Royal Assent provided that they are not deemed to "infringe the Royal prerogative nor be repugnant to the permanent political or fundamental laws of the island."[50] Triennial Regulations may not remain in force for more than three years, but are renewable. They were a significant instrument in the development of Jersey's political autonomy and were the only formal legislative instrument acknowledged by the Code of 1771. According to Le Hérissier the States "used perpetual re-enactment as one of the means of increasing the extent of their legislative power."[51] This practice was accepted as a legislative convention by the United Kingdom appointed Commissioners in 1847 and 1861.[52] The practice of perpetual re-enactment as a means of by-passing the Crown in legislative matters ceased to be effective after an objection to the renewal of a Triennial regulation by the Lieutenant Governor. This resulted in a report by a Committee of the States and an Order in Council which emphasised that Triennial Regulations should not be used to infringe prerogative powers.[53] The use of Triennial Regulations was restricted further by the use of vetoes by the Bailiff and the Lieutenant Governor when a regulation was thought to be *ultra vires*. The history of triennial regulations can be regarded as an initially successful, but ultimately failed, attempt to extend autonomy to the point where primary legislation could be passed without the United Kingdom's consent.

The most recent change in the legislative powers of the States has resulted from the large amount of European Community legislation which the island feels it is necessary to implement. Under a law passed in 1996, the States of Jersey took the power to implement by regulation any piece of European Community legislation regardless of whether it is covered by Protocol 3.[54] This law also streamlines the procedures involved in the adoption of European Community Law. It is hoped that this measure will reduce the burden of legislation required by the Protocol governing the island's relationship with the European Union. It will also allow Jersey to implement those elements of European legislation not covered by the Protocol but which the island wishes to adopt nonetheless. The adoption of such legislation can be advantageous in a way comparable to the use of Orders in Council to extend Acts of Parliament since a piece of legislation adopted in this manner may save the island considerable time and money should it attempt to draft its own comparable legislation.

The legislative powers available to the States and their operation reflect significant elements of the constitutional settlement in that the United Kingdom maintains constitutional conventions of non-interference in domestic and fiscal matters and does not extend Acts of Parliament without insular consent. These conventions rest on the mutual trust built up over time, but as with all uncodified constitutions, conventions are only as powerful as the stronger party is prepared to let them be. The arrangements also reflect both parties' preference for informal controls as, even though the United Kingdom has many formal powers to halt legislation on the island, informal vetting of legislation in draft form acts as the usual method of resolving disputes between Jersey and the United Kingdom.

Committees of the States

In a more complete way than the United Kingdom, Jersey has an executive embedded in a legislature. The executive is also highly and unusually fragmented. The core of the executive consists of thirty Committees of the States,[55] split into twelve standing and eighteen other committees. The number of standing committees tends to be stable over time, whereas the number of other committees varies. In 1997, the range of committees varied from Finance and Economics, which co-ordinates the government budget of £279 million, to the Cottage Homes Committee which administers ninety five units of accommodation for the elderly.[56] The Committees' authority is limited only by the States Assembly itself or, in exceptional circumstances, the Royal Court. The Committees of the States are supplemented by twenty three other committees, tribunals and boards which are appointed by the States and often include States members.[57] The evolution of committee responsibilities has been largely incremental and uncodified. The authors of the Peat Marwick review of the machinery of government in Jersey reported that "The terms of reference and remits of individual committees are not set out in Standing Orders, nor as far as we could discover, is there any central codification of the responsibilities of individual committees."[58] Further "most often committees rely for a definition of their responsibilities on the way that their remit has been built up traditionally and on specific powers and duties conferred on them by legislation."[59] Committee procedure is also based on precedent, although some elements are governed by the 1966 States of Jersey Law. At present a review is underway into the operation of the committee system. If the review recommendations are accepted, responsibilities and accountability within the system will be clarified and the number of committees reduced.[60] The acceptance of the need for reform highlights dissatisfaction with the fragmented nature of executive power which results from such a large and uncodified committee structure.

The proliferation of committees is explained in part by the fact that new committees are created to perform new functions, one such being the Jersey Transport Authority which is responsible for licensing the use of Jersey's airspace. Committees are also commissioned to prepare legislation on specific issues, an example being the Special Committee on Freedom of Information which is preparing a code of practice on Freedom of Information. Thus a tendency exists within the executive not only to govern by committees, but also to respond to problems by creating even more committees. The large number of committees further serves as an internal check within the executive to prevent too much power accruing in too few hands.

The fragmented executive in Jersey has resulted in a lack of overall coherence in the distribution of responsibilities. The Committees' structure does not match civil service departments. Thus the Defence Committee has partial responsibility for policing and the Immigration and Nationality Department, but complete responsibility for the Fire Service. Policing responsibility is shared with the parish based honorary police system and responsibility for immigration and nationality is shared with the Home Office via the Office of the Lieutenant Governor. The Defence Committee, however, does not have responsibility for the island's prison which is the responsibility of a single function Prison Board. The committees are, therefore, a mixture of large multifunctional committees and small, often single issue, committees, both of which can experience problems in developing policy. The multifunctional committees can lack the ability to develop policy in a focused manner across all their areas of responsibility. The small single issue committees can lack the administrative support to be effective. However, the existence of a large number of committees of varying size and responsibilities has its advantages. Firstly, it provides a means by which States members can learn the art of being a committee president on smaller committees before seeking promotion to larger ones. Secondly, the system also ensures that a large proportion of States members have presidencies. This wide distribution of power can be seen as promoting cohesion within the executive. Thirdly, the current structure ensures that most committee presidents do not have a workload which requires them to become full time politicians. This accords with the wishes of the majority of the States members to remain part-time.[61] Lastly, the current committee system militates against the development of a party system in the island as no formal hierarchy exists in the executive to match that of a party structure.

As the executive in Jersey is committee-based, it resembles in some ways the structures in English local government before 1974. However, some fundamental differences exist between the old local government model and Jersey's constitution. Firstly, Jersey has a powerful medieval element to its system, most apparent in the fused powers of the Bailiff. Secondly, the States Assembly is elected on three distinct franchises. Thirdly, the States operates within a quasi-federal system alongside twelve powerful Parishes whose Constables form a substantial voting block within the States. Fourthly, the island lacks a party system. Finally, but perhaps most importantly, local authorities lack the need for distinctive and developed external policies in the same way as required by Jersey. Therefore, for the purpose of this study the other Crown Dependencies and the United Kingdom Overseas Territories will be viewed as more effective comparators.

The Policy and Resources Committee was created in 1989 to address the lack of co-ordination within the system. Prior to its formation, all committees were regarded as equal.[62] The Policy and Resources Committee has developed co-ordination procedures which have allowed it to oversee the development of more coherent government, the most important being the institution of strategic policy reviews and action plans. These plans attempt to produce a document which can be regarded as comparable to the Queen's speech in the United Kingdom. The Committee can be accused of monopolising the Office of the Chief Adviser to the States, thereby effectively making it its own secretariat and no longer a resource available to the Assembly as one body. This resource is particularly important in a small state where expertise is in short supply. The fundamental difference between the United Kingdom and Jersey is that Jersey is not governed through a hierarchy and that there are no parties. As a result, any proposals put forward in the chamber rely on the States as a body resisting attempts from its own members to modify them. Co-ordination has been reinforced by the use of 'decision conferencing' in an attempt to bring committees together and prioritise issues across committee boundaries. It is as yet unclear whether this will be successful. Moreover, the continued existence of the Finance and Economics Committee and Establishment Committee has resulted in the Policy and Resources Committee attempting to co-ordinate policy without control over the budget or the civil service. The Committee's powers are therefore limited, forcing it to achieve co-ordination through exhortation. This is helped by the Presidency of the Committee having gained in prestige, becoming the most sought after committee post. But the Policy and Resources Committee's fundamental weakness as a co-ordinating body lies in its inability to enforce any of its decisions, whilst attempts to be more assertive are resisted by other committees who jealously guard their independence.

The States' members elect from amongst their number the presidents and members of each committee. No States' member may be president of more than one standing committee, nor a member of more than two. The election of presidents is the first task of the States after an election. The States does not view those politicians who top the Senatorial poll as automatically meriting the most senior presidencies. The two Senators who received the most votes in the 1993 Senatorial elections were not elected to presidencies. Presidents approach those individuals whom they wish to have on the Committee informally in the hope of receiving their consent before announcing their nomination. Some presidents will find competition exists to be on their committee and will, therefore, be able to select whom they wish to serve with them on the committee. However, with two hundred and ten committee posts to be filled by fifty three States members, some presidents may discover that it is hard to find six other States members to sit on their Committee. It must be noted, however, that the large amount of cross membership of committees by States members acts as a partial substitute for more formal co-ordination.

Any member of the States can be nominated to sit on a Committee in addition to those proposed by the president. This may seem to limit the power of appointment the president enjoys, but in practice, such nominations are rare. A president may regard the action as tantamount to the States imposing on their committee a member whom they do not wish to work with. In response, the president can resign, and by convention, if the president resigns the Committee is deemed to have resigned as a body. In practice, resignation of the individual nominated by the States is a more likely scenario as the president has a number of means of marginalising individuals.[63] The president prepares the agenda with the support of the relevant Chief Officer and the States Greffe and summarises the opinion of committee meetings which forms the basis of the minutes of the meeting. Thus, an opponent must formally minute opposition to have it recorded. Once this summary is agreed, committee responsibility applies and a member of the committee must, in theory, resign if he wishes to oppose the committee line. The convention of committee responsibility is a hindrance to opposition in the States as all proposals of the executive automatically have seven votes in their favour. In committee, all that the proposals need to become policy is the votes of the president and three other committee members. The position of president is further strengthened by the fact that committees, once elected, can only be removed by a vote of no confidence of the States. These votes are rare as, by convention, the proposers of the vote of no confidence must be prepared to form their own committee to replace the one they are seeking to oust. Furthermore, such a vote can also be interpreted as an attack on the ability of almost one seventh of States members.

The power of a committee president is enhanced by the fact that all the administrative support services work solely through the president. The president is also the committee's representative externally, thereby necessitating an element of delegation to the president to interpret policy in these situations. This delegation is particularly apparent when the President of Policy and Resources attends regular meetings with the Home Office and the other Crown Dependencies and must speak for the island and the Committee without having recourse to consultation. Moreover, the role of the media has forced presidents to adopt more of a ministerial approach by explaining policy in interviews and by responding to crises. In both cases policy can be subtly altered in response to questioning and the committee must then decide whether to challenge the president's interpretation of policy, not a step undertaken lightly particularly when the committee as a whole may be under considerable media pressure, or accept the president's view of committee policy.

A final power of the president, which distinguishes him from the rest of the committee, is the ability to select new members to replace anyone who resigns. A president, therefore, has the option to include only those who will agree with his views, rather than those with an interest in the field or a representative cross section of opinion. In other words, the three models of executive government available to any president are a committee reflecting his own views, a committee of all talents or an inclusive committee. The flexibility of the committee system to offer these options represents an advantage it has over some ministerial systems. The president remains, however, more powerful than the individual members in a way which has similarities to the concept of *primus inter pares* when applied to British Prime Ministers. On the other hand, the relative strength and security of the president of a committee does create some stability in what is a fragmented executive.

Judicial Autonomy

Judicial autonomy is expressed in a separate and distinct system of courts, a separate legal profession and a separate body of Norman customary law and tradition which is derived from medieval Norman practice and not from English common law. This legal distinctness has not only allowed the island to modify its legal system to suit the needs of an offshore finance centre, but has also prevented the intrusion of the English courts in a manner which would have eroded hard won political autonomy by enforcing English legal interpretations on the island. Indeed, without the combination of judicial and legislative autonomy acting to reinforce one another, Jersey's current level of political autonomy would have been virtually impossible to sustain.

Whilst the most significant limits on judicial autonomy stem from the authority which external courts exercise over the Royal Court, the most immediate threat comes from the Jersey Court of Appeal. The Court became operative from 1964 and consists of a panel of six English Q.C.s. and, by convention, retired Bailiffs of Jersey and Guernsey, should they wish to sit. The creation of the Court represented the first occasion on which English barristers were allowed to sit in a Jersey Court in their own right and might have led to a reduction of the island's judicial autonomy. However, the appointment of retired Bailiffs from Jersey and Guernsey to the court and the appointment of a Jersey-born English Q.C., Sir Godfrey Le Quesne, as President has helped to prevent the anglicisation of Jersey law which was feared when English barristers were introduced. Local Crown Officers and the local Bar have also retained the sole right to appear before the Court of Appeal as a further measure to protect local judicial autonomy.

The Judicial Committee of the Privy Council is the ultimate court of appeal for the Channel Islands and must be seen as a completely external constraint on judicial autonomy. This Committee must not be confused with a separate quasi-judicial right to appeal to a distinct special Committee on the Affairs of Jersey and Guernsey on constitutional grievances. The Judicial Committee is also the final court of appeal for eighteen independent Commonwealth Countries and all of Britain's remaining dependencies. [64] Four appeals have been made from the island since 1945.

The European Court of Justice has authority over Jersey, despite the island not being a full member of the European Union. The jurisdiction derives from the provisions of Protocol 3 of the United Kingdom's Treaty of Accession to the European Economic Community, but the extent of its jurisdiction is not made explicit in the Protocol. Therefore it is a source of controversy whether the jurisdiction of the court extends to all matters or just those areas specifically covered by the Protocol. This court's importance stems not only from the cases it hears originating in Jersey, but from the fact that its jurisdiction obliges Jersey to enforce any European Union legislation applicable to the island under the Protocol. The requirement to implement European Community legislation imposes a major burden on a small jurisdiction like Jersey.

48

The European Court of Human Rights may also hear cases originating in Jersey provided they are channelled through the United Kingdom as the sovereign power with responsibility for Jersey. [65] Rulings of the International Court of Justice also apply to the island but not in its own right, as the Court has ruled that Jersey is, as far as sovereignty is concerned, part of United Kingdom.[66] The Court's immediate significance in Jersey's context is its confirmation of the United Kingdom's, and hence Jersey's, jurisdiction over the Minquiers and Écréhos groups off the south and east coast of the island. This resolved a long running boundary dispute with France and helped define the extent of the territorial waters the United Kingdom could claim on Jersey's behalf.

Conclusion

A review of Jersey's internal political structures must highlight their stability over time, a facet of the constitution very attractive to offshore finance. The functions of government are highly disaggregated, a situation exaggerated by the lack of parties or committee hierarchies operating within the system. The non-hierarchical committee system, together with the lack of a formal opposition on the island, mean the checks and balances operate within the executive rather than between the executive and the legislature. The fusion of powers in the form of the Bailiff illustrates an anachronistic side to the constitution which may expose Jersey to actions in the European Court of Human Rights. In fact, the survival of a fused system government is evidence of the lack of crisis in Jersey's government and the fact that Jersey is small and dependent. Therefore there is little competition for the role of Bailiff and the United Kingdom provides an avenue of appeal against decisions of the Bailiff. Jersey's political stability has preserved the medieval aspects of the constitution and reform, when it has occurred, has been driven by external events. The partially modernised and uncodified nature of government in Jersey is comparable to the United Kingdom in that components of the constitution function as little more than façades for more efficient elements within it. The fact that the two constitutions are similar makes them more compatible. This is important in maintaining stability within the relationship as is both parties' preference for informal ways of managing the relationship. Moreover, in general, during the period under consideration, the insular authorities have shown considerable ability in managing the constitution with a view to avoiding conflict with the United Kingdom, developing the finance industry and promoting social cohesion.

References

[1] op. cit., Kilbrandon 1973, 441.

[2] Mathews rejects the claim that the Channel Islands are held by the Queen as Duke of Normandy see Mathews, P., "Lé Rouai, Nouot' Duc", Jersey Law Review, June 1999, vol.3, 177-204.

[3] Le Patourel, J., The Medieval Administration of the Channel Islands, Oxford University Press, London, 1937, 88, hereafter, Le Patourel.

[4] Jurats are elected lay officials who act as the sole judges of fact and assessors of damages in most cases before the Royal Court.

[5] op. cit., Le Patourel, 48. It must also be noted that over time the term Governor was used instead of Warden. The last Governor died in 1854 and from that date only a Lieutenant Governor has been appointed.

[6] The death of Sir Robert Houston was the most significant example of this practice. See op. cit., The Offshore Interface, 149.

[7] ibid., 148.

[8] The Superior Council consisted of the Presidents of each of the eight departments which the functions of government were divided into together with the Crown Officers under the Presidency of the Bailiff.

[9] Duret Aubin, C. W., "Recent Constitutional Changes in Jersey", Bulletin of the Société Jersiaise, 1954, Vol. XVI, Part II, 178.

[10] Jersey had experienced party politics in the first half of the nineteenth century; see op. cit., Kelleher, 173.

[11] op. cit., Le Hérissier, 120.

[12] Le Brocq, N. S., Jersey looks forward, The Communist Party, London, 1946, 84.

[13] Report of the Committee of the Privy Council on Proposed Reforms in the Channel Islands, Cmd.7074, HMSO, London, 1947, 2, hereafter, Report of Privy Council 1947.

[14] The term "States Jurats" was replaced by the term "Senator" when the reforms were implemented. The term Senator must not be confused with its more common use to denote a member of an upper chamber or Senate. Jersey retains a unicameral Parliament of which the Senators are members.

[15] The spoken language of the island had been Jersiaise, but from 1873 French and English were taught in schools. Jersiaise, although a dialect of French, is not close enough to allow easy translation, therefore education was in one of two languages foreign to most Jersiaise speakers. Large scale immigration and tourism led to English becoming the dominant language on the island and by 1900, the States had allowed debates in English, see op. cit., Kelleher, 260.

[16] This crises can be dated from a letter by Sir Philip Allen, Permanent Under Secretary of State at the Home Office, to the Lieutenant Governors of Jersey and Guernsey, 3/5/67, hereafter, Allen letter; see op. cit., Heyting.

[17] For details of the insular authority's position see Vibert, R., Memoirs of a Jerseyman, La Haule Books, Jersey, 1991, 139, hereafter, Vibert 1991.

[18] op. cit., Kilbrandon 1973.

[19] The Act cites Navigators and General Insurance Co. Ltd. v Ringrose, (1962) 1 All E. R. 97, C. A. as the precedent for this definition.

[20] Letter from Sir Charles Cunningham to Sir Frank Newsham, 24/9/57, HO284/3.

[21] ibid.

[22] ibid.

[23] Report of a discussion on Reform in Jersey, HO284/3.

[24] The Bailiff acts as Deputy to the Lieutenant Governor.

[25] Letter to the Secretary of State from the Lieutenant Governor of Jersey, 20/1/58, HO284/3.

[26] Vibert, R., Parliament without Parties The Committee System in The States of the Island of Jersey, States Greffe, Jersey, 1990, 3.

[27] States of Jersey Law 1966.

[28] op. cit., Vibert 1991, 165. The term Father of the House is used in the same way as the House

of Commons to denote the longest serving member of the Assembly.

[29] Bailiffs in this period have been Baron Coutanche of St Brelade and the City of Westminster (formerly Sir Alexander Moncrieff Coutanche) 1935-61, Cecil Stanley Harrison 1962, Sir Robert Hugh Le Masurier 1962-74, Sir Herbert Frank Cobbold Ereaut 1975-85, Sir Peter Leslie Crill 1986-95, Sir Philip Martin Bailhache 1995- . This list is derived from Crill, P., "The Ancient Role of the Bailiffs of Guernsey and Jersey as 'speakers'" in Société Jersiaise Annual Bulletin for 1997, vol. 27 pt. 1, 79-84.

[30] op. cit., Le Hérissier, 79.

[31] Interview with Sir Peter Crill, 10/4/97, hereafter, Crill interview.

[32] ibid.

[33] op. cit., Report of Privy Council 1947, 41 and op. cit., Kilbrandon 1973, 128.

[34] ibid.

[35] "Double role of Bailiff attacked", Jersey Evening Post, 4/3/97, 2.

[36] European Commission of Human Rights, Application No. 28488/95, Richard James McGonnell v United Kingdom, adopted 20/10/98.

[37] op. cit., Crill interview.

[38] The Parishes of St Clement, St Helier and St Saviour have population densities of 1,901, 3,200 and 1,363 persons per square kilometre. All other parishes have densities of less than 1,000 per square kilometre, op. cit., Census 1996, 26.

[39] In Jersey the term "Law" or "Loi" corresponds to Acts of Parliament in the United Kingdom.

[40] op. cit., Kilbrandon 1973, 103.

[41] op. cit., Heyting, 30.

[42] op. cit., Kilbrandon 1973, 103.

[43] ibid.

[44] ibid., 10.

[45] Although no legislation has been imposed, the Prime Minister blocked the operation of a separate Channel Island airline at the time of the 1946 Civil Aviation Act by stating that such an airline would be denied landing rights in the United Kingdom, op. cit., Le Hérissier, 186.

[46] op. cit., Kilbrandon 1973, 103.

[47] Interview with Deemster Cain, 17/5/96.

[48] op. cit., Heyting, 30.

[49] op. cit., Kilbrandon 1973, 103.

[50] ibid., 104.

[51] op. cit., Le Hérissier, 38.

[52] Report of the Commissioners appointed to inquire into the Civil, Municipal and Ecclesiastical Laws of the Island of Jersey, London, 1861, vii & First Report of the Commissioners appointed to inquire into the state of the Criminal Law in the Channel Islands, London, 1847, xi.

[53] Rapport du Comité pour prendre en considération les raisons donnée par Son Excellence le Lieutenant-Governor en apposant sa Voix négative au Règlement sur les Marchés, Jersey, 1882 & Ordre du Conseil relativement aux pouvoirs des Etats de passer des Règlement Provisoires Triennaux, R des L., T.IV-VI, 46.

[54] European Community Legislation (Implementation) (Jersey) Law 1996.

[55] Figure correct as at December 1996.

[56] States of Jersey, Budget Extract 1997, Jersey Evening Post, Jersey, 1997, 17.

[57] Figure correct as at December 1996.

[58] *KPMG* Peat Marwick McLintock, States Of Jersey: A review of the Machinery of government, States Greffe, Jersey, 1987, 51, hereafter, Peat Marwick.

[59] ibid.

[60] States of Jersey, Committees of the States: Reorganization, P. 107/96, States Greffe, Jersey, 1996.

[61] States Members Remuneration (P.31/96) Report, States Greffe, Jersey, 1996, 2. The report endorsed the belief "that the principle of honorary service should by maintained within the States".

[62] The terms of reference of the Committee were adopted on 24/1/89.

[63] One such conflict arose when Deputy Dorey was appointed to the Education Committee. The Deputy criticised the President for discussing with the local paper an audit of secondary schools without first discussing the issue with the Committee. This led to calls for the Deputy's resignation. See Herbert, C., "Resignation call after Deputy's outburst", Jersey Weekly Post, 22/2/96, 7 and Falle, P., "Deputy resigns from Education", Jersey Evening Post, 14/5/97, 1.

[64] op. cit., Whitaker's 1995, 370.

[65] For example Application No.8873/80, Michael Dun v United Kingdom, claiming that the applicant's rights were infringed by his inability to vote in United Kingdom elections. The application was declared inadmissible by the Commission.

[66] Rodwell, W., Les Écréhous Jersey, Société Jersiaise, Jersey, 1996, 333-344, hereafter, Rodwell.

Chapter 3 - External Policy Development: The Operation of Autonomy

Introduction

Jersey possesses autonomy over its domestic and fiscal agendas subject only to the good government powers claimed by the Home Office on behalf of the Crown. These arrangements are given flexibility by the normally good relationship between the Jersey and United Kingdom authorities. This flexibility has proved more and more necessary as international and European Union agreements have been concluded with increasing frequency in areas traditionally regarded as the province of the insular authorities. The island's autonomy is extensive; in fact, for many functions of government the situation is equivalent to independence with overt intervention by the United Kingdom being extremely rare.

Political autonomy is buttressed by Jersey's successful economy, based on the operation of an offshore finance centre, which allows the island to fund all government spending without recourse to the United Kingdom. If Jersey were to rely on its metropolitan power for financial assistance in meeting its public expenditure needs, autonomy would be reduced as the United Kingdom would expect a role in defining budgetary priorities. As the experience of other British dependencies indicates, economic self sufficiency is crucial. Once a dependency is self-supporting it can usually gain almost total political independence if it so desires. The only caveat is that Britain's own perceived interest must not be harmed and it must not be embarrassed internationally by the dependency, for example, through endemic corruption or fiscal crime. However, if a territory is economically dependent on Britain, strict criteria and conditions are attached to the aid and, in effect, the dependency's economy is taken over by the metropolitan power.[1] A vital aspect of fiscal autonomy is the fact that it enables Jersey to enter into regime competition with other offshore finance centres. This is achieved by attempting to maintain a superior business environment for the finance industry compared to other offshore finance centres. If Jersey were not able to vary its fiscal laws, this would be impossible.

External Policy Aims

Before assessing external policy in Jersey, it is necessary to recapitulate the context within which the term is used in this book. Jersey is not a state and therefore does not have the ability to enter into binding agreements with sovereign states. This represents both the legal orthodoxy and the formal position of other sovereign states to the island. The Home Office defined the position of the Crown Dependencies as "neither part of the United Kingdom nor independent sovereign states."[2] Strictly stated, the constitutional position is therefore that only the United Kingdom can formally represent Jersey abroad and enter into international agreements on its behalf. However, this statement does not represent the reality of Jersey's situation as a number of developments have required the island to have its own external policies.

Jersey is, however, allowed considerable autonomy by the United Kingdom with respect to whether international agreements should be extended to the island. The insular authorities also maintain informal contacts with the European Union, France, and other Commonwealth microstates. More important, however, are the links which Jersey maintains with other Crown Dependencies and the United Kingdom. These links may not be considered external in strictly legal terms, but if an attempt is to be made to study Jersey as a dependency and the extent to which that status is managed to ensure Jersey's continued prosperity, such a division is necessary. It also reflects the fact that policy derived from influences outside the island is perceived as alien and an externally derived threat to Jersey's distinct legal and political heritage.

The aims of Jersey's external policy can be derived from the Policy and Resources Committee's mission statement.[3] This includes several objectives which entail external policy action if they are to be achieved. One such aim is "A permanent resident population the same or less than the current level", another "the maintenance of the island's low tax status" and the third significant commitment is "the retention of the Island's existing relationship with the United Kingdom and the European Union." More detailed policy aims concern environmental protection, an objective requiring more co-operation with neighbours, and the implementation of international agreements. Another aim is to improve the island's infrastructure which involves maintaining excellent transport links with the United Kingdom.[4] The Strategic Policy Review also includes a specific section on international relations and in the list of agreed objectives it restates the aim of preserving the *status quo* with respect to the European Union and the United Kingdom. Policy on international agreements is summarised as "international conventions and agreements to be extended to the Island with proper regard for the circumstances and interests of the Island" and "to make more generally available information on international conventions and agreements to which the Island is or is not a party." [5] The Policy and Resources Committee is also considering the merits of a Bill of Rights for the island together with the possibility that three United Nations' Conventions, regarding Children's Rights, the Elimination of Racial Discrimination and Women's Rights, should be extended to the island.

The fundamental justification for having an external policy is, therefore, to maintain the viability of the finance industry which dominates the island's economy. It is because Jersey's external policy has different aims to those underlying British foreign policy that a distinctive external policy must be developed. The most common controversies in the area of external policy arise over the question whether individual international conventions or agreements should be extended to the island by the United Kingdom. The policy's geographical focus is on the relationships with the United Kingdom and the European Union. France, despite its historical connection, is economically of little significance and as a result little effort is put into promoting links. Consequently, any policy issues which arise tend to be caused by France's geographical proximity.

Relations with the United Kingdom and the European Union

The oldest justification for Jersey pursuing an external policy is to safeguard its autonomy from encroachment. Jersey's partially modernised medieval constitution is vulnerable to external pressure to reform its more archaic elements. Alf Dubs, MP has criticised the system as being akin to "benevolent paternalism." [6] However, the uncodified nature of Jersey's autonomy is also a strength in that it preserves the distinctive and flexible elements of the constitution while enabling modernisation by evolution where necessary. Any attempt to develop a rational codification would inevitability destroy some of the flexibility inherent in the current arrangement and reduce the ability of the relationship to evolve over time. The option of the replacement of evolution with reform by periodic constitutional conferences would automatically introduce political and financial instability into the relationship, thereby damaging the island's finance industry. Codification was rejected by the Royal Commission in 1973, despite Jersey requesting it. [7] The durability of the post-war settlement has been such that, fifty years on, the system established survives in something close to its original form. This suggests that Jersey's external policies have established a successful survival strategy.

The most significant external relationship Jersey has to manage is that with its metropolitan power. This is not only because of the constitutional and economic sway the United Kingdom has over the island, but also because all formal external contacts are carried out via the United Kingdom. The relationship is intimate and largely informal, and its success depends on the ability of the actors involved to maintain effective working relationships. In 1957 Sir Charles Cunningham described the relationship as "Business is normally transacted by means of semi official letters, it is very rarely indeed that a formal policy letter is sent to either of the Lieutenant Governors, and that is only sent after its terms have been informally agreed with the Bailiff." [8] The Policy and Resources Committee's stated aim of maintaining the existing relationship must be qualified because, as with all uncodified relationships, opinion can differ as to its exact nature. [9] Therefore, the Committee's aim is perhaps best described as preserving the interpretation of the relationship as it is currently understood by the insular authorities. Frequent and public intervention in insular affairs by the United Kingdom, even if constitutionally permissible, would not only lead to public hostility in Jersey towards the United

Kingdom but would also cause the kind of political instability which would precipitate the withdrawal of the finance industry.

From time to time, however, the island has perceived threats to its political stability. In 1981 the Labour MP George Foulkes sought to introduce a Bill targeting the use of the island's fiscal privileges to avoid tax in the United Kingdom.[10] Such calls to restrict the fiscal privileges of the island to prevent tax leakage from the United Kingdom economy have become more frequent in the mid-nineties.[11] They came to a head in an announcement by the Home Office on 20 January 1998 of "a wide ranging review of the financial legislation and regulatory system in Jersey, Guernsey and the Isle of Man." [12] These actions are perceived as threatening by the island, not only because of the threat they represent to the island's autonomy, but also because they damage the image of the offshore finance centre on which the island's economy is dependent. The island, therefore, tends to be wary of the Labour party as most attacks emanate from those on the left of that party. The insular authorities, however, are on the whole, satisfied with the current relationship which is demonstrated by their desire to maintain it.

Jersey wishes to preserve the current situation with respect to the European Community which adopts a similar policy towards Jersey to that of the United Kingdom, in that neither harbours any desire to alter the island's political status or damage the island economically. In his last statement as President of the Commission, Jacques Delors confirmed the constitutional *status quo*.[13] However, moves towards fiscal harmonisation or pressure to prevent funds leaking to offshore finance centres in general could cause damage, both directly through preventing funds being invested in the island and indirectly by eroding Jersey's fiscal autonomy.[14] At present all parties are satisfied with the current Protocol arrangements with respect to the relationship. However, Jersey employs a lawyer in Brussels to warn the island of potential threats originating from the European Union. The fact that any threats posed by the European Union are likely to result from collateral damage from policies not drafted with Jersey in mind makes reassurances about the status of the Protocol of limited value. Such threats would arise from more general moves towards fiscal harmonisation. The European Union is happy to reassure the Channel Islands that it has no wish to challenge their status.[15] This statement is used locally to reassure critics about potential threats from the European Union. Neither side is willing to discuss, at least in public, how to counter long-term attrition of Jersey's position by actions not targeted specifically at the island. The United Kingdom might be expected to use its veto to protect Jersey's status. However, such a willingness might not extend to an economic, rather than a constitutional, threat. It is also unclear whether the United Kingdom would be prepared to use its veto to protect Jersey if the use of the veto destroyed a wider agreement which it supported. At the time of the United Kingdom's accession, it was made clear that Jersey's hostility towards its own inclusion in the EEC would be sacrificed to gain the wider United Kingdom aim of membership.[16]

The Structure of the Economy and External Policy

The fact that Jersey hosts a major offshore finance centre requires it to maintain a separate external policy. The core of this policy is the protection and promotion of the finance industry based on the island. The preservation of the offshore finance centre is an essential policy aim as the island would not be economically viable without a finance industry. The dominance of the finance industry has led Mark Hampton to argue that international financial capital has captured the state in Jersey.[17] For the offshore finance centre to prosper, Jersey must attract financial institutions, often in competition with the United Kingdom or the other Crown Dependencies. To succeed in this involves not only interaction with multinational financial institutions, but also an awareness and a capacity to react to developments within international financial regulations by such bodies as the United States Federal Reserve or the Commission of the European Communities.

Jersey's tourism and agricultural industry require a limited degree of external policy management. Indeed, Jersey would be far less active in this field if these industries still constituted the island's economy as both are dependent on the British market.[18] Accession to the European Economic Community had the potential to create a customs boundary between Jersey and the United Kingdom. Jersey's decision to accept association with the European Union was dictated by the need to maintain free access to the United Kingdom market for its agricultural products.[19] The common agricultural policy also represents an external threat since Jersey is being forced to subsidise its own industry to enable it to compete with the heavily supported European industries. The insular tourist industry views fiscal harmonisation in the European Community as a threat too as one of its main marketing advantages is the existence of duty free products on the island.

Jersey's external policies with respect to the other Crown Dependencies are ambivalent. The United Kingdom and international bodies, such as the European Community, tend to treat the Crown Dependencies as a single entity and this practice tends to create a community of interest. However, the idea of integrating the Channel Islands, or even the Crown Dependencies, as one political entity has never received strong support in the islands, despite the United Kingdom administering the Crown Dependencies as one unit.[20] One of the very few combined Channel Island operations is the local independent television station. The ambivalence is derived from the fact that all the Crown Dependencies are economically dependent on offshore finance centres and compete with one another for business, but have a shared interest in preserving their peculiar constitutional links to the United Kingdom and the European Union. Without the financial autonomy derived from these links, there would be no finance industries offshore. Therefore, the Crown Dependencies may be seen as politically less integrated with one another than the United Kingdom is in relation to the European Union. This situation exists despite similar historical experiences and strong external links between the Crown Dependencies based on informal contacts and pooling of knowledge. Moreover, annual meetings between the Crown Dependencies occur which supplement the six-monthly meetings all attend at the Home Office. The informal nature of the relationship is a reflection of the small number of individuals involved and close working relationships developed.

The Influence of other International Bodies on Jersey

Jersey's policy towards France is notable by its absence. Despite recent attempts to revitalise the link, policy-making in this area lacks focus and direction. In economic terms there is little in the relationship to manage. This is due in part to the finance industry's dominant focus on English-speaking markets. The tendency is exaggerated by a French tradition of hostility to offshore finance centres. The French government has largely reciprocated Jersey's indifference. The lack of French interest in the island is best illustrated by the decision in 1993 to replace the full time French consul with an honorary official. The relationship is, however, stronger with neighbouring French regions and both Normandy and Brittany have sought to promote links with a Norman office operating in St Helier and a local civil servant seconded to Normandy for six months in 1997. The links between France concentrate on the proximity of French nuclear installations and disputes over shared fishing ground and airspace over the island. It could thus be said that the relationship with France is dominated by the management of a series of issues resulting from the island's geographical proximity with the traditional cultural links being peripheral.

The fact that the United States of America can be regarded as a threat to the island is a reflection of the global nature of Jersey's economy.[21] It is the United States' assertive and hostile attitude to offshore finance centres which is dangerous for Jersey.[22] The policy response of local authorities has been through membership of such groups as the Offshore Group of Banking Supervisors. This group seeks to reassure the regulatory authorities of larger nations that the offshore finance centres are well-regulated and do not represent a threat to other economies. Pressure is exerted by the United States ranking offshore finance centres and in recent tables Jersey has performed worse than Guernsey and the Isle of Man. This measure represents a serious threat by damaging investor confidence in Jersey's finance industry.

Jersey maintains relationships with other Crown Dependencies and Commonwealth small states through the Commonwealth Parliamentary Association. This group not only recognises a community of interests between these territories, but is also an attempt to pool experiences. The value of the group to all of the small states involved has been emphasised by Dr John Henderson of the Commonwealth Parliamentary Associations International Division - "The main reason is it gives them a unique platform. There they can talk to the rest of the Commonwealth on equal terms. They take the CPA meetings very seriously. They send high powered delegations and make a lot of effort on their main concerns."[23] Jersey was instrumental in founding the

58

Conference of Members from Small Countries; the aim of which is to gather together the parliaments of the smaller states and territories of the Commonwealth to pool ideas and information. Membership of the Commonwealth, therefore, allows Jersey to exchange ideas at both formal and informal meetings with countries whose scale may make their advice more relevant in certain circumstances than that of the United Kingdom. The Jersey delegate at the 1995 Commonwealth Parliamentary Association conference "strongly advocated co-operation among small states to prevent them from being marginalized."[24] Moreover, Jersey has sought to use this venue to promote its own political model to other small states and territories.[25] The Commonwealth Parliamentary Association also acts as a forum in which Jersey can have a presence on an international stage independently of the United Kingdom and appear to function as a state. Reginald Jeune, a former President of the Policy and Resources Committee, emphasised the importance of the Association as a forum for the island where it could maximise its external contacts.[26] The prestige associated with membership of the organisation is enhanced by the fact that in 1990 a local politician, Senator Jeune, was treasurer of the association. A final reason for support for the Commonwealth apparent on the island is that Jersey's somewhat archaic and uncodified constitutional settlement has more in common with many in the Commonwealth than with European codified constitutions, a factor which helps to make the idea of the Commonwealth more attractive than that of the European Union.

A major threat to the island's autonomy which the island shares with many other Commonwealth microstates is the trade in illegal narcotics. Jersey is fortunate in that, unlike many of Britain's Caribbean Dependencies, it is not on a major drugs transhipment route. Jersey does, however, have a relatively rich population and therefore makes a tempting target for those seeking to sell illegal drugs. Jersey is also vulnerable to the allegation that as an offshore finance centre the profits from the trade are being laundered on the island. Moreover, a widespread perception exists that the operation of offshore finance centres and drugs trafficking are linked. Julia Pascal argues that "sex lines, arms deals, drug and money laundering"[27] all benefit from the United Kingdom's toleration of Jersey operating as an offshore finance centre. Consequently, while the simplistic perception of such a link must be challenged, the authorities in Jersey see the importation and use of illegal drugs as a threat, not only because of the damage the trade may do to the social fabric of the island, but also because of allegations being made about the origin of the funds being deposited in the island and the damage done to the image of the offshore finance centre.[28]

The Influence of Jersey's Demographic Structure on External Policy

The existence of significant French, Portuguese and Irish minorities in Jersey gives these nations an interest in the internal affairs of the island, if only to protect the rights of their citizens.[29] The Portuguese community, in particular, tends to be concentrated in lower status and lower paid occupations and their welfare is more likely to be monitored by the Portuguese government. Britain's membership of the European Union has enhanced the potential influence France, Ireland and Portugal have over the island. In particular, it has increased the possible benefits to the United Kingdom of not defending Jersey's position against a group of nations with which the United Kingdom has many shared economic and political interests.

Only fifty-two per cent of the population of Jersey were born there and this has profound implications for external policy.[30] The most likely cause of conflict between those locally born and those born outside the island has been on the subject of housing rights. The island's Housing Law renders the right to buy and rent property dependent on birth and can, therefore, be regarded as discriminatory. It creates what are in terms of housing rights, and hence *de facto* right of abode, second class citizens. As thirty-seven per cent of Jersey's population are United Kingdom born and thus citizens of the country of which Jersey is a dependency, the island is particularly vulnerable to British born citizens appealing to their own government to use its influence to overturn the Housing Law. An example of such an appeal occurred in 1994 when the Labour MP David Hanson tabled a motion in the Commons "condemning Jersey's 'discriminatory' residence policy for UK citizen's employed on fixed term contracts."[31] The motion derived from a complaint by two of the MP's constituents whose daughter was on a contract which granted her housing rights for the duration of the contract only. The ability of such a large proportion of the population to appeal to the island's metropolitan power for protection creates a situation where decisions, which in other jurisdictions would be viewed as entirely domestic, have the potential to provoke external intervention.

The operation of the Housing Law also demonstrates the effective management of Jersey's dependency status. It succeeds in maintaining a form of immigration control acceptable to external authorities, whilst maintaining the benefits of British nationality for the island's citizens.[32] Further, neither the European Union, nor the United Kingdom have challenged the housing regulations in Jersey.[33] Shared nationality is a vital part of Jersey's population policy as it allows Jersey to import the specialist employees necessary to operate an offshore finance centre from the United Kingdom using short term contracts. It also allows Jersey-born people to move to the United Kingdom, should they wish to do so. This is important as Jersey still suffers from a considerable amount of emigration. The ability of Jersey-born workers to move across what would otherwise be an immigration boundary allows those individuals to gain experience outside of Jersey. As illustrated by the last slow down in economic growth, it effectively reduces social problems since it allows Jersey to export its unemployment to the United Kingdom which has more comprehensive unemployment provision.[34] Thus dependency status allows Jersey citizens to have the rights associated with full British nationality while, via the Housing Law, maintaining *de facto* immigration controls through denying the right to buy or rent property on the island, thereby reducing the population pressure.

Options to the *Status Quo*: Independence or Absorption

It should be emphasised that Jersey's autonomy is not without advantages for the United Kingdom. While the *status quo* is maintained, Jersey is prosperous and politically stable. If the United Kingdom were to absorb Jersey, and this has never been United Kingdom government policy, it would not only cause resentment on the island as it has never been part of the United Kingdom, but also remove the basis of Jersey's dominant industry, finance. Barring finance, it is difficult to envisage another industry which could ensure full employment for such a geographically peripheral society. Therefore, if Jersey were to be integrated which, although unlikely, must be within the scope of the good government powers, it would have to fall back on its far weaker tourism and agricultural sectors. The United Kingdom would thus acquire an island with a collapsing economy with the resulting effect that the United Kingdom would have to subsidise the insular economy, at the very least in the form of welfare payments. Additionally, a degree of political instability would result from such an economic collapse and the United Kingdom might well have to absorb large-scale emigration from the island.

The other alternative to the *status quo* is to offer the island independence. However, it is difficult to see how this option would be of more benefit than the present situation. Independence would allow the United Kingdom to formally distance itself from any actions of the island. As such, it would no longer be responsible for an offshore finance centre towards which both the European Union and the United States, together with some back bench Labour MPs, have expressed hostility. However, at present it has the influence and ultimately the power to ensure that Jersey does not become an embarrassment to the United Kingdom internationally. If Jersey were independent, the United Kingdom would be left in a situation where it would be assumed to have power over the island due to its long historical links, but in fact would lack the power to change insular policy without provoking an international dispute with Jersey. It is also likely that the finance industry would decline. Past experience seems to indicate a preference amongst financial institutions to invest in British dependencies rather than in newly independent states. The most vivid example was the flow of funds from the Bahamas to the Cayman Islands when the Bahamas were granted independence.[35] If Jersey's economy were to decline as a result of independence it would result in emigration to the United Kingdom as thirty seven per cent of the population are United Kingdom born. This would be supplemented by those individuals who would move to the United Kingdom fearing that the change in the relationship would impede the free movement of individuals which currently exists between the two islands. It is also likely that any funds leaving Jersey would flow to other offshore finance centres instead of being repatriated to the United Kingdom. This would mean that the United Kingdom, rather than having some influence over capital movements, would have none at all. If Jersey were to be granted independence, the United Kingdom and the European Union would lose sovereignty over a significant area of the English Channel. While there is no evidence of oil bearing strata near Jersey, the waters do contain important stocks of fish and shellfish. Jersey's territorial waters, if set at twelve miles, would amount to over one thousand square miles and under international law Jersey would be able to claim up to two hundred miles, where appropriate. Jersey's independence would, therefore, exacerbate the current fishing disputes within Europe. In addition, in periods of geopolitical instability, the United Kingdom's security would decrease as the island occupies a strategic position at the mouth of the English Channel and the United Kingdom would no longer be able to rely automatically on the island not being sympathetic to a hostile power.

The United Kingdom has not excluded independence as an option for the island. If Jersey wants absolute control over its external affairs it must seek independence. This option is little discussed by either party although, when the issue is raised, neither side views it as remotely desirable at present.[36] Both sides, however, acknowledge it is a possibility. The last offer of independence as an alternative was made at the time of the United Kingdom's accession to the European Economic Community. The action of Her Majesty's Government in offering independence as an option when the island felt its political and fiscal rights were threatened would seem to confirm this view.[37] The island considered Protocol 3 to be a far better option than independence at the time. However, independence would have been considered more seriously if the alternative had been full membership which was viewed as destroying Jersey's constitutional autonomy with respect to the United Kingdom. As the Protocol was accepted, it is difficult to judge the extent to which the highlighting of the option of independence was in part an attempt to scare the island into line on an issue the United Kingdom was not prepared to compromise on as the island would have been regarded at the time as too small to be a viable independent state. Recent developments in the European Union, including the introduction of the Euro, have rekindled insular interest in independence as an option, should the burdens these developments impose prove detrimental to the island's interests. The issues were discussed at a conference entitled "Jersey in or out of Europe" held on 11 September 1997. In his presentation to the conference, Colin Powell recalled that Jersey was offered independence in 1971 in relation to Britain's accession to the EEC and argued that "Jersey could consider becoming independent if the European Community sought to impose burdens on the Island".[38]

The Home Office's and Foreign and Commonwealth Office's evidence to the Kilbrandon Commission give the reasons why independence is not favoured by the United Kingdom. Four considerations were cited when assessing what constitutional arrangements were desirable, "the ultimate responsibility of the Crown for the good government of the islands, their geographical proximity, the economic relationships and the need to avoid submerging such small communities under administrative burdens."[39] The submission also emphasised the Crown Dependencies' distinctive status due to their ancient links and propinquity to the Crown. Thus a parameter of maintaining international coherence in the British Islands is defined by the Home Office. Further, "the British Islands are an entity in the eyes of the world and Her Majesty's Government would be held responsible internationally if practices in the Islands were to overstep the limits of acceptability."[40] The evidence also points to the economic interrelation of the Crown Dependencies and argues that "without some compatibility of legislation it would be easy for practices to develop in the Islands, particularly in the commercial field, that would be detrimental to the economic well-being of the British Islands as a whole."[41] Despite the modern Jersey economy being more global in nature than at the time of the Royal Commission, the latter phrase may be seen as more as more relevant today in that it is in the United Kingdom's interest to have some control over three major offshore finance centres to protect both its own image abroad and its own economy.

Independence, therefore, would be potentially disastrous for Jersey and also to the United Kingdom's disadvantage. It is therefore in the United Kingdom's interest to allow a high degree of autonomy in return for the island's acceptance of the United Kingdom as a sovereign power. These statements would seem to reinforce the policy already seen to apply in the field of international relations where the island will be allowed full autonomy except where exercising autonomy runs counter to the United Kingdom's interests. At that stage Jersey will be informed of the conflict and, only if Jersey does not accept the United Kingdom's position, will the United Kingdom intervene. Accordingly, such interventions are rare and not undertaken without informal warnings. Events which are perceived as external interventions by the United Kingdom may also be, at least in part, the result of internal requests. Jersey's inclusion in the Kilbrandon report are examples of this process. Jersey's inclusion in Kilbrandon is widely attributed to its representations to the Home Office on the constitutional effects of the United Kingdom's membership of the European Economic Community. As the request had become vociferous, the decision was made to include the Crown Dependencies in the Royal Commission to look into the complaints.[42]

It is difficult to see what Jersey could gain from independence beyond what it has already. In terms of defence, even if Jersey funded its own separate forces at considerable expense, it would still rely on help from the United Kingdom against any substantial emergency. In terms of external relationships, any move to independence would mean renegotiating Protocol 3 and it is unlikely that the member states of the European Union would allow Jersey as generous a deal as it was offered in 1973, now that the island is a major finance centre. More broadly, in all international discussions it would lose the support of the United Kingdom which has been very useful, despite the fact that in such negotiations Jersey's interests have to compete with many other factors for the United Kingdom's attention. Independence would also create a barrier between

Jersey and its largest market threatening tourism and agriculture. Just as importantly, the United Kingdom is a vital source of labour for the island and a place where islanders can develop careers before returning home. A separate citizenship which would result from independence, would reduce all these advantages currently enjoyed by the island. Moreover, it would create a situation in which a large number of families would be divided by nationality. On the other hand, Jersey would acquire a freedom of manoeuvre in international affairs, but at the cost of very little positive influence on events. This would give it full notional control of its economy, although it would be cut off from automatic access to its European neighbours and thus rendered very vulnerable to every shift in the world economy. It would take a very small currency movement to absorb any insular reserves which could be built up to defend the home currency. Perhaps, however, the worst consequence would be to cut the island off from links which date back hundreds of years and at present dominate both the economy and culture of the island.

International Agreements

The equating of external policy developments with threats to the island's autonomy is particularly evident in the debate surrounding international agreements where those seeking the adoption of such agreements face the charge that they are diluting the island's autonomy.[43] This phenomenon, which effectively amounts to an appeal to nationalism, also restricts the ability of any opposition to appeal for external support, be it from the media or the constitutional avenues of appeal which form part of the island's dependency relationship. Any such actions are viewed as fundamentally disloyal. The discussion of internal problems outside the island is seen as damaging the island's image and possibly threatening its autonomy. As a result, individuals embarking on this course of action face strong pressure to desist.[44]

International law with reference to the island is complex and its beneficial application to the island requires effective co-ordination with the United Kingdom. With regard to international agreements, Jersey's interests are not always identical to those of its sovereign power. In these cases Jersey may wish to adopt a different position. The United Kingdom alone has the authority to represent Jersey abroad. Jersey is thus unable to represent itself formally and must channel its international communications through the Home Office. The Home Office will then via the Foreign and Commonwealth Office present these views to the governments involved. In 1950, the Home Office created the space for this to happen by separating the Crown Dependencies from the United Kingdom with respect to international agreements by declaring that "His Majesty's Government has come to the conclusion that it would be more consistent with the constitutional position of these Islands to regard them for international purposes as not forming part of the United Kingdom of Great Britain and Northern Ireland."[45] The result of the decision was that "any treaty or international agreement to which His Majesty's Government in the United

Kingdom may become a party after the date of the present dispatch will not be considered as applying to the Channel Islands or the Isle of Man by reason only of the fact it applies to the United Kingdom of Great Britain and Northern Ireland, and any signature, ratification, acceptance or accession on behalf of the United Kingdom will not extend to the Islands unless they are expressly included."[46]

The United Kingdom allows the Crown Dependencies the right to determine the application of international agreement to their own territories.[47] This right is not, however, absolute. Though the right to independent and leisurely consideration of the application of conventions to the island has been a consistent post-war aspiration of island politicians, it has not been granted.[48] In his oral evidence to the Kilbrandon

Commission, Professor Jennings argued on behalf of the States of Jersey that if the United Kingdom was unable to sign an international agreement without securing for Jersey the ability to opt out of the agreement "for constitutional reasons it would be in the circumstances not be possible for the United Kingdom, without a breach of constitutional understandings and convention, to become a party unless Jersey were to co-operate".[49] This was supported in the memorandum submitted to the Commission by the States of Jersey which stated that "Apprehensions would be allayed if the United Kingdom Government were in a position to give an assurance that it would not ratify, except with the concurrence of the States, any international agreement requiring legislative implementation in Jersey on domestic matters."[50] The United Kingdom has refused to give the island what would be in effect a veto over elements of British foreign policy. However, it has sought to reassure Jersey that it would be given as much notice as possible of pending agreements and that efforts would be made wherever possible to insert territorial application clauses or their equivalent.[51] This circular has been interpreted in practice to mean that Jersey may determine whether it wishes an international agreement to be ratified on its behalf by the United Kingdom, except in four circumstances. First, agreements which do not permit the insertion of territorial application articles allowing the United Kingdom to specify which of its dependencies wish to ratify the treaty; second, the United Kingdom may feel that it is contrary to its national interest to allow Jersey to exclude itself from ratification, for example, for security reasons or the rapid consideration and implementation of a treaty; third, the United Kingdom also reserves the right to impose an agreement on the island should it deem that agreement to be in Jersey's best interests. This power derives from the good government provisions of the constitution and has not yet been formally exercised. A fourth area where the United Kingdom may seek to impose an agreement is when Jersey's accession is dictated by its geographical proximity to its metropolitan power. Hence the United Kingdom's accession to the European Economic Community required special arrangements with respect to Jersey. The policy of the insular authorities towards conventions remains that they are "to be extended to the Island with proper regard for the circumstances and interests of the Island".[52] However, it must be emphasised that the possibility of opting out of all international agreements no longer exists and attempts by Sark to refuse to allow the extension of such international agreements as Maastricht have been blocked by the United Kingdom.

The agreement on international agreements reached in 1950 was challenged by the Vienna Convention on the Law of Treaties of 1969. Article 29 states that "Unless a different intention appears from the treaty, a treaty is binding upon each party in respect of its entire territory."[53] This clause required the United Kingdom to seek to negotiate, rather than just declare, a territorial application article on behalf of its dependencies in each new international agreement. Such declarations had been normal practice prior to the signing of the Vienna Convention. Both the treaty itself and the difficulties the United Kingdom faced in adding territorial application articles after the Vienna Convention's signature derived from the interplay of Jersey's anomalous constitutional status, the cold war and the burgeoning anti-colonial lobby. It was an easy assumption to make, in particular for the newly independent colonies, that Jersey was another British colony ripe for independence. Furthermore, the idea of a territory preferring to remain a dependency, let alone benefiting from such status, had very little currency, the concept being anathema, not only to communist states and many of the newly independent states, but also to sections of Western opinion. The inclusion of territorial application clauses was therefore opposed by many states, in the view of the Foreign and Commonwealth Office's legal advisers on the basis that "the spurious argument that they [territorial application clauses] somehow condoned the existence of non-metropolitan territories of a colonial nature."[54] The United Kingdom sought to finesse the problem from 1967 by submitting Notes to the Depository to institutions unwilling to allow territorial application clauses.[55] These notes specified the extent of application of individual international agreements. The practice has also been adopted by the Netherlands and Denmark in respect of their dependencies which are granted similar autonomy in this area. A fundamental problem, however, remains with this policy in that it is only feasible if it is compatible with the object and purpose of a treaty. Thus a class of treaties still exists which the United Kingdom feels it is necessary for it to ratify and where no means exist to prevent Jersey from being automatically included. One such case was the European Convention on Extradition which states in Article 27 that the Convention shall apply to the Channel Islands and the Isle of Man.

It would be easy to portray the insular authorities' worries with respect to international agreements as a manifestation of insular and parochial hostility to the wider world. However, such agreements present genuine problems for small dependencies. At a practical level international agreements tend to assume the resources of a large state with a civil service to match. The report on the Office of the Chief Adviser suggests that administering these agreements should form part of the duties of one civil servant.[56] This staffing level indicates the average level of resources made available for the processing of international agreements since the war. The amount of agreements to be processed, however, does not decline proportionately to Jersey's size. In the period from April 1 to September 30 1996, eleven agreements were submitted to the island for consideration for the first time, eleven agreements were pending action by the insular authorities, twenty-three had been considered and decisions reached and thirteen were awaiting insular legislation.[57] These figures do not include any European Community directives extended to the island in the period. The agreements are not only numerous, but also often not relevant to Jersey. In the period under consideration a Draft United Nations Declaration on the Rights of Indigenous Peoples was considered by the insular authorities. The matter was resolved by accepting the advice of the Home Office Legal Adviser's Branch "that the Bailiwick has no "indigenous people" as defined in the United Nations' Declaration."[58] Agreements can also require legislation to be implemented to take effect. This argument was used by the Policy and Resources Committee for Jersey not seeking to extend the United Nations' Convention on the elimination of all forms of discrimination against women as this would have required Jersey to introduce comprehensive equality legislation whereas the States tends to prefer Codes of Practice to legislation on these matters. Moreover, agreements can contain detailed and time-consuming reporting provisions which Jersey can find difficult to undertake as it lacks a government statistical office. Together with what might be termed the more practical considerations listed above, the proliferation of international agreements has led to constitutional difficulties. The problem is that many international agreements transcend the constitutional compromise at the heart of Jersey's relationship with the United Kingdom in that they cover issues which are domestic or fiscal in nature. Accordingly, the island should have complete independence on the decision but, as they are international agreements, the United Kingdom assumes responsibility in the role of Jersey's sovereign power. Thus international agreements can be portrayed as eroding Jersey's autonomy. This danger was most apparent in 1967 when, in a letter to the insular authorities, Sir Philip Allen made it clear that should it not be possible to secure special arrangements for the island, Jersey would have to become part of the European Economic Community, a move which would have severely curtailed Jersey's domestic autonomy.

The development of international law is not, however, entirely contrary to the island's interests. International agreements and their implications for Jersey have provoked so much interest that an index of agreements under consideration or applying to the island is available at the public library. This index was produced in spite of the significant staff constraints apparent in this area of policy development. Dispute settlement through international law represents a means by which smaller communities can overcome some of the problems of scale and resolve disputes with larger neighbours on a more equal footing. It further increases the pressure which Jersey is able to exert in disputes as the island can use the extension of the relevant agreements which also cover larger neighbours to reinforce its own policies in certain areas. Therefore, Jersey has had many international agreements relating to nuclear power extended to it, not because it has any intention of initiating a nuclear power programme, but because it wishes to have leverage over the neighbouring French nuclear industry should an accident occur. International conventions and agreements have gained their significance on the island for a further reason. In a way which is comparable with the support many members of the Opposition gave to the European Union when the Conservatives were in power, those who wish to initiate social change on the island, but are blocked by the majority opinion in the States, have sought to use international agreements to achieve what they desire.[59] This practice is an extension of the tactic of those seeking to challenge established positions on the island by seeking support in the United Kingdom; with the development of international law a new source of external support has evolved.

The arrangement the authorities in Jersey and the United Kingdom have reached with respect to international agreements reflects the way in which, by mutual consent, space has been created for Jersey to have its own distinctive external policies. This right, as with all aspects of Jersey's constitution, is constrained in theory by the United Kingdom, but in practice this control is little used as both sides operate within well understood parameters. This area of external policy remains, however, potentially contentious as many international agreements are perceived as undermining Jersey's autonomy whilst others, which deal with controversial moral or social issues, provoke debate on the island as to the best policy to adopt. If the threat of imposition by the United Kingdom becomes part of this debate, it serves to increase the intensity of the discussion by adding another perceived threat to the island's autonomy.

Management of External Affairs

The remarkable element in the relationship between Jersey and the United Kingdom is its stability. That this has been achieved is in part a tribute to the insular authorities' ability to manage their dependency relationship though a number of tactics. These strategies have been predicated on an attempt to maintain a clear understanding of the parameters of Jersey's autonomy and how that autonomy might be endangered. Knowledge of these parameters has been sought through active efforts to maintain good personal relationships with Home Office staff.[60] The relationships are maintained through formal six-monthly meetings at the Home Office, periodic ministerial visits, and informal contact on issues such as legislation requiring the Royal Assent. In 1996, the Jersey delegation to the Home Office was led by Senator Jeune, who emphasised his commitment to maintaining good and close relations with the Home Office when in office as President of the Policy and Resources Committee.[61]

The insular authorities must receive as much warning as possible of any conflict with the United Kingdom. This is because Jersey's ability to resist an ultimatum from the United Kingdom is limited. For example, the United Kingdom dominates visible trade with the island and could choose to use the threat of economic sanctions, rather than constitutional provisions, to enforce its will.[62] Bearing in mind the ultimately overwhelming dominance of the United Kingdom, Jersey does not seek to provoke conflict in areas where its metropolitan power is determined to have its way. The island must concentrate on seeking to resolve any conflicts by persuasion. An example of such an issue was the passing of the law legalising homosexuality in 1990. The United Kingdom authorities felt that pressure from lobbyists would result in an appeal to the European Court of Human Rights and therefore, despite the fact the States did not wish to pass this reform, the United Kingdom was prepared to use its dominance to force the issue. In view of this, the island preferred to avoid the damage to the relationship as well as the finance industry which might be caused if a public conflict took place. In the debate itself the President of the Legislation Committee, Deputy Edgar Becquet, justified the actions of the States as Jersey was not a sovereign state and the United Kingdom could impose its will if it wished. The capacity to know which battles to fight and which defeats to accept is fundamental to managing Jersey's dependency.

Jersey has also sought to avoid being either a burden or an embarrassment to the United Kingdom. In the event Jersey were to prove to be either, an issue involving the island would become more of a priority for the United Kingdom government and would not present Jersey in a positive light. Consequently Jersey has, apart from an initial post-war grant, avoided seeking any financial assistance from the United Kingdom. The fear is that United Kingdom loans granted to the island would only be sanctioned in return for some Treasury oversight over the island's finances in a way analogous to the Department for International Development's policy towards those remaining United Kingdom Overseas Territories requiring financial support from the United Kingdom.[63] The legislation on homosexuality and the abolition of capital punishment were both undertaken when it was felt that the lack of such reforms in the island was becoming an embarrassment to the United Kingdom government. The Home Office made clear when the States was resisting pressure to reform the island's laws on homosexuality that "Jersey's stand on the issue is embarrassing the British Government in its relations with its European partners, because local laws are viewed as being in contravention of the European Convention on Human Rights."[64]

Jersey thus manages its end of the relationship by seeking to avoid confrontation with the Home Office and any undermining of the United Kingdom's interests. The United Kingdom has reciprocated by seeking to allow the island as much autonomy as possible. Hence the complex and time-consuming procedures used in respect of international agreements which allow the Crown Dependencies and Overseas Territories a degree of autonomy in this area. Even more significantly the operation of an offshore finance centre is permitted provided certain minimum regulatory standards are met, as the United

Kingdom could, by expressing its displeasure, cripple the island's finance industry. Another facet of the relationship can be used to the advantage of the insular authorities. Insular issues are often seen, at best, as being of marginal importance in the United Kingdom or the European Union which can work in Jersey's favour. As an illustration, the Protocol defining the Crown Dependencies' relationship with the Community itself was so generous, in part, because of the island's perceived irrelevance to the treaty as a whole. Ralph Vibert, when interviewed, noted that "Jersey benefited from being a very small thing, England was the big prize."[65] The disadvantage inherent in this position is that it distinctly limits the extent to which Jersey can make its views heard in the relevant corridors of power. Its views are also unlikely to be heard where they contradict European Community or United Kingdom policy. This makes good intelligence with respect to the actions of its neighbours essential so that, what influence the island has, can be brought to bear.

Jersey's relative insignificance does open up another policy option, obstruction. This is quite significant given that Jersey usually has a different agenda compared with the United Kingdom. For example, the extension to the island of most international agreements is not a priority for the United Kingdom whereas the freedom to determine whether these agreements should be extended to the island is seen by most States members as essential in defending Jersey's autonomy. Even if Jersey is ordered to embark on a policy, the United Kingdom or the European Union may give a low priority to ensuring compliance. This advantage can extend to more contentious policy areas in as much as a favoured policy in Jersey may initially be blocked by the United Kingdom. However, it is highly unlikely that the political support for continuing opposition will have the long-term strength and support to match that of Jersey, where the policy is seen to be relevant.[66] Thus a policy aim, such as population control, will be achieved via circuitous routes since direct methods, such as immigration control, are not practical. As Jersey is not allowed to control its own immigration policy, it has developed the ability to control its population by means of its Housing Law.

Jersey is vulnerable due to its size. This is especially true if its interest conflicts with those of its metropolitan power. This situation occurred in 1996 when the interest of the finance industry clashed with the wishes of the United Kingdom. The dilemma resulted from the desire of accountancy firms to introduce legislation to allow them to restrict their liability in the same way as limited companies, whilst continuing to operate as partnerships. Such legislation would limit the maximum amount for potential claims against accountancy partnerships as, at present, partners are jointly and severally liable for all claims. The United Kingdom did not, however, wish Jersey to enact such legislation as it was unwilling to introduce similar measures to prevent accountancy firms from leaving the United Kingdom.[67] The law also provoked bitter debate in the island, both regarding perceived flaws in the law and the wisdom in provoking the United Kingdom.[68] However, after a bitter debate, in which a member of the States was excluded from the chamber, the States passed the law. The United Kingdom has not sought to use any of its constitutional powers to block it and has announced that it will enact similar legislation in 1999, thus suggesting that Jersey has forced a change of policy by the United Kingdom government.[69] This action may not be without its consequences. Prem Sikka alleges that the financial review announced by the United Kingdom government was, in part, a consequence of Jersey seeking to enact limited liabilities partnership legislation[70]. It is unclear what benefits the island has gained from supporting the finance industry beyond its essential, but unquantifiable, goodwill. No new accountancy firms have moved to the island and there is no evidence of directly related investment moving to the island. The episode does illustrate the robustness of the United Kingdom's respect for the island's autonomy as constitutional methods were not used to block the legislation. The enactment has, however, led to conflict between the wishes of the island and those of the United Kingdom.

Conclusion

The ability of Jersey to define policy with respect to territories external to itself is predicated on the resilience of the constitutional conventions at the heart of the relationship between Jersey and the United Kingdom. This accounts for the essentially conservative and defensive nature of Jersey's external policies. The most fundamental of these is the convention of non-interference in domestic and fiscal affairs. This convention is both undermined by developments in international law and limited by the existence of the good government powers of the United Kingdom. Thus the core compromise at the heart of Jersey's autonomy, that of domestic and fiscal independence in exchange for the United Kingdom controlling foreign affairs and defence, must be seen as increasingly anachronistic in the face of developments since the war. Part of Jersey's response to these developments has been the formulation of policies which increasingly resemble an embryonic foreign policy. The fact that the United Kingdom has not only tolerated, but at times actively collaborated, in the evolution of this area of policy illustrates a commitment on behalf of both parties to use the inherent flexibility in what is an uncodified relationship to ensure its continued viability. Jersey has also been forced to develop external policies in response to the global nature of its own finance industry. This industry's reputation must be ensured by interaction with both external regulatory authorities and multinational companies. It is against this background of the increasing internationalisation of both its economy and the blurring of the distinction between domestic and international law that the United Kingdom has given Jersey the political space required to develop its own distinctive *de facto* foreign policy.

Jersey's external relationships have been remarkably stable since the war. The insular authorities have preserved the fiscal autonomy necessary to allow a booming finance industry to develop, avoided full membership of the European Union and ensured that the constitutional relationship with the United

Kingdom has remained intact. The stability of this relationship in the long term depends in part on the ability of the insular authorities to manage their external relationship and in part on the nature of the exogenous threats to the island. If such threats were derived from policy imperatives which were significant to the United Kingdom and the European Union, Jersey could have difficulties in its stated aim of preserving the *status quo* in its relationships with these powers. A significant threat which Jersey faces from the United Kingdom is that the government seeks to impose substantial constitutional reform upon the island and as a result of this process the position of the insular authorities becomes fundamentally weakened. A second threat faced by the island is that the United Kingdom or the European Union or both will seek to restrict the operation of Jersey's offshore finance centre and hence harm the island's economy. The moves towards fiscal harmonisation by the European Union and the financial review instigated by the United Kingdom are both evidence of developments in this direction.

References

[1] Kermode, D. G., Devolution at Work: A Case Study of the Isle of Man, Saxon House, Farnborough, 1979, 112-120, hereafter, Kermode.

[2] op. cit., Kilbrandon 1973, 8, para 6.

[3] Policy and Resources Committee, Strategic Policy Review & Action Plan 1996, Policy and Resources Committee, Jersey, 1996, 3, hereafter, Strategic Policy Report 1996.

[4] ibid., 28.

[5] ibid., 54-55

[6] Falle, P., "What you've got is a non-critical political system", Jersey Evening Post, 17/9/86, 11.

[7] op. cit., Kilbrandon 1973, 452, para 1494.

[8] Letter from Sir Charles Cunningham to Sir Frank Newsham, 24/9/57, Public Record Office HO284/3.

[9] op. cit., Strategic Policy Report 1996, 3.

[10] "C.I. tax Bill rejected, but MP 'encouraged' by Commons support', Jersey Evening Post, 21/10/81.

[11] An example is Pascal, J., "Islands awash with ill-gotten gains", The Guardian, 1/11/97, 21.

[12] Home Office Press Release, 20/1/98.

[13] Answer given by Jacques Delors on behalf of the Commission cited in Jersey and the European Community An Update 1992, Policy and Resources Committee, Jersey, 1992, 22, hereafter, Jersey and the EU 1992.

[14] Barber, "The big catch", Financial Times, 29/7/97.

[15] op. cit., Jersey and the EU 1992, 22.

[16] op. cit., Allen letter.

[17] Hampton, M., "'Treasure Island' Revisited. Jersey's Offshore Finance Centre crisis: implications for other Small Island Economies", University of Portsmouth, September 1997, 22, hereafter, Jersey's Offshore Finance Centre crisis.

[18] Seventy five per cent of agricultural production is exported to the United Kingdom and eighty

per cent of tourists are from the United Kingdom. Source Office of the Chief Adviser, <u>Budget extract 1996</u>, States of Jersey, Jersey, 1996, 13.

[19] <u>Report and Recommendations of the Special Committee of the States of Jersey appointed to consult with Her Majesty's Government in the United Kingdom on all matters relating to the Government's application to join the European Economic Community</u>, States Greffe, Jersey, 1967, 11, hereafter, EEC Report 1967.

[20] The Crown Dependencies are the responsibility of the Constitutional Unit at the Home Office.

[21] Two thirds of bank deposits in Jersey are held in currencies other than sterling. Source "Jersey bank deposits top £90 billion", <u>Jersey Weekly Post</u>, 16/5/96, 1.

[22] Corbridge, S., Martin, R. & Thrift, N., <u>Money, Power and Space</u>, Oxford, Blackwell, 1994, 97.

[23] Dower, G., <u>Britain's Dependent Territories</u>, Dartmouth, Aldershot, 1992, 61.

[24] <u>The Parliamentarian Journal of the Parliaments of the Commonwealth</u>, LXXVVII,. No. 1, Jan. 1996, 51.

[25] Vibert, R., <u>Parliament without Parties The Committee System in the States of the Island of Jersey</u>, States Greffe, Jersey, 1990 & Wettenhall, R., "Using *All* the Talents of a Legislature in Governing a Conversation with Ralph Vibert OBE", <u>Australian Journal of Public Administration</u>, vol. 53, No. 1, March 1994, 107-115.

[26] Interview with ex-Senator R. Jeune, C.B.E., States Member 1962-96 and former President, Policy and Resources Committee, 26/3/97, hereafter, Jeune interview.

[27] Pascal, J., "Islands awash with ill-gotten gains", <u>The Guardian</u>, 1/11/97, 21.

[28] ibid.

[29] Nationals of the Irish Republic made up 2% of the population, French citizens 1% and Portuguese citizens 5%. Source <u>Report on the Census for 1996</u>, States of Jersey, Jersey, 1997, 33, hereafter, Census 1996.

[30] ibid., 32.

[31] Pedley, R. & Peters, L., "Contracts System: MP tables motion", <u>Jersey Evening Post</u>, 25/5/94, 1, hereafter, Pedley & Peters.

[32] ECHR ruling in <u>Gillow v UK</u>, 5 EHRR, 581.

[33] The EEC's exclusion of the Crown Dependencies was to allow the islands the option to maintain measures to limit population. The United Kingdom had the power to refuse the Royal Assent to the Housing Law and did not.

[34] This is illustrated by a decline in the economically active population of 111 people. This period coincides with a slowing down of economic growth on the island; op. cit., Census 1996, 15.

[35] op. cit., The Offshore Interface, 99.

[36] Interview with Senator Frank Walker, 5/8/98, hereafter, Walker interview. No interviewee consulted has suggested this to be a preferable option.

[37] ibid.

[38] Powell, G. C., "Future holds no real threat to us", <u>Jersey Evening Post</u>, 12/9/97, 9.

[39] op. cit., Kilbrandon 1973, 7, para 4.

[40] ibid.

[41] Memorandum by the Home Office and Foreign and Commonwealth Office, op. cit., Kilbrandon 1973, 7, para 4.

[42] Interview with John Rothwell, 6/8/98.

[43] Body, P., "We can't opt out", <u>Jersey Evening Post</u>, 19/6/96, 3.

[44] Falle, P., "Senator voices fear for Jersey's future", <u>Jersey Evening Post</u>, 10/9/96, 3.

[45] Circular No. 0118 Foreign Office 16th October 1950 cited in <u>Treaties: Application to Crown Dependencies</u>, R.C. 24/93, States Greffe, Jersey, 1993, 8, hereafter, Treaties 1993.

[46] ibid.

[47] This right is confirmed in a memorandum prepared by the Legal Advisers in the Foreign and Commonwealth Office dated May 1993 cited in Treaties 1993.

[48] op. cit., Kilbrandon 1973, 140.

[49] ibid., 141.

[50] ibid., 106.

[51] ibid., 8.

[52] op. cit., Strategic Policy Report 1996, 54.

[53] op. cit., Treaties 1993, 3.

[54] ibid., 6.

[55] For example, the Council of Europe and the Hague Conventions on International Law.

[56] States of Jersey Review of the Office of the Chief Adviser Final Report and Recommendations, Deloitte and Touche, 1997.

[57] International Conventions and Agreements: Progress Report for the Period Ended 30th September 1996, R.C.38/96, Policy and Resources Committee, 10/12/96, States Greffe, Jersey, 1996.

[58] ibid., 24.

[59] Campaign Manifesto of Michael Dun in the Jersey Evening Post supplement for the 1996 Senatorial Elections, 15/10/96.

[60] op. cit., Jeune interview.

[61] ibid.

[62] An example of this occurring was during the Imperial Contributions Conflict, which arose from a request in 1923 by the United Kingdom government for a contribution towards the expenses of Empire. When Jersey refused to make a contribution the United Kingdom threatened to curtail the island's fiscal privileges.

[63] Interview with Richard Stoneman, Consultant on Overseas Territories, 4/2/97 & Speech to the Dependent Territories Association by the Rt. Hon. Robin Cook MP, London, 4/2/98.

[64] Marett-Crosby, H., "Sodomy: Pressure from Home Office", Jersey Evening Post, 20/4/90, 1.

[65] Interview with ex-Senator Ralph Vibert, Solicitor General 1948, States Member 1957-87, President of the Committee charged with negotiating the island's arrangements with respect to the European Economic Community at the time of the United Kingdom's accession to that body, hereafter, Vibert interview.

[66] The use of Housing regulations to control immigration is the most pertinent example of this.

[67] Jeune, P., "Concern over Jersey law shrift", The Independent, 9/10/96, 26 & Leonard, C., "Partners law: MPs protest to Privy Council", Jersey Evening Post, 31/10/96, 1.

[68] Minutes of the States of Jersey 3/9/97 & Cousins, J., Mitchell, A., Sikka, P. & Willmott, H., Auditors: Holding the Public to Ransom, Association for Accountancy & Business Affairs, Basildon, 1998.

[69] ibid., 37.

[70] Sikka, P., A Comment on: 'Limited Liability Partnerships (Insolvent Partnerships) (Jersey) Regulations 199', University of Essex, 1998, 11.

Chapter 4 – The Economic Context: Jersey as an Offshore Finance Centre

Introduction

Jersey's economic structure is a product of its political autonomy. The finance industry, in particular, only exists because Jersey's political autonomy allows the island's government to modify its laws to create the correct fiscal environment for an offshore finance centre to develop. Finance, therefore, represents the most important area in which the island must manage its dependency. The purpose of this chapter is to describe the structure of Jersey's economy as well as highlighting the areas where government action has been influential.

The managed dependency school provides the essential framework to understand the operation of Jersey's economy. Although it accepts the orthodox economic contention that microstates exhibit a form of dependency, it asserts that this dependency is neither passive, nor necessarily harmful. Instead, the successful microstate will nurture and exploit a dependency relationship to its own advantage. Orthodox economists, including Jalan[1] and Knox,[2] concentrate on identifying economic constraints of scale because "size was seen as a structural inhibitor to the prerequisites of the development path"[3] and as such cannot provide the necessary framework for understanding Jersey's economy. Knox[4] lists the features of a small economy as less diverse resources, smaller domestic markets, high degrees of specialisation and concentration on a limited range of products with other essential needs met through imports. Small states, therefore, require free trade or economic union with a larger state to allow the inexpensive importation of essential goods and must also have a product to offer in exchange for these essential imports. Therefore, although the orthodox theories, in particular the analysis of the importance of obstacles to growth in small states, are very persuasive, they cannot explain why Jersey's economy has been so successful. This explanation can only be found within the framework of managed dependency.

Jersey's economy is not passively dependent on the United Kingdom but, instead, the insular authorities and businesses seek to manage the dependency relationship with the United Kingdom and, indirectly the European Union, as this is necessary to maintain free trade on which Jersey's industries are dependent. Diseconomies of scale are inevitable in a microstate and have widespread economic and social ramifications. In Jersey such apparently fundamental infrastructure projects as hospitals suffer from diseconomies of scale.[5] The innovative solutions developed illustrate some of the advantages of the dependency relationship with the United Kingdom and the fundamentally different approaches a microstate must take to sustain a developed economy.

Jersey's economy is small in absolute terms. The Gross Domestic Product in 1996 was £1,350 million.[6] Yet Jersey's economy, although minute when compared with the United Kingdom's, is considerably richer in terms of income per capita. Comparative figures available for 1993 estimate Jersey's Gross Domestic Product per capita as £15,955 and the United Kingdom's as £9,385.[7] The success of the Jersey economy is further illustrated by the low level of unemployment. It is even possible to argue that endemic labour shortages are characteristic of the insular economy. Unemployment in Jersey peaked in January 1993 at 1,214 individuals[8] or 2.55% of the economically active workforce. Unemployment over the past twenty years has been significantly lower than both the United Kingdom and European Union averages. Inflation, however, has a tendency to be higher than in the United Kingdom.[9] These figures together may describe a successful economy but can also, due to the island's scale, illustrate an economy experiencing unsustainable growth. The insular economy experienced severe resource shortages in the 1980s as regards land, water and population. In addition, the capacity limit of elements of the local infrastructure was reached. It is physical resource limitations, not money, which represent the fundamental constraint on development. The major policy issue facing Jersey, therefore, becomes how to ensure continuing prosperity in a community hostile to further population growth or urban development.

The island has internal fiscal autonomy as regards taxation and spending. Jersey's economy will produce an estimated income available to the States of Jersey of £340 million for the year 1999 with net budgeted expenditure being £323 million.[10] The island has no public debt and maintains a strategic reserve which is estimated in 1999 to stand at £308 million, representing ninety five per cent of annual revenue expenditure.[11] This gives the government instant access to funding for capital projects, although it was originally created as an insurance against the vulnerability to exceptional events from which all microstates suffer, an example being the loss of a supertanker near to the island. The States of Jersey have viewed the lack of public debt as an essential policy aim.[12] This is partly because a reputation for financial probity is seen as attractive by the finance industry and partly because most States members are ideologically hostile to this scenario.

Jersey has been in a monetary union with the United Kingdom since 1876. The island issues its own local currency which circulates in parallel and at par with Bank of England notes. The arrangement has proved very profitable with £2.4 million accruing in 1995.[13] Jersey's continued membership of the Sterling Area, at the time of the rescheduling in 1972, was in Mark Hampton's opinion a major reason for the initial expansion of the island's finance industry as the exclusion of the Caribbean centres resulted in a flood of banks applying to operate on the island.[14] Thus the island was able to benefit from a relatively minor change in United Kingdom policy to gain a competitive advantage over

Caribbean competitors and ensure the expansion of the finance sector. The island's experience of the redefinition of the Sterling Area highlights a potential threat posed by the Euro. The introduction of a single currency could exclude the local finance industry from major markets. The insular authorities, therefore, must seek to preserve access to European markets while resisting attempts by the European Union to restrict the scope of the finance industry in the island.

The Finance Centre

Jersey's economic structure is dominated by the finance industry which in 1996 accounted for fifty five per cent of national income. The finance industry represented thirty per cent of gross domestic product in 1983 and has grown at the expense of all other sectors. The finance industry, also, has a close symbiosis with investment holding on the island as both share much of the same professional infrastructure. Investment holding accounts for fourteen per cent of the national income, thus, activities directly associated with the island's finance infrastructure contributed sixty nine per cent of the national income in 1996. The island's other significant industry is tourism which accounts for twenty four per cent of national income. This industry is in long term decline and large scale investment is planned to attempt to revitalise it. The remainder of the economy consists of farming and manufacturing for export which respectively account for five and two per cent of national income.[15] Thus Jersey's economic structure can be summarised as essentially a dominant finance sector operating alongside a smaller and weaker tourist sector. Although the finance industry is internally diverse and sells a wide range of financial products to individuals and companies, Jersey's high cost base has created a situation where a tendency towards specialisation in private banking for wealthy individuals has developed. However, the high cost base makes operating conditions difficult for Jersey's other industries.

Due to the secrecy inherent in maintaining such a finance centre, it is impossible to calculate the exact size of the local finance industry. The figures available, however, indicate that bank deposits in Jersey reached £90.4 billion in the first quarter of 1996 which represents a two hundred per cent increase over the 1992 figures.[16] Two thirds of these deposits are held in foreign currencies and this tendency to further globalisation of the deposit base was illustrated by a 166 per cent increase in foreign currency deposits over the same period while sterling deposits rose by only twenty-six per cent.[17] This, however, does not include money held in trust on the island; conservative informed guesses of this total vary from £35 billion[18] to £190 billion.[19] These figures serve to emphasise both the dominance of finance within Jersey's economy and Jersey's position as a major offshore financial centre in global terms. Thus, at least in the financial community, Jersey's influence far outweighs its small geographical size.

Jersey is an offshore finance centre and not a tax haven. Jersey has comparatively low taxation, but the funds benefiting from the taxation regime are administered in Jersey, not onshore as in a tax haven. This means that Jersey benefits from the taxation of the funds resident on the island and, unlike a tax haven, the administration of these funds provides employment for a considerable part of the population, in Jersey's case twenty per cent. Offshore finance centres, as opposed to tax havens, do not attract business solely on low rates of taxation but through the quality and diversity of financial services on offer to a potential investor. This has profound implications for the structure of an offshore finance sector economy which must be structured to provide these services.

Hampton identifies four spaces necessary for an offshore finance centre to develop: the secrecy, fiscal, regulatory and political spaces.[20] Jersey maintains its secrecy space via the assumption of client confidentiality as laid down in Jersey common law. Further, the high degree of autonomy which the United Kingdom allows the island enables the States to create the fiscal, regulatory and political environment required for the offshore finance centre to thrive.

The competitive manipulation of fiscal law, both between offshore finance centres themselves and with onshore centres, is a fundamental area in which governments hosting offshore finance centres seek to gain competitive advantages for their respective finance industries and hence maximise tax yields. Richard Pirouet, Managing Partner at Ernst &Young in Jersey, used the analogy of it being akin to a "game between tax lawyers and the United Kingdom authorities";[21] the governments of onshore jurisdictions seeking to maximise their own tax yields and offshore governments seeking to maximise the legal opportunities for tax management. The competitive manipulation of fiscal laws is not, however, without risk. This was illustrated by the bitter debate surrounding proposals to allow accountancy firms to set up limited liability partnerships on the island. This law allowed the creation of accountancy partnerships in which the firm, not individual partners, was liable for the losses of the partnership. This law was designed to attract accountancy partnerships to relocate from jurisdictions such as the United Kingdom where partners, if sued, may suffer personal bankruptcy. This type of legislation was rejected by Guernsey which correctly predicted the hostile reaction it would provoke from the United Kingdom.[22] Its has also failed to attract new accountancy partnerships to the island.

Jersey's attractions as an offshore finance centre largely derive from the island being viewed as politically and economically stable. The industry is consulted on all measures likely to affect it and the government is extremely unlikely to take fiscal measures which are deliberately detrimental to the finance industry.[23] It is also essential that the island is perceived to have stable international relationships.[24] In this area, the significance of Protocol 3 in excluding fiscal directives from applying to the island, cannot be overestimated. The island, also, benefits from an image of stable, non-party domestic politics. The combination of stable internal politics and what, in fiscal terms, is effectively non-membership of the European Union has proved very attractive to investors who fear changes in taxation and regulation within the European Union.

Effective regulation of the finance industry by government is vital. Both Powell and Pirouet[25] believed that strict regulation, which has the effect of driving away doubtful business, was essential for business confidence and the island's media image. The promotion of the island as a well regulated offshore finance centre is considered so important that the Finance and Economics Committee maintain the services of the London based consultants Shandwick for this purpose.[26] The need to maintain the image of a stable well-regulated offshore finance centre, together with the social cohesion already apparent in a small community, has created a political environment which has promoted a degree of self censorship in areas deemed to damage the island's image as an offshore finance centre. This can be illustrated by the response of the President of the influential Jersey Chamber of Commerce who was "absolutely staggered"[27] that a local Senator would criticise the finance sector in an international finance journal. The President went on to state that "there are times to close ranks and show a united front in the interests of mutual benefit and for the common good."[28]

Effective regulation is, also, essential to prevent bank failures, a situation successfully avoided in Jersey for thirty years. Such a failure would cause substantial damage to the local industry and Pirouet argued that the failure of the Savings and Investment Bank in the Isle of Man in 1982 was a major reason for the Isle of Man having a relatively small finance industry compared to Jersey and Guernsey.[29] Good regulation is also essential to prevent criminal activities as widespread financial crime has the potential to cripple any offshore finance centre, particularly if, like Jersey, it is trying to promote itself as a "quality centre." In 1996 thirty two cases involving money suspected of originating from organised crime were being investigated by the local police.[30] This figure, when considered in the context of a multi-billion pound industry, must be regarded as acceptable. It must also be accepted that some crime will always occur in such a large industry and if no crime were reported it would more likely be due to lack of regulation than the centre being crime free. The government success in effectively regulating the local finance industry was confirmed for the journal "Accountancy"[31] by the Bank of Credit and Commerce International (BCCI) being refused entry to Jersey. The journal's view of the offshore finance centres in the Channel Islands was emphasised by the decision to entitle the article "The Blue Chip Islands".[32] The exceptional demand by banks to locate in Jersey has allowed the island the luxury of setting very high quality thresholds with only banks in the top five hundred, as measured by net assets, being allowed entry.[33] Therefore, the island adopts policies which have the effect of driving away certain businesses seeking to establish themselves on Jersey, the aim being to develop an exclusive image for the island's finance industry and benefit from what Powell has deemed a "flight to quality".[34] The rationale is that the industry will increasingly rationalise its activities on the more respectable offshore finance centres.

The fear that microstates are especially vulnerable to crime associated with tourism or finance is apparent in the Commonwealth secretariat's report which highlights "the weak power and administration of small states and the encouragement these activities [tourism and finance] give to corruption, fraud, commercial crime, drug trafficking, prostitution and political interference."[35] Panama is alleged to be an example of a small offshore finance centre which has been overwhelmed and corrupted by the Latin American drug cartels.[36] International fears about the ability of microstates to regulate their own finance industries have led to the evolution of international organisations such as the Offshore Group of Banking Supervisors created by the offshore finance centres themselves. These bodies aim to work with larger economies to create structures which placate international fears about the level of regulation in microstate offshore finance centres. This is necessary because, if onshore regulators and investors came to regard Jersey as poorly regulated and hence vulnerable to fiscal crime investments, jobs would quickly flow to other offshore finance centres. This is despite the fact that most illegal activities originate and are controlled onshore.

The external relationship with the United Kingdom is fundamental to the stability of the local finance industry as it is through this relationship all other relationships must be managed. The very existence of the offshore finance centre is seen by Hampton as predicated on Britain's role as a metropolitan power.[37] Only Britain and the Netherlands have dependencies operating as major offshore finance centres, in part due to the fact that English is essential to the operation of an offshore finance centre, but more importantly, due to the United Kingdom's relatively benevolent attitude towards offshore finance centres. The Foreign and Commonwealth Office has even promoted the creation of offshore finance centres in dependencies to facilitate self sufficiency.[38] The tolerant attitude of the United Kingdom towards offshore finance can be contrasted to that of the United States and France. The United States' policy toward offshore finance centres is exemplified by the subpoenaing and fining of the Bank of Nova Scotia in 1983 to gain access to information held at a Cayman Islands branch. This action was undertaken despite protests from the governments of Canada, the United Kingdom and the Cayman Islands, who each felt that their sovereignty was being violated.[39] The benevolence of the United Kingdom is thus essential and, despite insular fears about the attitude of a future Labour government[40] on this issue, United Kingdom governments have, since 1927,[41] refrained from direct confrontation with Jersey on the issue of its fiscal autonomy.

Hampton posits a Marxist influenced interpretation that offshore finance centres are tolerated as an extension of the paramount power of the City in the British economy.[42]

Jersey must, therefore, be seen as an extension of the London based leg of a tripartite global market and, thus, in economic, if not political terms, an extension of the City. Hence Jersey's status is protected and promoted by the political and economic power of the City. Johns and Le Marchant[43] and Roberts[44] have also noted that offshore finance centres perform a vital role for the global finance markets in that they compete to provide entities such as transnational corporations or wealthy individuals with a means of managing their global finances in ways which both minimise cost and maximise investment opportunities. The demand for such centres by powerful investors mean, in the current deregulated financial environment, that these centres will continue to exist regardless. Thus if Jersey were to close as a market, the money would just go elsewhere. If this occurred, Powell asserts that the United Kingdom would lose the element of control over its own offshore markets. [45] This control is real, if informal, and consists largely of self-limitation by the Crown Dependencies. It is illustrated by the description of the vetting procedure used by John Roper, Director-General of the Guernsey Financial Services Commission, towards applications submitted by banks to operate on Guernsey, "we will ring up our contacts at the Federal Reserve or the Bank of England and if there is a sharp intake of breath when we mention the name, then we say "Right, forget it"".[46] Jersey's finance industry is also tolerated as it ensures that Jersey is not only self-sufficient, but also a net contributor to the United Kingdom Exchequer for services shared with the United Kingdom. The attraction of a prosperous and stable Jersey contributing to the Exchequer and, more importantly, not imposing financial costs or causing political problems for the United Kingdom must not be underestimated.

External relations are complicated by the fact that Luxembourg and the Irish Republic have a status within the European Union which allows them to compete directly with offshore finance centres. This allows them, not only to trade within the European Union, but also the option of seeking to use their powers as members of the European Union to undermine offshore finance centres outside the European Union. This complicates Jersey's relationship with the European Union. Although the Luxembourg government is wary of seeking advantage over external competitors by using the tools of the European Union for fear that they will be turned by the other member states against Luxembourg itself, it is not inconceivable that the European Union could perceive it to be in its interest to create a situation where it promotes its own internal finance centres at the expense of others beyond its control. The most dangerous competition, for Jersey, however, was defined by Pirouet as a reduction in world wide direct taxation.[47] This policy was promoted by the last United Kingdom Conservative government. If, in particular, capital gains and inheritance taxes in the United Kingdom were abolished, the United Kingdom would have similar tax advantages to Jersey. Thus, the threat exists of Jersey's onshore metropolitan power becoming a competitor in offshore finance.

High Net Worth Individuals
The attracting of wealthy immigrants to Jersey by the insular authorities is a long established policy and is seen as a way of increasing government taxation

revenues whilst minimising immigration. It provided one of the necessary conditions for the development of the offshore finance centre as it provided the core of the necessary financial skills to enable 'the pinstripe' infrastructure for the offshore finance centre to develop. Once other necessary conditions occurred, the island was able to develop rapidly as an offshore finance centre. Immigration is controlled by the granting of limited licences to carefully screened individuals to allow the acquisition of housing rights on the island. Wealthy immigrants are screened by the Chief Adviser's Office and are expected to contract to pay a guaranteed sum of taxation every year, currently believed to be in the region of £180,000. John Christensen emphasised that recent measures had been taken to make this procedure more stringent.[48] This may be in response to persistent rumours, which, due to the secrecy inherent in the finance industry, are impossible to confirm, that certain individuals were arranging their affairs to avoid paying any tax to the island once they had been granted residence.

The wealthy immigrants' spending can be a mixed blessing to the economy. It is beneficial to local restaurants, but creates inflationary pressures on building prices.[49] Wealthy immigrants can also attract bad publicity as the British press often alleges that they are tax exiles. There is further a danger that they will seek to use their financial resources to influence local politics. This threat is currently exemplified by the Barclay brothers who are seeking to challenge the Seigneur of Sark's authority over Brecqhou and thus exclude Brecqhou from the jurisdiction of Sark.[50] The seriousness of the threat is illustrated by the fact that estimates of the Barclay brothers' personal wealth are double that of government spending in the Bailiwick of Guernsey.[51] Thus, despite the considerable financial advantage wealthy individuals represent for the island, the policy must be used with care as it has the potential to affect internal policy decisions as well as harm the external image of the island.

Tourism

Tourism has been a major island industry since the introduction of steam packets to the island in 1824. It has taken advantage of the combination of a warmer climate combined with a shared currency, and later the language, to attract the British visitors who account for almost eighty per cent of staying visitors in 1994.[52] The industry is in decline, both in absolute terms since 1990 and in the proportion of national income, which has halved over the past thirty years.[53] The local industry's decline has been accelerated by staff recruitment problems as employees opt for better paid non-seasonal work on offer in the finance sector. Jersey has, also, been in competition with guaranteed sunshine destinations, such as Majorca, because of a focus on charter rather than high income visitors, when the cost of air travel between the two destinations is little different. In addition, the tourism industry has poor wet weather facilities. The need to remedy this situation has been acknowledged by the investment of £10 million from the Strategic Reserve in an attempt by the States to diversify the economy away from dependence on the finance industry.[54] A degree of symbiosis exists between finance, tourism and the attraction of wealthy investors. All require good global communications and, owing to the poor economies of scale which exist in Jersey, these have to be provided by the States. The necessity of these links was emphasised by Pirouet as of great importance in enabling potential investors to visit the island and financial advisers to travel to clients abroad.[55] Moreover, good quality hotels and restaurants allow potential investors and wealthy immigrants to be entertained at the highest standards. However, the requirement of rich investors and charter tourists are different and so the extent of the symbiosis is difficult to assess.

Diversification, due to labour shortages on the island, means the diversion of resources from one sector to another. Thus any expansion in tourism must produce a decline in the labour available to another sector, essentially the offshore finance centre. Such an expansion could prove to be a poisoned chalice, however, as the increase in tourist spending would not offset the loss of income from business luncheons. In addition, tourism provides a positive external image for the island as something more than a banking centre, and adds an economic rationale to the preservation of the insular environment and agricultural industry. It is unclear whether government support will reverse tourism's long term decline. The tourism industry may also not be the most beneficial industry for the state, in effect, to subsidise, as it is seasonal, tends to pay comparatively low wages, and relies on imported labour. The tourism industry, in the world at large, is also very competitive and Jersey, given its high transport costs and small scale, may find it increasingly difficult to compete successfully.

Agriculture and Fisheries

The agricultural industry, although now of limited economic significance, is deeply embedded in the national identity. Kelleher's whole thesis is concerned with illustrating the ability of the local rural elite to dominate politics.[56] Farming in Jersey is intensive, specialised, export orientated and based on small units. Fifty five per cent of the island's area is devoted to agriculture and in 1990 the industry exported approximately seventy five per cent of production to the United Kingdom.[57] The industry is dominated by the Jersey Royal new potatoes, which accounted for sixty nine percent by value of all production, while dairy farming represented twenty five percent.[58] The industry received a net injection of revenue from the States of Jersey of £6.9 million in 1995.[59] Agriculture in Jersey can, therefore, be summarised as a modern export industry reliant on access to government subsidies and United Kingdom markets. An analysis of the influence of the economy on external policy would be incomplete without the inclusion of the small local fishing industry. The industry only produced a catch in 1990 valued at £5.3 million.[60] Its significance lies not in its relatively small contribution to the economy, but the related dispute over the extent of the island's territorial waters.

The agriculture and fisheries sector in the island is of great importance when considering the relationship with the European Union. The Protocol governing the relationship with the European Union covers agriculture and fishing, but not tourism and finance. The United Kingdom's accession introduced direct competition from the Continent on equal terms, thus removing the island's traditional climatic advantages over its competitors. The existence of European Union subsidies has also required Jersey to subsidise its agricultural industry to an equivalent degree to ensure the viability of local farming.[61] It is therefore the only sector of Jersey's economy to have suffered as a result of Jersey's decision not to integrate fully with the European Union.[62] Protocol 3 precludes the island from paying higher agricultural subsidies than the European Union, but allows it to maintain subsidies at the levels ruling in the European Union. Therefore, the direct influence of the European Union on the local agriculture and fishing industries is considerable. This relationship creates a potential conflict of interest with the finance industry's preferred policy of minimising the European Union's influence on the island. The agricultural sector, in particular, has benefited from association with the European Union. A recent example of such a benefit is the European Union's recognition of Jersey's exclusive right to market potatoes as the Jersey Royal New potatoes.[63] The industries also require access to the markets of the European Union to survive. Thus the interests of the agriculture and fisheries industries in this field can be seen as providing a counter-weight to the financial sector's desire to disassociate the island as far as possible from the European Union.

Other Industries

Manufacturing for export currently represents only two per cent of national income. Manufacturing industry is not, however, seen as a possible area for diversification of the island's economy. This is despite the fact that eleven per cent of the Isle of Man's income is generated by manufacturing industry.[64] A number of factors have contributed to produce this situation. The success of the financial sector has increased land and labour costs to levels which are unsustainable for most industries. The costs of importing and then exporting goods to a dominant market ninety miles away makes the production of bulk products unlikely to be viable and the fact that Jersey is outside the European Union Value Added Tax regime imposes considerable administrative and financial burdens on manufacturing industry. The Isle of Man is inside this area and this status is considered essential to the health of its industrial sector.[65] The Isle of Man is also five times the size of Jersey and so land is cheaper. Light industry in Jersey can be regarded as a casualty of deliberate policy decisions in the management of the island's relationship with the European Union and the United Kingdom. In 1971 a small diversified industrial sector operated on the island.[66] Exclusion from value added taxation provisions was seen as beneficial to the island's tourism industry and the finance industry, but has only added to the burdens of the local light industrial sector.[67]

The Office of the Chief Adviser is actively promoting information technology and information services as part of the attempt to diversify Jersey's industrial base. It is believed that these industries have the potential to evolve from the infrastructure already in existence to support the finance industry and would utilise the island's excellent communications infrastructure and proximity to Europe. It is too early to draw any firm conclusion about the success of this initiative, but Jersey has a well educated, computer literate workforce and low taxation which could be attractive to such firms. Jersey, however, remains a relatively high cost area for companies to operate from and this may present problems for the initiative.

Conclusion

To recapitulate, Jersey's economy is dominated by its finance industry. This industry provides the financial stability to guarantee the island's continuing autonomy. It is dependent on the island's political autonomy, both through the island's ability to define its own fiscal laws and its access to global markets via economic union with the United Kingdom. Therefore, Jersey's economic structure can be viewed as the result of successful management of its autonomy. The creation of an offshore finance centre has proved to be the most profitable use of the limited resources available to Jersey as the finance industry produces a relatively high income per employee while utilising few physical resources. However, fears about over-dependence on the finance industry have led to a policy of diversification as planned by the insular authorities.[68] The offshore finance centre also requires greater integration in world markets than in alternative industries. This makes the island more vulnerable to global economic events and perhaps too dependent on effective management of external policy. This diversification is to be achieved by reversing the long term decline of the tourist industry and promoting new industries. Such a diversification has the potential to result in economic decline as the alternatives proposed produce both lower tax yields and pays lower wages. Therefore, the dilemma presented for island policy-makers is how to create a more diversified, and hence less vulnerable, economy without causing an unacceptable decline in the size of the island's economy as the high wages and rents paid by the offshore finance centre crowd out all other industries. The success of this policy will provide both an illustration of the ability of the insular authorities to manage the island's dependency and evidence as to whether the island's politicians are willing, or able, to move away from an economy based on financial services.

References

[1] Jalan, B., Problems and Polices in Small Economies, Croom Helm, London, 1982.

[2] Knox, A. D., "Some Economic Problems of Small Countries" in op. cit., Benedict, 35-44, hereafter, Knox.

[3] op. cit., Baldacchino, 34.

[4] op. cit., Knox, 35.

[5] Specialist health care is provided via a reciprocal health care agreement with the United Kingdom, mainly using facilities in Southampton.

[6] Finance and Economics Committee, Statistical Review 1997, Office of the Chief Adviser, Jersey, 1997, iii, hereafter, Statistical Review 1997.

[7] Finance and Economics Committee, Statistical Review 1994, Office of the Chief Adviser, Jersey, 1994.

[8] Policy and Resources Committee, 2000 & Beyond: Strategic Policy Review 1995 Part 1, States Greffe, Jersey, 1995, 5, hereafter, 2000 & Beyond Part 1.

[9] ibid., 6.

[10] Budget 1999, Finance and Economics Committee, Jersey, 1999, 3.

[11] ibid., x.

[12] op. cit., Vibert 1991, 159.

[13] Office of the Chief Adviser, Budget Extract 1996, States of Jersey, Jersey, 1996, 20.

[14] op. cit., Treasure Island, 241. 26 banks were reported to be on the waiting list.

[15] op. cit., Statistical Review 1997, 50.

[16] "Jersey bank deposits top £90 billion", Jersey Weekly Post, 16/5/96, 1.

[17] ibid.

[18] Jersey Evening Post Economic Review 1996, 7/3/96, 7, hereafter, JEP Economic Review 1996.

[19] op. cit., The Offshore Interface, 143.

[20] Hampton, M.P. "Creating Spaces. The Political Economy of Island Offshore Finance Centres: the case of Jersey." Geographische Zeitschrift, 84 vol.2, 103-113.

[21] Interview with Mr R. Pirouet, Managing Partner, Ernst & Young (Jersey), 28/3/96, hereafter, Pirouet interview.

[22] Falle, P., "New Law: Members to see Bailiff", Jersey Evening Post, 25/7/96, 1.

[23] op. cit., Pirouet interview.

[24] States of Jersey, The International Finance Centre, Financial Services Department, Jersey, 5

[25] op. cit., Pirouet interview and interview with Mr G.C. Powell, O.B.E., Chief Adviser to the States of Jersey, 25/3/96, hereafter, Powell interview.

[26] "Big Boost planned for offshore status", Jersey Evening Post, 7/3/96,1.

[27] Falle, P., "Stop rocking the boat!", Jersey Weekly Post, 17/1/0/96, 1.

[28] ibid.

[29] op. cit., Pirouet interview.

[30] "Shock admission: Jersey hooked on drugs money", Jersey Weekly Post, 30/5/96, 3.

[31] Grey, S., "The Blue Chip Islands", Accountancy: The Journal of The Institute of Chartered Accountants in England and Wales, September 1994, vol.114, no.1213, 1994, 35, hereafter, The Blue Chip Islands.

[32] ibid., 34.

[33] op. cit., Treasure Island, 240.

[34] op. cit., Powell interview.

[35] Commonwealth Secretariat, Vulnerability: Small States in Global Society, Commonwealth Secretariat, London, 1985, 35.

[36] Rohter, L., "Panamanian drug scandal poses dilemma for US ally" in Guardian, 13/6/96, 14.

[37] op. cit., The Offshore Interface, 77.

[38] ibid.

[39] Roberts, S., "Fictitious Capital, Fictitious Spaces: the Geography of Offshore Financial Flows",

109, in Corbridge, S., Martin, R. & Thrift, N. eds., <u>Money, Power and Space</u>, Oxford, Blackwell, 1984.

[40] Neale, T., "Tax and a Labour Government? Make the first move, CI urged" <u>Jersey Weekly Post</u>, 8/2/96, 11.

[41] op. cit., Le Hérissier, 51-53.

[42] op. cit., The Offshore Interface, 73.

[43] Johns, R. A., & Le Marchant, C. M., <u>Finance Centres: British Isle Offshore Development since 1979</u>, Francis Pinter, London, 1979.

[44] Roberts, S. M., "Small Place, Big Money: The Cayman Islands and the International Finance System" in <u>Economic Geography</u>, vol.16, no. 1, June 1994, 3-14.

[45] Powell, G. C., <u>Economic Survey of Jersey</u>, States Greffe, Jersey, 1971, 18, hereafter, Economic Survey.

[46] op. cit., The Blue Chip Islands, 35.

[47] op. cit., Pirouet interview.

[48] Interview with John Christensen, Assistant Adviser (Economics), 30/8/96.

[49] ibid.

[50] Sweeney, J., "Lords of the Island", <u>The Guardian Section 2</u>, 23/4/96, 4.

[51] States Advisory and Finance Committee, <u>Guernsey Statistics 1996</u>, States of Guernsey, Guernsey, 1996, 19. Public expenditure in 1995 was £194.7 million pounds. The Barclay brothers are alleged to have a personal fortune of £650 million, see: Jeune, P., "Barclay brothers move in to Brecqhou castle", <u>Jersey Evening Post</u>, 3/8/96, 3.

[52] op. cit., Budget Extract 1996, 13.

[53] op. cit., 2000 & Beyond, part 1, 7.

[54] op. cit., JEP Economic Review 1996, 11.

[55] op. cit., Pirouet interview.

[56] op. cit., Kelleher.

[57] op. cit., Budget Extract 1996, 13.

[58] op. cit., JEP Economic Review 1996, 23.

[59] op. cit., Budget Extract 1996, 13.

[60] Economic Adviser, <u>An Introduction to Jersey</u>, Economic's Adviser's Office, Jersey, 1991, Section 18.

[61] Policy and Resources Committee, <u>Strategic Policy Review and Action Plan 1994</u>, States Greffe, Jersey, 1994, 12.

[62] op. cit., Vibert interview.

[63] "EU extends Royal welcome to potato protection", <u>Jersey Weekly Post</u>, 14/3/96, 5.

[64] <u>The Official Isle of Man Yearbook 1996</u>, Executive Publications, Isle of Man, 1996, 69.

[65] Interview with Mr Steven Carse, Economic Adviser to the Economic Affairs Division of the Isle of Man Treasury, 14/5/1996.

[66] op. cit., Economic Survey, 181.

[67] op. cit., EEC Report 1967, 54.

[68] op. cit., 2000 & Beyond Part 1, 36.

Chapter 5 - The United Kingdom:
The Pivotal Link

Introduction

The relationship between Jersey and the United Kingdom is pivotal to the island. Jersey's constitution, economy and ability to interact with the rest of the world is dependent on it. To understand the long term stability of this relationship it is necessary to assess why it is in the interest of both parties to preserve the association. This chapter will examine how the United Kingdom views the relationship, the arrangements facilitating its operation and the extent to which service-provision is shared.

In studying the United Kingdom's attitude to the relationship it is important to assess whether the United Kingdom benefits from it and why it not only tolerates, but also prefers, the *status quo*. A fear exists in Jersey that the current constitutional arrangement will only survive as long as it is convenient for the United Kingdom to allow it to do so. While this is no doubt the case, a strong argument exists that the benefits of the management of a formal dependency relationship flow both ways. The United Kingdom has maintained significant, if rarely used, powers over Jersey. It has also maintained a formal bureaucratic structure to communicate with Jersey and to informally guide decision-making on the island, should this become necessary. The dependency relationship thus allows the United Kingdom to exert informal and covert pressure. This avoids the danger of a public confrontation which, although it would be far more damaging to Jersey, nevertheless would place the United Kingdom in the embarrassing position of being perceived as bullying a smaller jurisdiction. In addition, it preserves the political stability as neither side needs to acknowledge any disagreements in public.

The economic benefits which each side derives from the relationship are more difficult to quantify. No official figures exists for Jersey's contribution to the British economy although defenders of the finance industry suggest as much as £150 billion is invested in the City of London via Jersey.[1] Certainly the offshore finance centre funnels money into the City of London. However, its opponents argue that the offshore finance centre causes leakage of tax receipts out of the United Kingdom making Jersey a drain on the British economy. What is easier to conclude is that the island is a major market for British goods and that Jersey relies on the United Kingdom as a market for its agricultural exports and as a source of tourism. In addition, Jersey makes a contribution towards the services provided by the United Kingdom, although in the case of defence the contribution is not remotely equivalent to the spending per capita of the United Kingdom.

A hostile interpretation of the relationship is that it is based on neglect, an analysis supported by the low level and infrequent contacts the Crown Dependencies have with the Home Office. This is particularly so when comparison is made with the Dutch Dependencies which have representation at Cabinet level. The United Kingdom's paramount objective in its relationship with Jersey, namely that the island should not become a problem, is similar to that which the United Kingdom has in relation to its other dependencies. Beyond this, it has no interest in insular events. Jersey has been able to exploit this neglect over the past forty years to create its offshore finance industry. However, the fact that Jersey has been able to manage the relationship to ensure its prosperity does not necessarily mean that the relationship is benign. The decline of the Manx economy in the early post war years suggest that the United Kingdom's lack of intervention was not because of Jersey's economic success, but rather part of a general policy of non intervention. Evidence of the neglect is illustrated by the scarce Home Office resources devoted to overseeing the affairs of all the Crown Dependencies, the lack of any proposals to develop the relationship and ministerial statements regarding the island which have amounted to little more than platitudes.[2] This view of the relationship has worked to the extent that Jersey has not yet seriously embarrassed the United Kingdom on the international stage. The disputes which have entered the international arena are those which have resulted from the late implementation of international agreements or the operation of the offshore finance centre. With respect to international agreements, it can be argued that such occurrences are as much the fault of the United Kingdom authorities in not devoting sufficient time to the management of an issue over which they have ultimate jurisdiction. However, the existence of an offshore finance centre represents a more likely source of conflict. In this area, however, the United Kingdom might find it difficult to curtail Jersey's operations, not only because the City of London operates in a similar way, but also because the two finance centres have a symbiotic relationship.[3]

If the United Kingdom, in particular Parliament, were to take a more active interest in Jersey's affairs, pressure would build on the Home Office to take a more pro-active stance in its management of the relationship. Issues might be of concern, not because of illegality or immorality, but rather due to the different political outlooks of the authorities in Jersey and the United Kingdom. Such attention would place strains on the relationship since Jersey would resent what it saw as unwarranted interventions in its internal affairs. The United Kingdom's policy of neglect thus has the advantage that it is seen not to be meddling in Jersey's affairs.

On the other hand, the disadvantage of the relationship is that Jersey only appears on the policy agenda when a crisis has occurred and this does not create a propensity in the Home Office for addressing Jersey's problems. In fact, the United Kingdom seems to discourage issues being sent to it. The relationship can be characterised as the United Kingdom allowing the island self-government by setting a very high threshold before intervening. However, when intervention is deemed necessary, the United Kingdom reserves the right to use its good government powers to their fullest extent. The implication of the above policy is that if Jersey cannot sort out its own problem and thereby requires action by the United Kingdom, part of the outcome will be some form of punishment for the island. The Home Office would, however, argue that their actions would only be to correct behaviour on the island's part. Despite this, they would be perceived on the island as punitive. The relationship can therefore be seen to resemble that of a parent's attitude to an adolescent. Jersey is allowed responsibility within defined parameters, but problems arise in defining where these are set. In an arrangement of this form it is to the United Kingdom's advantage for Jersey to learn to manage its dependency. This is because the metropolitan power's attitude of *laissez faire* depends on Jersey knowing the parameters of its autonomy in a changing international climate and using this autonomy to ensure its own prosperity.

The core conventions of the relationship are, in the eyes of the United Kingdom, defined in the Kilbrandon report.[4] The report cites the areas in which the United Kingdom would be prepared to override the island's wishes as defence, matters common to British people throughout the world, good government, international responsibilities and preservation of the United Kingdom's own external interests.[5] This list seems to be potentially all encompassing while contradicting the convention of non-interference in the island's domestic and fiscal affairs. This description of the relationship must therefore be regarded as a simplified façade. Instead, each element of the relationship reflects the uncodified and often *ad hoc* way it has developed.

The interpretation of the good government power by the United Kingdom is essential to any discussion of the relationship. Kilbrandon's view was that "the United Kingdom Government ... ought to be very slow to seek to impose their will on the Islands merely on the grounds that they know better than the Islands what is good for them."[6] The report goes on to note that "the UK should be very careful not to confuse its essential interests with its own convenience and preference or the damage to those essential interests with mere irritation or annoyance".[7] This attitude would seem to reflect British policy during the post-war period and is a different interpretation of the apparent neglect shown towards the island by the United Kingdom. What must be assessed, however, is how far these noble sentiments represent a façade and how far they represent the reality of the relationship. This policy does not extend to Jersey's external affairs and amounts to an acknowledgement of Jersey's informal domestic autonomy. However, the extent of such autonomy has declined with the development of the offshore finance centre and the evolution of international law. It is in the field of international law that the most potential for conflict occurs, in part because interests diverge and in part because it is the area where the United

Kingdom asserts its authority over the island. Even the Royal Commission noted that "circumstances may arise in which an international agreement will be applied to the Islands against their wishes",[8] the most significant of these being Jersey creating any form of association with the European Union.

The relationship has bound Britain to Jersey in a form of uncodified, multi-level government. Both domestically and internationally, many formal and informal influences and avenues of appeal exist. Domestically, each islander has at least fourteen elected representatives at his disposal together with legal and administrative channels which include appeals directly to the Bailiff. In terms of external influences, regular appeals are made to the Lieutenant Governor, the Queen, the Home Office, the European Court of Justice, the European Court of Human Rights or, if the appellant has links with the United Kingdom, via Members of Parliament or the European Union. These external avenues of appeal serve as very useful escape valves for internal dissent on the island. As many of these appeals involve the United Kingdom, no matter how little the United Kingdom desires to intervene in Jersey's domestic affairs, its role as metropolitan power ensures it will. The Home Office is further constrained by the view, held both in the island and other nations, that non-intervention on an issue signals consent. Further, the media assume that Jersey is under the control of the United Kingdom authorities. All these factors necessitate the United Kingdom to maintain an interest in insular affairs and the ability to intervene to prevent damage to its own image abroad or in the media.

The Kilbrandon Commission reflected United Kingdom policy in strongly resisting codification of the island's constitution.[9] This was despite submissions from Jersey, Alderney and the Isle of Man proposing codification. Codification would tend to limit the island's autonomy and Jersey has since reversed its position on this matter. The act of drafting or revising the constitutional elements of the relationship would put the Dependencies at a disadvantage as the far larger United Kingdom civil service could be brought into play for the time necessary to define the relationship. Moreover, at a superficial level it would seem that an uncodified constitution tends to favour the stronger party in a dispute. However, this is not true where the stronger party has less of an interest in the relationship. The United Kingdom may have far more, and even abler, legal minds at its disposal, but, as any potential changes in the relationship would affect the United Kingdom much less than Jersey even in absolute terms, far less effort is put into understanding and managing the island's relationship. Further, people with constitutional expertise are almost entirely concentrated in the island. Therefore both sides in the relationship now prefer to keep the relationship informal and flexible.[10] It should be noted that a more formal definition of powers could require the United Kingdom to legislate in areas which would be better left to the States, either due to their controversial nature or the fact that the United Kingdom does not have a view on whether legislation is required.

The United Kingdom's attitude was best illustrated by the negotiation surrounding the United Kingdom's accession to the European Economic Community where Jersey, in association with the other Crown Dependencies, presented a proposal which was adopted with little debate as all the other parties had other priorities. These negotiations, however, highlighted a limitation on the advantages which an informal and flexible constitution bestows on Jersey. Should an issue arise which the United Kingdom attaches importance to, the flexibility and informality of the relationship allows the United Kingdom to rapidly bring unchecked pressure to bear on the island. Thus the United Kingdom was able to dictate that it was joining the European Economic Community and if the United Kingdom's membership forced the Crown Dependencies to join against their will, it was not considered an obstacle.

The option of adopting a more modern federal system might give the island more security as it would gain parity of status with the other units of the federation. However, such a situation, while technically producing equality, would expose Jersey's political weakness as the one Member of Parliament which Jersey could hope to obtain in a federal arrangement would effectively minimise its current influence. At present, the island has larger informal influence exaggerated by it having no direct access to Parliament, instead its views must be represented by a major department of state.

Constitutional Position of the Crown Dependencies

Jersey, Guernsey and the Isle of Man form the Crown Dependencies. Crown Dependencies can be distinguished from United Kingdom Overseas Territories by not being acquired by conquest or discovery. Additionally, their good government is the responsibility of the Home Office, as opposed to the Foreign and Commonwealth Office, and their constitutions retain significant medieval elements. Their title emphasises that the Channel Islands predate England as a possession of the Crown. Further, Jersey's links with the United Kingdom predate the evolution of Parliament as a modern legislature and therefore no direct link with Westminster is acknowledged in that the Channel Islands were formally annexed to the Crown of England in 1254 by Henry III.

The distinction between the Crown Dependencies and the United Kingdom Overseas Territories is, to a degree, a product of historical inertia and the desire of the islands themselves in the past to have such status. However, it also maintains a useful distinction for the United Kingdom. The United Kingdom Overseas Territories, with the exception of the special cases of Gibraltar and the Sovereign Base Area in Cyprus, are not geographically proximate to the United Kingdom. Therefore the amount of interaction the Crown Dependencies have with the United Kingdom on a day-to-day basis is of a different order to that of United Kingdom Overseas Territories. Given this, the responsibility for the Crown Dependencies in many ways fits more accurately into the British-focused Home Office than the overseas-focused Foreign and Commonwealth Office. It has also long been the assumption behind the operation of the Foreign and Commonwealth Office that independence was to be encouraged and granted to all territories under its control, wherever viable. However, despite all of the Crown Dependencies being larger and richer than many of the Caribbean colonies which have thus far been granted independence, the different assumptions about independence, due to the high level of cultural and economic interdependence existing between the United Kingdom and the Dependencies, have resulted in both sides always viewing this as a last resort.

The distinction also has the advantage of helping to reduce the difficulties faced by the island with respect to the United Nations. The United Nations established a Special Committee as a result of a 1960 General Assembly Resolution entitled "Declaration on the Granting of Independence to Colonial Countries and Peoples."[11] The special committee established saw its role as ensuring that independence was granted to all remaining dependencies regardless of size.[12] The refusal of the United Nations to recognise entities other than sovereign states therefore not only causes problems for Jersey in the field of international agreements, but has the potential to create a situation where the metropolitan power is put under pressure to grant Jersey independence regardless of the wishes of either party. Were the United Kingdom to come under sustained pressure at the United Nations to grant Jersey independence, this option would become more attractive, if only to relieve pressure in that forum. However, Jersey's status as a Crown Dependency seems to have exempted it from the regular visits by the Committee of Twenty Four which the United Kingdom Overseas Territories have to endure.[13] Thomas Russell's description of one visit describes how "they came and they really lifted up the carpets to find one Caymanian underneath that wanted to be independent. They couldn't find one".[14] Such visits would serve to damage the finance industry on the island which would see them as threatening the island's political stability. Thus no evidence exists that the Committee of Twenty Four is interested in attempting to impose independence on the island. However, it must be noted that the United Nations has been approached by politicians from the Isle of Man examining the option of Manx independence.

In light of the recent move towards devolution within the United Kingdom, consideration must be given to how far the Crown Dependencies fit into such a model. Constitutionally the islands do not fit into any modern model of devolution. The islands are for most purposes fully autonomous which suggests a willingness on behalf of the United Kingdom to tolerate the loss of direct control required for devolution to work. However, the fundamental difference between this and the modern form of devolved powers is that, as the powers were never formally devolved by a modern Act of Parliament, it would be more difficult to legally revoke the core elements of the constitution as no Act of Parliament exists to be revoked. Moreover, in the current situation, the Crown Dependencies would be likely to seek independence if the United Kingdom attempted to revoke their autonomy.

Fiscal Autonomy

The view that taxation should be viewed as purely a local concern is problematic as Jersey's economy is not totally self-contained but global, and actions by Jersey have ramifications beyond its borders. Insular fiscal policy therefore cannot be seen as an entirely domestic issue and any claim by Jersey to have independence in this field must be viewed on its own merits. Jersey's fiscal independence, from which it chose to develop a successful offshore finance centre, also forms the basis for its domestic autonomy. Thus both fiscal and domestic independence must be defended as both are necessary for Jersey's survival. This constrains the ability of the Home Office and the Treasury to press for any changes in the island's fiscal independence, as doing so would cripple the offshore finance centre and leave the United Kingdom with the responsibility for Jersey's collapsed economy.

It must also be remembered there are reasons for the United Kingdom to tolerate Jersey's current position. The Kilbrandon Commission, despite a dissenting memorandum prepared by Crowther-Hunt and Peacook,[15] merely confirmed the island's pre-existing fiscal privileges.[16] Jersey is politically stable and not only requires no funding, but actually provides a small contribution to the Treasury. Jersey's offshore finance centre is in a symbiotic relationship with the City of London which is one of the United Kingdom's largest industries. To impose a different solution would not only damage the interests of the City but would involve Treasury expenditure. Furthermore, it would cause political instability in the island which might have international ramifications for the United Kingdom as it would be seen to be imposing its will on a small, but very old, political entity. Therefore the preservation of the *status quo* is attractive to the United Kingdom authorities and becomes more attractive the less Jersey impinges on United Kingdom policy-making. Thus the United Kingdom's policy towards the island is characterised by a conservative approach aimed at preserving the existing situation where Jersey is not an economic or political burden.

The fundamental weakness in the current situation is that Jersey's dominant industry can be seen as a major burden on the United Kingdom since some commentators argue that the removal of offshore finance would prevent tax leakage from larger states. The salience of this issue is illustrated by the fact that some of the most bitter disputes in the relationship arose over financial matters. Whatever the merits of this argument, its support by members of the Labour Party could undermine the relationship. The offshore finance centre has therefore fundamentally changed the nature of Jersey's fiscal independence as, when it was granted, such independence was largely an issue domestic to Jersey. Since the war a large, legal and visible industry has developed exploiting this element of Jersey's constitution thereby changing the nature of the autonomy granted.

The development of Jersey's offshore finance centre has also added a new element to the United Kingdom's relationship in ideological terms. All the Crown

Dependencies have traditionally been conservative. With the development of a finance industry, this political bias has been overlaid with the knowledge that the Conservative Party tends to be ideologically more sympathetic to offshore finance than Labour. This, together with the close links developed between the Conservative Party and the island's elites during the eighteen years of the last Conservative government, left both sides of the relationship wary when the Labour Party was returned to power in 1997.[17] One justification for the Edwards review into the island's financial legislation and regulation is the Labour Party's uncertainties about offshore finance. The situation may have been worsened by the allegations about Lord Simon and Geoffrey Robinson having offshore interests in Jersey and Guernsey and the use of this information by the opposition to try to embarrass the government.

The hostile attitude to Jersey in sections of the British press and the Labour Party towards offshore finance is well known. Austin Mitchell, MP commented in an article about whether the United Kingdom should extend its own Bill of Rights to the island that "now at long last human rights are to accompany the floods of funny money, the tax fiddlers and the wealthy exiles who pour out of Britain to the Channel Islands and the Isle of Man."[18] Such comments by a member of the governing party, even one very unlikely to ever be granted ministerial office, do not build goodwill and trust. However, the United Kingdom does feel it to be necessary to monitor the operation of Jersey's offshore finance centre. This is due to worries about tax leakage and the use of such territories in ways which might damage the United Kingdom's own economy, for example the threatened exodus of accountancy firms from the United Kingdom when Jersey introduced legislation allowing for limited liability partnerships to be set up. The need for sensitive monitoring of the situation is heightened by the fact that Jersey feels its very existence as a separate political entity is at stake and hence prepared to use public relations firms and lobbyists at all available opportunities to defend its fiscal position.

The relationship may, however, be enhanced by the fact that members of both the last and current governments have investments in the island, the most significant being Michael Heseltine whose publishing company, with an estimated value of £150 million, has three directors, two of whom are listed as being based in Jersey.[19] These investments illustrate how integrated Jersey is into the London global finance markets and perhaps guarantee a degree of understanding of how offshore finance operates.

Services Provided by the United Kingdom from which Jersey Benefits

Jersey's small size makes it not only vulnerable to events, but also creates substantial diseconomies of scale in providing certain services. In overcoming these two problems, Jersey's dependency relationship with the United Kingdom is a critical element. Since the 1980s, Jersey has been expected to contribute to the costs of shared services or provide such services independently. This has required Jersey to expand its provision, particularly as the United Kingdom's provision of fishery protection services and search and rescue cover has progressively been separated from defence.

The Amoco Cadiz incident exemplifies Jersey's vulnerability as a small community. It also highlights the advantages of being in a formal dependency relationship with a larger power in that the United Kingdom felt obliged to assist the island. In 1978, the supertanker Amoco Cadiz ran aground off Brittany. The Channel Islands were immediately threatened by an oil slick which local resources proved inadequate to deal with. The United Kingdom therefore had to provide the resources required to disperse the oil. The overall operation was under United Kingdom control and support was provided by five Royal Navy ships. Resources available on the islands were pooled with those sent by the United Kingdom. The effort to disperse the oil was therefore the responsibility of the Parliamentary Under Secretary of State to the Board of Trade. Although formal channels of communication with the islands are conducted through the Home Office, a meeting between the minister and the island's government was organised to co-ordinate the dispersal effort.[20] Jersey escaped pollution from the oil spill in the end, but the United Kingdom agreed with the authorities in the Channel Islands that Jersey and Guernsey would pay £716,540 towards the cost of the operation, split equally. These costs are in addition to those incurred by the island independently of the United Kingdom, such as the purchase of oil dispersants and booms to protect harbours. The President of the Harbour and Airport Committee summed up Jersey's response to the United Kingdom's request for the contribution by arguing that "it would be "short sighted and stupid" not to pay, as the next time the island could be in real need."[21]

As it is felt that Jersey is unable to sustain a diverse higher education sector, nearly all higher and postgraduate education occurs in the United Kingdom. For this the island pays a fee to cover tuition to the Home Office. This acknowledges that Jersey makes no contribution to the United Kingdom spending and thus the fee negotiated is above the so-called Home rate paid by local education authorities, but below the overseas rate. The fee itself is subject to annual negotiations between the Home Office, the Universities' Vice-Chancellors and the Crown Dependencies with Jersey represented by the Education Committee.[22]

The fact that a reciprocal health care convention is deemed necessary reflects the operation of Jersey as a separate jurisdiction to the United Kingdom as regards health care in that a convention exists in the same way as it would between neighbouring sovereign states.[23] The nature of this agreement is that Jersey treats United Kingdom residents free of charge if they require immediate treatment. This includes medical and nursing services, including those dental, ophthalmic and pharmaceutical services provided via the hospital, together with the operation of a visitors' clinic which offers free consultations with a doctor, a service not available to islanders. Jersey therefore offers the United

Kingdom emergency care both for tourists and those British citizens who move to the island but have not yet paid any insular taxation. In exchange, islanders who, either are temporarily resident in the United Kingdom or require tertiary or superregional treatments not available in Jersey, can be referred to the National Health Service. This provision includes virtually all of the island's students in higher education. The convention allows the Channel Islands access to specialist treatment they could never provide on their own due to diseconomies of scale. The agreement, which has the United Kingdom and the Isle of Man as one party and the Channel Islands as the other, is monitored annually to ensure the costs to each party are roughly similar.

Jersey purchases a number of services from the United Kingdom. The Police, Fire Brigade and, until recently, schools are all inspected by the appropriate United Kingdom inspection services. This not only avoids the costs of maintaining such a service on the island, but also ensures the regular input of external advice. The use of external advisors is common throughout these organisations, in particular in areas where Jersey has little experience. The Customs and Excise and Immigration and Nationality departments must also work in close co-operation with their mainland counterparts, partly because they are effectively enforcing United Kingdom or European Union regulations and partly because of the international nature of the criminal activities they deal with. The United Kingdom controls the activity of the Immigration and Nationality Department even though the island pays its costs. This arrangement represents the concession which Jersey made in order to be allowed to remain within the Common Travel Area.

Despite the fact that overseas aid was considered part of the responsibilities of the Foreign and Commonwealth Office under the Conservative administrations of Margaret Thatcher and John Major, Jersey has a separate distinct overseas aid policy and budget.[24] That this is tolerated reflects the low priority which the United Kingdom gives to control of this policy area. The United Kingdom's position allows the island to develop a distinct policy within this field enabling Jersey to make immediate responses to international emergencies rather than operating via the United Kingdom. As the aid is targeted at a few small countries, the overseas aid budget allows the island to build a high profile in these regions which embodies the strong feeling of solidarity which Jersey has with these countries. Jersey's external policy can therefore be seen to reflect the aim of promoting solidarity, or at least mutual assistance, between small communities.

Constitutionally defence issues would seem to fall totally within the United Kingdom's ambit, yet Jersey makes a defence contribution. The lack of such a contribution between 1940 and 1986 was described by Ralph Vibert as the constitution's Achilles's heel as it left the island open to allegations of benefiting from the United Kingdom's defence umbrella without contributing to it.[25] Jersey has made only six contributions to external defence until 1987.[26] Prior to 1940, Jersey had a militia unit raised solely for local defence. The States, traditionally, made a contribution to the cost of maintaining this unit in the form of paying for the unit's powder, whilst the United Kingdom paid for uniforms and weapons. The division of costs, like the issue of defence, has been a regular source of discontent in the relationship between the island and the United Kingdom.[27] The defence contribution created in 1987 is an integral part of the British army and takes the form of a Territorial Army Field Squadron of the Royal Engineers. As it constitutes a part of the British Army, the insular authorities have no control over its actions, although it is paid for out of the island's budget. This contribution, while important symbolically, must be put into context. It represents 0.07% of Jersey's GDP compared with the United Kingdom's spending of 2.7% and is even less than the spending of the other Crown Dependencies.[28] The low level of Jersey's contribution has meant that the insular authorities have been advised that they are unable to request any reduction in the size of the unit to reflect post cold war defence cuts.[29] The defence contribution's form was established by agreement between the island and the United Kingdom and was to last for a minimum of ten years with no termination date specified. The fact that the contribution took the form of a unit, rather than a cash payment, has had the advantage that the cost of the unit has fallen in real terms since its inception.[30]

The issue of a defence contribution, when raised in the 1920s, caused what Roy Le Hérissier describes as "the most important constitutional conflict of the period."[31] The United Kingdom Committee on National Expenditure, while acknowledging the two gifts Jersey had made towards the costs of the war, noted that "The Channel Islands require and raise comparatively little revenue, and are very lightly taxed"[32] and suggested the island should make a contribution of £275,000 per annum for the benefits in the form of imperial services. The island's reply emphasised its fiscal autonomy and hence the inability of the United Kingdom Parliament to impose such a tax. The dispute led to a Privy Council Report which concluded with a ringing endorsement of absolute parliamentary sovereignty over the island by stating that "Parliament has unquestionably the power to impose financial legislation on the Islands with or without their consent."[33] This threat was, however, not used to enforce payment and the insular authorities continued to resist any payment for services "which the Island had freely enjoyed for centuries."[34] Instead the United Kingdom resorted to less formal economic pressure. The Chancellor of the Exchequer announced plans to prevent United Kingdom residents from avoiding the payment of United Kingdom tax by moving their residence and financial assets to the Channel Islands. Although no formal linkage of the issues was ever made, the Chancellor's proposals were revised once the islands resolved to make a one off lump sum payment.

The most recent defence contribution was precipitated by a letter from the Home Secretary dated 4 June 1984. Earlier flagging of the issue of a defence contribution was made by the Solicitor General in 1981 when he, in a rare and controversial political speech made in the budget debate, urged the States "to make sure that Jersey was seen to "Pay its way" in the eyes of the British Government".[35] There is evidence of unofficial prompting prior to the 1953 contribution and the motivation behind such a request is shown in a Home Office minute:

> In view of the economic difficulties with which the United Kingdom is confronted at the present it may be thought a suitable moment for inviting the Channel Islands to make a contribution to United Kingdom funds in recognition of the benefits which the Islands derive from the participation of the United Kingdom in European defence activities and from consular facilities.[36]

It would seem logical that the same route was taken in the early eighties of beginning by informal soundings via the Crown appointed Crown Officers. However, in the event more direct pressure was necessary in the form of a letter from the Home Secretary. The Bailiff's response was to request the "Father of the House" to propose a Committee composed of senior members of the assembly to look into the matter. It was a reflection of the serious constitutional implications of the issue that such a powerful committee was created to deal with a request for a relatively small sum of money. The request for a contribution to international representation made on behalf of Jersey proved less controversial as the sum of money involved was smaller, reflecting the overall budget of the Foreign and Commonwealth Office, and the fact that the direct cost attributable to the island could be identified. It was agreed that Jersey would meet its direct costs of overseas representation and maintain the funding of the Immigration and Nationality Department but make no specific payments to the general Foreign and Commonwealth budget. The controversy therefore focused on the defence contribution.

The establishment of a defence contribution was a source of intense controversy on the island, both as regards whether such a contribution should be made and what the nature of the contribution should be. This debate highlighted some of the bones of contention in the island's relationship with the United Kingdom. It was felt the United Kingdom was dictating the form of the contribution and resisting the overwhelming choice of the island.[37] A more emotional argument was that, due to the failure of the defence guarantee in 1940, the United Kingdom neither deserved, nor merited, a defence contribution. Moreover, it was felt that the request for a defence contribution would not have occurred if the island had not flaunted its wealth by offering a gift of five million pounds to the Falkland Islands following their occupation in 1982.[38]

The Committee rejected the option favoured by the Isle of Man of a cash contribution as "It would merely, improve, to an infinitesimal degree, the cash position of HM Treasury."[39] A more concrete option was for a reserve unit to be based in Jersey. Three options were given consideration: a search and rescue helicopter unit, a territorial army unit or a sea training unit centred on a minesweeper. The option favoured by the public was the helicopter.[40] This was rejected by the Ministry of Defence, thereby revealing that as far as the defence contribution was concerned the United Kingdom was prepared to ignore the wishes of the island. The military no longer regarded the provision of search and rescue cover as a military function and this option was, and still is, therefore considered unacceptable.[41] The alternative chosen by the Committee and supported by the Ministry of Defence as making the greatest contribution to national defence was a minesweeper. This choice was unpopular as it was viewed as both too expensive and too labour-intensive for the island to sustain. It was felt that the Ministry of Defence, as always, was seeking to obtain the most money possible out of the island. This view feeds off a feeling of impotence generated by the island's lack of control over the issue. The debate surrounding the minesweeper proved so contentious that the option was taken of making a one-off payment in 1987 while consideration began of the third alternative, the Territorial Army unit. This proposal was finally accepted by the United Kingdom since the preferred option in Jersey, the search and rescue unit, was still deemed unacceptable.

The issue of defence has always been at the core of Jersey's relationship with the United Kingdom, indeed its privileges are based on the need to keep a frontier province loyal. Even in the twentieth century, despite Jersey no longer being on the boundary between two hostile powers, defence issues have been responsible for conflicts within the relationship. On three occasions in 1927, 1953 and 1986 the issue of how far Jersey should fund the cost of the United Kingdom's defence budget and the representation provided on Jersey's behalf by the British government abroad has arisen. The issue led to tension in the relationship, in particular in the first and last case, due to the constitutional issues which such a request raises. The practice before 1940 of Jersey defending itself with a militia consisting, during the majority of its existence, of all adult males had proved acceptable as it suited the island's traditions of honorary service and was confined to the island. Further, insular feeling is that a general contribution to the British defence budget could easily be increased by the United Kingdom without Jersey's consent. Jersey's view of defence has always been more local than that of its metropolitan power. While service in the militia for defence of the island was compulsory, service outside the island was always voluntary and no islander can be conscripted into the British armed forces. The defence controversy created resentment because consideration of the issues ceased to be in the confidential informal arena. The public and politicians dislike such issues being public as well as the resulting instability caused to the relationship. However, in this case it is unclear whether the insular authorities themselves forced the issues into the open by not responding to earlier, confidential prompting. The concept of a defence contribution raises the question of whether such a contribution amounts to a form of taxation and thus run counter to Jersey's fiscal autonomy by creating a situation where Jersey pays taxation to the United Kingdom Parliament without being represented in it. This led Guernsey historian L. James Marr to declare that "One thing is crystal clear. Regular subventions to the British Exchequer would mean the end of our autonomy, as to pay a tax is to recognise one's subordination to its recipient."[42] This view was accepted by the insular authorities in 1927 but rejected by Jersey's Crown Officers in 1985.[43] Jersey's defence contribution, however, can be seen as a significant reversion to the Victorian model when the United Kingdom, although responsible for the island's defence, required Jersey to make a contribution to the costs.

Jersey made no formal contribution to defence spending, nor to the cost of representing the island abroad until 1987. This, together with the island having no public debt, has significantly reduced the financial burden on the island when compared to that of the United Kingdom. The United Kingdom provides defence to which Jersey makes a contribution. In all other areas Jersey either purchases the service from the United Kingdom or has a reciprocal arrangement in which Jersey pays the same amount as a United Kingdom authority. However, increasingly Jersey arranges its own services, the prime reason being the introduction of more market mechanisms and privatisation in the United Kingdom. Both factors make the billing of Jersey for specific services easier as well as encouraging institutions to seek new sources of income outside the Treasury thus making Jersey, a rich community, an obvious target. This could either be viewed as increasing Jersey's autonomy or as a worrying sign of reduction of the United Kingdom's commitment to the relationship. However, it does avoid potential tension developing when it is felt that Jersey benefits excessively from a British spending priority to which it does not contribute.

Limits to Autonomy

The United Kingdom imposes few, if any, limitations on Jersey's autonomy since the island is seen as largely irrelevant by the British government. Lord Williams of Mostyn on his first visit to the island repeated the Home Office view that "We have no intention of reviewing the position. Both parties appear content with the current arrangements, and they would appear to work well from what I have seen."[44] However, the Minister, when asked about Jersey's offshore finance centre, acknowledged Jersey's independent right to set its own fiscal laws but argued that issues of tax leakage fell under the ambit of the Treasury, not the Home Office.

Much of the management of the relationship occurs beneath a façade of high politics, a pertinent example being that the island's official links are to the Privy Council, though in reality to the Home Office. The fact that the relationship is stable and prosperous is not, however, entirely down to luck. The relationship is managed via meetings and procedures, such as the assent procedure for Jersey Laws, which have plenty of scope for instability were the management of the relationship to be unsuccessful, given its uncodified and asymmetrical nature.

Jersey's relationship with the United Kingdom may be different under the

101

Labour party because the party finds the notion of dependencies embarrassing. The Labour government renamed the former British Dependencies United Kingdom Overseas Territories because it did not like the implications of the term "dependencies".[45] Jersey, being a Crown Dependency, may find itself vulnerable due to this name since the assumption is that a dependency is financially dependent on the United Kingdom, a situation which is untrue of any of the Crown Dependencies and of a majority of the former British Dependencies. Rather, it could be argued that Jersey is a Crown Dependency because this is an accurate description of its status under international law. The problem which must be resolved within the Labour Party is whether it is acceptable for the party in government to maintain dependencies or overseas territories or whether they should be granted independence irrespective of their wishes, a position in many ways similar to that of the United Nations Special Committee on the situation with regard to the Implementation of the Declaration on the Granting of Independence to Colonial Countries and Peoples. The problem, if the latter course is to be taken, is that such an action may not prevent these territories from remaining offshore finance centres. In addition, the Crown Dependencies are so proximate to the United Kingdom that independence may cause more, rather than less, problems for a United Kingdom government. The option favoured by some members of the Labour party is absorption which is justified by the tax leakage damaging the United Kingdom economy.

Crown in Council

The apex of government is the Privy Council via its "Committee of the Privy Council for the Affairs of Jersey and Guernsey and for the Isle of Man". This Committee has long been the active link between the island and the United Kingdom and constitutes the ultimate arena for constitutional debate and conflict resolution. The Committee is dominated by the Home Secretary who advises the Crown on the appointment of fellow Committee members.

The Committee consists of the Lord President, the Home Secretary and two or three other Privy Councillors nominated by them. The Council delegates major issues to Royal Commissions. Both the Committee as well as any Royal Commissions are effectively selected by the government of the day which gives the United Kingdom government the ability to select, not only which issues go before the Committee, but also who adjudicates on the matter. An appeal to the Privy Council is therefore not an appeal to the Queen for non-political adjudication of a wrong, as its image in Jersey would suggest, but an appeal to the Home Secretary, not only as a politician but also as a Member of Parliament.

The Privy Council's Committee for the affairs of Jersey and Guernsey is appointed at each succession and acts as the advisory body to the Crown. The Committee's remit is defined as covering –

All Acts passed, or to be passed, by the States of the Islands of

Jersey and Guernsey and its Dependencies, and submitted to Her Majesty in Council for Her Majesty's approval, and all petitions received from these Islands be, and the same are hereby, referred to the said Committee for their consideration and report.[46]

In their evidence to Kilbrandon, the Jersey Constitutional Association suggested that the Committee should consist of a majority of the Privy Councillors nominated by the States, as in its current form it represents a very real expression of the United Kingdom government's power over the island.[47] The Home Office strongly objected to these proposals on constitutional grounds as:

> It would be intolerable for differing advice to be tendered to Her Majesty on a single subject and inevitable therefore both that the Privy Counsellors appointed to the Committee to hear the petition should be members of Her Majesty's Government and they would seek guidance from the Home Secretary and the Ministers directly concerned with the matter.[48]

The Jersey Constitutional Association's proposal would, in effect, allow Jersey to appoint its own sovereign body which would fundamentally change Jersey's present position. The result would be *de facto* independence as the United Kingdom would have no sovereign authority over the island. The United Kingdom would consider it preferable for the island to seek independence rather than modifying the operation of the Privy Council. An even more unsatisfactory model could emerge if the Home Secretary used his power to block all petitions to the Privy Council for fear of the outcome going against the government. This would place the Channel Islands totally under Home Office control and, while they are prepared to accept this position as the normal state of affairs, they might not be prepared to lose the right of appeal.

Islanders value the right to petition Her Majesty in Council as a practical expression of the belief that the island's fundamental relationship is with the Crown, not with Parliament. This general right of appeal can be viewed as a double-edged sword as far as the United Kingdom authorities are concerned as it does threaten to involve the United Kingdom in many domestic disputes. The right of petition to the Privy Council is another element of the constitution where the façade appears much more impressive than reality. Petitions are channelled through the Home Secretary who has the power, nearly always used, to prevent the petition going any further. If the Home Secretary deems the petition worthy of consideration, it is heard by the Committee of the Privy Council for the Affairs of Jersey and Guernsey.

The Privy Council Committee which heard the petition from Tynwald with respect to United Kingdom's plan to extend the Marine Broadcasting Offences Act to the Isle of Man was entirely composed of ministers. This led to a feeling that the island could not receive a fair hearing when complaining about the actions of the United Kingdom Parliament as the Privy Council and the British government had become virtually identical. Although this may be the case, to expect to have a veto over the appointment of Privy Council Committees is unreasonable as the United Kingdom would not tolerate a diminution of its ability to control the Crown Dependencies.

The idea that Jersey remains the personal property of the Crown is of little relevance to the operation of the relationship today. The most important residual element is that the Judicial Committee of the Privy Council acts as the final court of appeal while the Committee of the Privy Council for the Affairs of Jersey and Guernsey is the supreme executive and legislative body. The Queen has delegated her powers to the Home Secretary, who further delegates the oversight of the Crown Dependencies to a minister of state. This development amounts to a pragmatic acknowledgement of the constitutional changes that have occurred in the United Kingdom in the past century. Before that, it was possible to use the Crown to counter-balance attempts by the United Kingdom Parliament to assert control over the island. This is no longer true as, even though the institutional façade of Crown prerogative remains, the reality is that it is exercised by the Home Secretary.

Parliamentary Sovereignty

Jersey's links with the United Kingdom remain mediated via the Crown as direct links with Parliament, via an elected MP, have never existed. There have been only two attempts to instruct Jersey to send MPs to the English Parliament. In 1541, a letter was sent to the Privy Council requesting the election of two MPs, but no election occurred. In 1652, Parliament declared Jersey an English county and later, when Cromwell was made Protector, it was decreed that Jersey should have one seat in all future Parliaments. However, this was effectively annulled at the Restoration when all Jersey's ancient privileges were restored in recognition of its loyalty to the Crown in the Civil War. The United Kingdom Parliament has never imposed direct taxation on the island. Jersey's autonomy is thus theoretically buttressed by the fact that the only formal democratic representation available to the island is that provided by its own legislature. Direct rule by the United Kingdom Parliament without representation therein would be tantamount to colonial rule and would pave the way for an appeal to be made to such bodies as the European Court of Human Rights.

Jersey's lobbying of Parliament is informal in nature and by tradition, unlike Gibraltar or the Falkland Islands, there is no backbench group of MPs lobbying on the island's behalf.[49] A danger exists that such a grouping might be seen as acknowledging parliamentary sovereignty over the island. Instead, personal links between those in power in Jersey and the United Kingdom are promoted. Moreover, in the Commonwealth Parliamentary Association parliamentarians meet as equals which allows the island's politicians to cultivate links with MPs away from the glare of media attention. The Labour MP George Foulkes was in the early eighties a major critic of the island's offshore activities and is now a junior government minister. Through his membership of the Commonwealth Parliamentary Association, local politicians have sought to convince him that his criticism of the past was unfounded and Foulkes has made no hostile comments about the island since. Perhaps more importantly, efforts have been made since the occupation to cultivate a good relationship between the relevant United Kingdom civil servants and their Jersey counterparts. This practice has been promoted by both sides to ensure the smooth functioning of a largely uncodified relationship.[50]

The traditional view of Jersey's parliamentary sovereignty is summed up by Charles Le Quesne:

> The [Channel] Islands are not represented in Parliament; they do not derive their laws or constitution from Parliament; they belong to the Crown, but do not form part of the realm of England. They are not a portion of the United Kingdom. This position is derived from their being a part and parcel of the ancient Duchy of Normandy, which, although governed by Kings of England after the Conquest, was not subject to the Parliament of England, but to its own peculiar constitution, their Dukes sitting on the English throne.[51]

However, the extent or existence of parliamentary sovereignty over Jersey is a source of dispute. Parliament's influence over the island must be divided into two elements. There is no dispute that members of the Commons, and more directly the Lords, are in a position of power over the island, either by membership of the Privy Council or the Home Office. The distinct debate is more theoretical and centres on whether Parliament has that power in its own right or purely by the coincidence that many of its members are in the Privy Council. In terms of behaviour, Parliament has acted as if it has authority over the island and throughout the nineteenth and twentieth century members of both houses have asked questions which directly infringed on the island's presumed independence in domestic and fiscal affairs. Nineteenth century interventions peaked with attempts by Sergeant Piggott MP in 1861 and John Locke MP in 1864 to impose reforms on Jersey's Royal Court through parliamentary Bills. These were in part instigated by a local reform group under Abraham Le Cras. The first Jersey Court Bill was halted by the government in its second reading to allow the island to reform itself. The second Bill, which was introduced when it was felt the island was failing to do this, was dropped after its second reading as the island had both illustrated popular hostility to Parliament's intervention by means of a petition and undertaken some internal reforms.[52]

Similar questions have arisen which have given the opposition a chance to embarrass the government, such as William Hague's questions with respect to Lord Simon's and Geoffrey Robinson's investments in the Channel Islands.[53] Other questions have been aimed more specifically against the island by focusing on Jersey's low tax or housing policies.[54] The response of the Home Office has been an explanation of the constitutional relationship.[55] The Home Office can therefore be seen as protecting the constitutional *status quo* from backbenchers' hostility. However, the very tabling of such questions causes concern on the island and exerts pressure for change. It also suggests that some peers and MPs believe that Parliament has authority over the island. Indeed Lord Lester of Herne Hill citing Kilbrandon argued that "Constitutionally, there is nothing to prevent the United Kingdom Parliament legislating for the Channel Islands and the Isle of Man."[56]

It is not only Members of Parliament who seek to use the United Kingdom parliament to influence affairs in Jersey. When Labour is in power, Jersey-based trade unions use their links with their United Kingdom counterparts to achieve their objectives on the island. Thus within a month of Labour gaining power in 1997, the Transport and General Workers' Union leader, Bill Morris, was in contact with the Home Secretary. This was alleged to have resulted in a ministerial investigation into why the union had been excluded from consultation on legislation proposed by the Employment and Social Security Committee of the States, a matter which would seem to fall entirely within Jersey's ambit in formulating its own domestic policies.[57] Such rumours of informal Home Office interventions are not uncommon and, because of the informal nature of the relationship, difficult to quantify.[58]

The United Kingdom's willingness to overrule local wishes to impose parliamentary policy was illustrated by the introduction of the Civil Aviation Act of 1946. The Act, introduced to nationalise the airlines, was forced through against the wishes of the island.[59] Jersey Airways had local support due to its efforts to maintain the air-link with the United Kingdom from the outbreak of the war until the island was occupied. In the process, it helped in the evacuation of those who wished to leave while assisting the insular authorities in maintaining communication with the mainland. Attempts in the House of Lords to exclude the Channel Islands failed and what was an element of United Kingdom economic policy was imposed. This was due to the significance of the legislation to the new government and its unwillingness to see any airline continue to function privately by transferring its operations to the Channel Islands. Unfortunately, the Act also had the effect of nationalising those airlines already operating from the Channel Islands. The United Kingdom government of the day saw no constitutional objection to extending the Act to Jersey. The island's attempt to form a separate airline was halted by the United Kingdom's use of economic, rather than constitutional, tools with the United Kingdom stating it would deny such an airline landing rights thereby making such a project financially untenable. Jersey was allowed to keep control over its airport and a Channel Island Air Advisory Council was created in recognition that the Act was forced on the Channel Islands. This compromise allowed the outcome to be presented as not being a complete defeat for the island, the United Kingdom preserved its nationalisation policy intact while Jersey kept control of its airport, even if it was obliged to follow United Kingdom rules on how it operated. Control of the airport was of emotional importance as evidenced by a States member at the time arguing that "no one will consider a proposition that will abandon some small part of Jersey soil to the British Government."[60] The Act also created the first and only statutory body which represents the interest of all the Channel Islands on a specific topic to the United Kingdom. The group has access at ministerial and Select Committee level leading to the first address by a member of the States to a parliamentary body.

Jersey's Law Officers have accepted that Parliament not only has the paramount right to legislate with respect to the island, but also that this right covers all fields of legislation and does not require the consent of the States.[61] However, the Law Officers, at Kilbrandon qualified their submission:

But in relation to self-governing territories outside the United Kingdom, parliamentary sovereignty is, to a very large extent, a legal abstraction, having only a remote connection with political realities. Far more important than the theoretical omni-competence of Parliament is the fact that sovereignty is qualified by a duty to observe constitutional conventions or binding usages.[62]

In his evidence to the Kilbrandon Commission, Dr. William Heyting disputed the view that Parliament had ever enjoyed legislative authority over the island as the link with the Crown predates Parliament.[63]

Parliament's power is enhanced in that Royal Assent is required for Acts of the States which gives the Home Office a veto over all insular legislation. This right is viewed by the Home Office as necessary because forsaking it "would remove one of the means whereby institutions and practices in the islands may be kept in close harmony with those in the United Kingdom."[64] Open disputes are avoided by prior consultation on legislation while it is being drafted and it is difficult to judge the influence of this procedure. However, the fact that Jersey submits its legislation to the United Kingdom at all suggests that the United Kingdom has authority in this area. Notably, the United Kingdom has only committed itself to consult the insular authorities when it seeks to extend an Order in Council to the island when possible, thereby suggesting an absolute right to legislate without consent when necessary. The power to withhold the Royal Assent is still real, leading the Lieutenant Governor in 1997 to remark that "This is a very real power…It is not just a case of them being rubber stamped."[65] The power of non-registration has never been invoked in the Channel Islands, but only in respect of the Isle of Man.[66]

Heyting argues that "It has been a long established rule of Construction of Acts of Parliament that they are only presumed to extend or apply to those parts of the realm that are represented in Parliament".[67] The argument that there can be no legislation without representation, while powerful, is flawed; Parliament could and did legislate with respect to colonies and still does when necessary. The fact that the United Kingdom prefers not to use this power does not mean it does not exist, nor does it mean the power is not valued as an essential element in the relationship should a crisis appear.

It is possible to argue that the Crown Dependencies, being excluded from representation in Parliament by predating Parliament in their accession to the Royal House, are not covered by parliamentary sovereignty.[68] Such an argument, however, fails to acknowledge the constitutional realities of late twentieth century Britain. The Crown has, *de facto*, derogated its powers to Parliament which includes its powers over Crown Dependencies, among them Jersey. The Crown is advised by the Home Secretary on Jersey matters and the Queen always defers to this advice. Even if the Queen wished to attempt to defy her ministers, which in itself is highly improbable, it is unlikely to be over Jersey which is a relatively minor possession of the Crown. Thus there is already a pragmatic acknowledgement of parliamentary sovereignty, made palatable by the fact that little or no direct parliamentary scrutiny occurs. English constitutional theory would seem to assert that the High Court of Parliament has automatic supremacy over all dependencies of the Crown. The good government provisions would seem to assert that all insular authority now derives from Parliament. Therefore, although historically unprecedented, the notional power exists for Parliament to remove insular autonomy.

The view taken by the insular authorities has always been that parliamentary power to legislate over the island exists, but a constitutional convention dictates that this will not occur in domestic or fiscal matters without the consent of the States.[69] It must be noted here that the applicability of constitutional conventions in Jersey is as problematic. The main justification for constitutional conventions is an appeal to past practice, although the definition of domestic affairs is difficult, as suggested by Kilbrandon when Jersey attempted to have the distinction as part of the proposed Jersey Bill.[70] This belief in the absolute duty of Parliament to observe constitutional conventions indefinitely is optimistic. In fact, Simon Horner submits that "by insisting on its continued legal capacity to intervene, the United Kingdom is explicitly denying the existence of a binding convention."[71]

The issue of whether Parliament has sovereignty over the island is dealt with by both sides ignoring the slightly different positions held on the subject. Moreover when appeals are made by islanders to post-medieval concepts, such as no taxation without representation, the United Kingdom maintains a position that it will only accept the relationship in its current form. In this way, it challenges the island to request independence if it does not like the current relationship, knowing that the island is highly unlikely to do this. Thus the options presented to the island are independence or maintaining the archaic relationship. The core issue implicit in the sovereignty debate is not the sovereignty of Parliament, but how far the United Kingdom government is willing to exercise its control in any particular area.

Administration of the Relationship

Maintenance of the United Kingdom's relations with Jersey has in the twentieth century formed part of the responsibilities of the Home Office. This distinction originated in 1801. Jersey's position is anomalous and complicated by the rarity, until recently, of such devolution in Britain. This results in the Home Office having little experience in dealing with such a situation and, perhaps, little sympathy. This attitude of neglect, although not entirely to Jersey's disadvantage, does create problems due to misunderstandings of the island's position both in Parliament and the civil service. Such events as the failure to consult the States before announcing the review of the island's fiscal legislation or the island's membership of the British-Irish Council, create both annoyance and doubts on the island as to how effective the relationship would be, should a real crisis develop.

It must be remembered that, although the relationship with the United Kingdom government is channelled through the Home Office, this is not the only department involved. The Foreign and Commonwealth Office and Ministry of Agriculture, Fisheries and Food are also required to regularly advise on insular affairs. The Home Office, or indirectly the insular authorities, will seek advice from the relevant British government department. Furthermore in specific areas certain departments will keep a close interest in Jersey's affairs. The Foreign and Commonwealth Office, as the department responsible for ensuring Britain's compliance with international agreements, must ensure the Home Office and the island are aware of, and have implemented, any relevant legislation. Moreover, Jersey being an offshore finance centre ensures that the Treasury is interested in the operation of the finance industry. In fact, the close and good relations between the insular authorities, the Treasury and the Bank of England were essential to its development. Examples of the Treasury's involvement include assistance in preparing the United Kingdom's appendix to the Report of the Privy Council prepared as a result of the Imperial Contributions Controversy. A further illustration is that the 1947 Exchange Control Act required detailed returns from banks dealing in foreign currency. Until the Act was revoked in 1979, Bank of England supervisory staff would visit the island on a monthly basis. This was due to the fact that as far as the legislation was concerned, Jersey banks were covered by the same provisions as United Kingdom banks.

A convention has evolved that the minister responsible for the Crown Dependencies is a member of the Lords. This convention hides a too visible expression of parliamentary control as the post, if held by an MP, might be viewed as more political. The presence of a peer as minister ensures that the fiction is maintained of the Commons having no power over the islands. In this respect the façade is maintained by the Home Secretary acting as a Privy Councillor. The fact that the post is held by a member of the House of Lords may well also illustrate the status of the island as a quiet backwater in Whitehall's eyes. This situation may also apply to internal postings within the Home Office as there are few opportunities to develop a high profile career by specialising in Crown Dependency issues. This may give the island the advantage of having larger and better briefed delegations when issues are discussed with the Home

Office, but also means that United Kingdom officials and the minister may have little influence in the department or government. The lack of consultation at a level where decisions can be made is a constant complaint by Jersey's authorities.[72]

The unit responsible for the Crown Dependencies is the Constitutional Unit, which is part of the Constitutional and Community Policy Directorate. It has a staff of eight, including two grade seven civil servants. The Unit is one of the many responsibilities the Home Office has acquired by virtue of its function as the Department which "deals with those internal affairs to England and Wales which have not been assigned to other Government Departments."[73] As it does not fit into any obvious larger portion of the department's responsibilities, it finds itself included in a directorate with other similar sized, but fundamentally different entities, such as the Gaming Board for Great Britain, and elections. A senior civil servant in 1997 sought to reassure the island by saying that "The unit understands the constitutional position and ensures that Jersey's views are properly represented. We also arrange a series of briefings for Island officials and politicians on matters such as EC issues which affect the island."[74] Whilst the Unit may have a thorough understanding of its own perception of the constitutional position, there exists doubt in the island as to whether the Unit fails to understand or chooses to ignore Jersey's perception of its constitutional position. However, the position taken by the Unit can be explained by it seeking not to raise issues of dissent between the Home Office and Jersey by clarifying areas of conflict.

Jersey is caught in the dilemma of finding it useful to be considered a low priority by the Home Office, and therefore more or less left to its own devices, while wishing to have its views presented at a higher level of government. For this to occur it would be necessary for Jersey to be of higher priority and therefore more vulnerable to intervention from the United Kingdom. The Unit is responsible for arranging the six-monthly meetings between the Home Office and the Crown Dependencies. There is, however, a further annual meeting of the Crown Dependencies which does not include the Home Office which partly indicates the ambivalent attitude by the Crown Dependencies towards the Home Office.

One advantage in the relationship for Jersey is the amount of experience of the insular authorities in operating the relationship. Each Crown Dependency maintains its own advisory services, government secretariats and legal advisers. The Constitutional Unit may have recourse to the United Kingdom government machine for advice, but its requests must compete for priority in a system with many others. The staff of the Constitutional Unit also tends to be in post for a shorter period than their counterparts in the Dependencies and thus have less experience of the issues involved.[75] Both sides, however, seek to develop an informal relationship between the civil servants and the Crown Officers who manage the relationship on a day to day basis. The effectiveness of the relationship is illustrated by the fact that the head of the Constitutional Unit can contact the appropriate member of the insular authorities without prior notice.[76]

The main characteristic of the Constitutional Unit's operation is that it is rarely proactive, seeking instead to preserve the *status quo* and reacting to crises, should they arise. It is largely focused on ensuring uniformity with the United Kingdom in such areas of high policy as defence and foreign affairs. The major exception to this rule regards the island's fiscal autonomy. Although the Unit cannot directly intervene in this area, the Home Office can, and does indirectly, on behalf of the Treasury, as in the case of the Edwards review.

It must be remembered that the Crown Officers owe a loyalty to the Crown which appoints them. "The Home Office considers that it would not be consistent with the responsibility of the Crown for the good government of Jersey for the Insular Authorities to be able to dictate in the matter of appointment to Crown Offices."[77] The Crown Officers are defined by the Home Office as being directly responsible for the island's good government. As they are required to give advice to the Crown, they cannot be appointed by the States. The right to appoint, and if necessary remove, Crown Officers is one of the non-negotiable aspects of the relationship in the Home Office's view.[78] This is to give the United Kingdom control over the appointment, a power rarely exercised. However, such an arrangement does not remove the problems of conflicts of loyalty and the lack of separation of powers inherent in the post.

The most dramatic recent use of the Crown's authority over the Crown Officers was the decision to sack the Deputy Bailiff in 1992. Vernon Tomes was sacked and not re-instated despite popular demonstrations in the Royal Square, a rare event, and the despatch of a delegation of States members to the Home Office to reflect the hostility felt in the island to such a move. The dispute began in 1988 and was triggered by problems the Deputy Bailiff encountered in keeping up to date with judgements in the Royal Court. In October 1991, the Deputy Bailiff had agreed with the Home Office to keep up to date and provide six-monthly reports on his progress which would be prepared by the Bailiff. These discussions were held in confidence as the Home Office threatened to move unilaterally if the details were released. However, on 17 February a letter was received from Sir Clive Whitmore, Permanent Under Secretary of State at the Home Office, informing Tomes that two judgements were late. The letter went on "I must therefore consider reporting to the Home Secretary that you have failed to satisfy the conditions which he set, and you accepted, for your continuance in office".[79] Tomes was given ten days to justify the delays which he attempted to do in a letter dated 28 February. The explanation given was not accepted by the Home Office and instead the Deputy Bailiff was summoned and informed that "the Home Secretary has decided you must cease to be Deputy Bailiff of Jersey".[80] Two options were proposed. The Deputy Bailiff was given the opportunity to retire quietly, but if it became necessary to dismiss him it "would of necessity refer to the facts and history of your continued failure to perform your judicial duties satisfactorily."[81] This point emphasises that the Home Office, despite acting within the parameters of the constitutional relationship, did not wish to be seen intervening in Jersey politics by sacking a popular individual. This illustrates the informal operation of the relationship but also one of its drawbacks in that, when the decision became public as Tomes refused to resign quietly, there was no time to prepare the island's public by presenting the Home Office's case for its actions.

The decision to remove the Deputy Bailiff may not have been entirely externally driven. A rift had developed between the Bailiff and his deputy which, due to the nature of Jersey's constitution, had implications in both political and judicial spheres. The dispute centred around the workload required of the Deputy Bailiff and his differing preference of working methods compared to the Bailiff. It was summarised by Tomes as "Sir Peter's [the Bailiff's] preference is for the speed of ex tempore judgements, whereas his own is for reserved judgements, for 'accuracy, structure, quality, the build up of case law, and to eliminate the need for appeals'".[82] The Home Secretary did review the situation in response to the delegation of States members, but did not change his mind.

International Relations

Jersey's proximity to the United Kingdom obliges the island to keep its international obligations broadly in line with that in force in the United Kingdom. This is partly the result of international pressure from bodies, such as the European Court of Human Rights, but also from the United Kingdom media and backbench politicians. At present, this pressure can be seen in freedom of information legislation and Bill of Rights proposals. In the sphere of Freedom of Information legislation a real danger exists that if the two jurisdictions do not co-ordinate their approaches, information concerning one jurisdiction will be released under the other's legislation. The most visible pressure from the United Kingdom has been in the field of a proposal for a Bill of Rights. The media pressure is exemplified by statements given by Austin Mitchell, MP and by Ian Mather in The European.[83] Parliamentary pressure was exemplified by an attempt by Austin Mitchell in the Commons and Lord Lester of Herne Hill in the Lords to extend the Act of Parliament incorporating the European Convention of Human Rights and Fundamental Freedoms to the islands. These amendments were rejected, although Jersey introduced proposals for a Bill of Rights in 1998. The motivation for these interventions is viewed as deriving from the good government powers of the United Kingdom and an interpretation of the Kilbrandon idea of "matters common to British people throughout the world". Thus Mather argues that "Their citizens [those of the Crown Dependencies] have the right to expect the same protection as other British citizens."[84] Lord Lester argues that non-extension will leave the United Kingdom in breach of Article 14 of the Convention, when read in conjunction with Article 6, in that the United Kingdom would be "discriminating in the provision of remedies".[85] Lord Williams of Mostyn for the government rejected the argument on the ground that "the jurisdictions are different."[86]

112

The United Kingdom has created space for Jersey to develop a distinctive external policy. However, the United Kingdom insists on retaining absolute sovereignty rejecting any division of sovereignty on the grounds that "Her Majesty's Government is not to be placed in the impossible position of having responsibility without power."[87] Thus, as long as the United Kingdom is responsible for Jersey's international relations, it reserves the right to maintain the powers necessary to ensure it can force Jersey to undertake its obligations. In their evidence given to the Kilbrandon Commission, many in Jersey and the Isle of Man have been hostile to the United Kingdom's position on this matter and have sought the right to leisurely consideration of international agreements or a situation similar to the associated statehood offered under the 1967 West Indies Act. Under this arrangement, the United Kingdom would in most cases act as agent for the island.[88] However, the United Kingdom has always argued that it either has, or it has not, full sovereignty over the island. Nevertheless, the United Kingdom has been willing to allow Jersey considerable autonomy in its external affairs. Jersey's economy is based on global trade and the very size of its economy means that it has regional significance giving Jersey separate, and perhaps contradictory, external policy requirements to the United Kingdom. The United Kingdom therefore needs to allow Jersey the flexibility to enter into regional agreements with its neighbouring departments in France and the other Crown Dependencies as well as, perhaps more significantly, the ability to respond to the increasing influence of international law and bodies over both the United Kingdom and the island. Otherwise, there would be a real risk of destroying Jersey's economy, which would create an additional burden for the Treasury. Thus the United Kingdom has tolerated the development of a limited degree of international legal personality for the island. The United Kingdom allows for this distinct legal personality by allowing the island as much freedom as possible with respect to international law and organisations.

Conclusion

The United Kingdom's relationship with Jersey is based on a combination of factors, which have produced a relationship which has been stable and seen to be advantageous to both sides. The stability of this relationship has been less due to any specific aspect of the constitutional relationship, but rather to the circumstances underpinning it. Western Europe has enjoyed a remarkable period of political stability and prosperity since the Second World War and both Jersey and the United Kingdom have shared in this. Their relationship has therefore been insulated by favourable geopolitical and economic circumstances. Moreover, Jersey's geographical and cultural proximity is exemplified by the fact that its students attend United Kingdom universities and British media are readily available in the island. All this enables the insular population to understand the political imperatives in the United Kingdom, thereby giving Jersey an advantage in seeking to manage its relationship with the United Kingdom. More generally, a common attitude has developed and been maintained through most of the post-war years between the officials and politicians responsible for maintaining the relationship with respect to how it should be managed. This is based on a desire to maintain the constitutional element in an uncodified form while seeking to manage the relationship in an informal way. This autonomy relies on the United Kingdom upholding a convention of non-interference in domestic and fiscal matters or, perhaps more precisely, allowing Jersey a very high degree of freedom before intervening. Interventions are therefore rare and thus, the implicit dispute at the core of the relationship between the insular view that it has full domestic and fiscal autonomy and the United Kingdom's belief that its good government powers cover all areas, rarely comes to the fore. Not only was this convention felt to be weak by Kilbrandon, but its edges are blurred by the nature of international agreements and the global nature of Jersey's finance centre. Jersey's autonomy is further limited by the British government's absolute insistence on maintaining an overarching right to maintain good government in the island, the right to deny the Royal Assent to laws and the right to appoint the Crown Officers and therefore control the appointment of the senior law officers, judiciary and the President of the States. These rights, although rarely used, are preserved by the United Kingdom to ensure it can enforce its will, should it become necessary. However, in exchange the authorities in Jersey are allowed to operate with little intervention and a high degree of tolerance from the United Kingdom. This freedom from interference is maximised even in the area of external affairs, by allowing the island a limited right to opt out of international agreements signed by the United Kingdom.

References

[1] "The City's satellite", Jersey Weekly Post, 23/4/98, 4.

[2] An example is Scriven, S., "The constant message: We shall not intervene", Jersey Evening Post, 10/4/96, 9.

[3] op. cit., Walker interview, in which Senator Walker conservatively estimates the value of investment from Jersey into London from outside the United Kingdom at £150 billion.

[4] op. cit., Kilbrandon 1973. See also correspondence with R. Miles, Constitutional Unit of the Home Office, 29/9/98 and notes of an interview with R. M. Morris, Assistant Under Secretary of State, Home Office, 1991-96, 2/10/98, hereafter, Morris interview.

[5] op. cit., Kilbrandon 1973, 453, para 1499.

[6] ibid., 454, para 1502.

[7] ibid, 457, para 1511.

[8] ibid., 455, 1504.

[9] ibid., 465, para 1539.

[10] op. cit., Le Hérissier, 184.

[11] United Nations Resolution 1514(xv) adopted 14/12/60.

[12] United Nations Resolution 14/12/70, "Programme of Action for the Full Implementation of the

Declaration".

[13] Interview with Thomas Russell, Cayman Island Representative in the United Kingdom and former Governor, 21/4/97.

[14] ibid.

[15] Memorandum of Dissent by Lord Crowther-Hunt and Professor A. T. Peacock, an extract from which is attached to op. cit., Kilbrandon 1973.

[16] ibid., 461, para 1528.

[17] op. cit., Jeune interview and op. cit., Walker interview.

[18] Mitchell, A., "Power of Persuasion", Guardian, 17/6/98, 1.

[19] Hunt, T., "Germany press Brussels to ban UK tax havens", Sunday Business, 29/1/97.

[20] "Fishermen to fight use of dispersants", Jersey Evening Post, 23/3/78, 1.

[21] "Island to pay over £350,000 in wake of oil tanker disaster", Jersey Evening Post, 5/12/80, 3.

[22] Information about the annual fees payable are available from the States Greffe. In 1997 they were £4,450 for class based courses, £6,645 for laboratory based courses and £11,958 for clinical courses.

[23] The Health Service Convention between the Governments of the United Kingdom of Great Britain and Northern Ireland and the Isle of Man and the States of Jersey, Guernsey, Alderney and the Chief Pleas of Sark, 1976, No. 6286.

[24] The budget of the Committee in 1993 was £2,612,000, see States of Jersey Overseas Aid Committee, States Greffe, 1994, 1.

[25] op. cit., Vibert 1991, 165.

[26] £25,000 in 1917, £50,000 in 1918, £25,000 in 1919, £300,000 in 1927, £100,000 in 1940 and £150,000 in 1953.

[27] An example of an earlier dispute is described in op. cit., Syvret & Stevens, 100, which led to a Commission under Sir Edward Conway in 1617 to examine Jersey's defences.

[28] Defence Contribution: Territorial Army Unit (P. 124/97) - Report, Defence Committee, 3/2/98, States Greffe, 9, hereafter, Defence Report 1998.

[29] ibid.

[30] ibid., 5.

[31] op. cit., Le Hérissier, 51.

[32] Report of the Privy Council on the question of Contributions to Imperial Funds from the Islands of Jersey, Guernsey and Man, Cmd. 2586, London, HMSO, 1926, 5, hereafter, Imperial Contributions Report 1926.

[33] ibid., 9.

[34] Pocock, H. R. S., The Memoirs of Lord Coutanche, Philimore, Chichester, 1975, 63, hereafter, Coutanche 1975.

[35] Smith, D., "Jersey should pay its way", Jersey Evening Post, 2/12/81, 1.

[36] Minute dated 4/2/52, PRO file HO45/25272.

[37] "Helicopter - 4,113 Minesweeper - 83", Jersey Evening Post, 19/6/86, 1, hereafter, Helicopter.

[38] "Defence Contributions under fire", Jersey Evening Post, 22/6/84,13.

[39] op. cit., Vibert 1991, 166.

[40] op. cit., Helicopter, 1.

[41] op. cit., Defence Report 1998, 17.

[42] James Marr, L., "A UK Defence contribution", Jersey Evening Post, 25/1/85, 11.

[43] "Defence contribution not a tax, say Crown Officers", Jersey Evening Post, 5/2/85, 1.

[44] McRandle, H., "Change? Only if the Island desires it", Jersey Evening Post, 14/7/97, 8.

[45] Speech to the Dependent Territories Association by Rt Hon Robin Cook, MP, delivered 4/2/98.

[46] Order in Council, 22/2/52, cited in Le Hérissier 1972, 36.

[47] Minutes of Evidence, Jersey, op. cit., Kilbrandon 1973, 210, para 202.

[48] Memorandum from the Home Office and Foreign and Commonwealth Office, op. cit., Kilbrandon 1973, 11, para 27.

[49] Although an article entitled " Lobbyists target MPs to support Channel Islands", Sunday Business, 9/8/98, 1, indicates Jersey and/or Guernsey are considering setting up a group of MPs entitled Friends of the Channel Islands.

[50] op. cit., Walker interview and op. cit., Jeune interview.

[51] op. cit., Heyting, 24, citing Le Quesne, C., Constitutional History of Jersey, Longmans, London, 1856, 389.

[52] op. cit., Heyting, 27 and op. cit., Kelleher, 164.

[53] Oral Answers, 17/12/97, Weekly Hansard, Issue No. 1771, December 1997, 15-22 with respect to Geoffrey Robinson, MP. For Lord Simon's investments in Jersey see Bevins, A., "Minister's tax break attacked", The Independent, 30/7/97, 1.

[54] For an example of an attack on the Finance Industry by Austin Mitchell MP see Petters, L., "Labour MP attacks Island again", Jersey Evening Post, 27/3/98, 4. For a motion by David Hansen, MP on Jersey's Housing Laws see op. cit., Pedley & Peters, 1.

[55] Hansard, 19/1/98 (980119-17), column 1307.

[56] ibid., column 1303.

[57] "UK government to study new job laws", Jersey Evening Post, 23/5/97, 3.

[58] A further example was the allegation that it was Home Office intervention which led to the prosecution of Robert Young for a $27million fraud in what became known as the Cantrade case, see "Home Office intervention led to $27m fraud charges", Jersey Evening Post, 31/5/98, 2.

[59] op. cit., Le Hérissier, 186.

[60] ibid.

[61] op. cit., Kilbrandon 1973, 202, para 174.

[62] ibid., 103.

[63] ibid., 177.

[64] ibid., 10.

[65] "Our friends in Whitehall", Jersey Evening Post, 14/7/97, 9, hereafter, Our friends.

[66] This case concerned the refusal by the United Kingdom authorities to grant the Royal Assent to the Wireless Telegraphy (Isle of Man) Act, 1962.

[67] op. cit., Heyting, 68.

[68] ibid., 1.

[69] op. cit., Kilbrandon 1973, 103, para 2.

[70] ibid., 465, para 1539.

[71] op. cit., Horner 1984, 24.

[72] op. cit., Walker interview.

[73] DOD'S Parliamentary Companion, 1997, DOD'S Parliamentary Companion Ltd, London, 948.

[74] op. cit., Our friends, 9.

[75] op. cit., Jeune interview.

[76] op. cit., Morris interview.

[77] op. cit., Kilbrandon 1973, 11, para 25.

[78] op. cit., Morris interview.

[79] Bisson, M., "The letter that spelled trouble for Mr Tomes", <u>Jersey Evening Post</u>, 23/3/92.

[80] ibid.

[81] ibid.

[82] "Mr Tomes and the Bailiff: Documenting the rift", <u>Jersey Evening Post</u>, 25/3/92, 12.

[83] Mather, I., "Human Rights for some", <u>The European</u>, 18-24/5/98, 7.

[84] ibid.

[85] <u>Hansard</u>, 19/1/98 (980119 - 17), column number 1308.

[86] ibid.

[87] Memorandum by the Home Office and Foreign and Commonwealth office, op. cit., Kilbrandon 1973, 8, para 6

[88] Minutes of Evidence, Isle of Man, op. cit., Kilbrandon 1973, 67, para 184.

Chapter 6 - The European Union:
A New Dependency to Manage

Introduction

Jersey's relationship with the European Union represents the most significant change in its dependency relationships this century. Although Jersey is not a full member of the European Union, it is nevertheless required under its agreement with the Community to adopt certain European legislation. Additional European legislation has been adopted to assist the island in maintaining its close economic integration with the United Kingdom. The United Kingdom's application for membership of the EEC was seen as part of a more general problem concerning the encroachment of international law on areas where Jersey traditionally had autonomy. Much of the evidence which the island presented to the Kilbrandon Commission was an attempt to resolve this problem.

Protocol 3 defines the relationship between the Crown Dependencies and the European Union.[1] It is a six clause agreement and therefore defines only the broad parameters within which the relationship operates. The first article deals with the extent of the application of the customs and agricultural rules to the Crown Dependencies. Article 2 guarantees existing rights but excludes islanders from the free movement provisions of the Treaty of Rome. Article 3 extends the rules of Euroatom to the islands. Article 4 requires the island to treat all European Union nationals equally. Article 5 allows the Council to review the operation of the Protocol. Article 6 gives definitions of a Jerseyman, Guernseyman and Manxman. The overall effect of the Protocol was described by Colin Powell as "Although the Island is 'within' the European Community only for free trade in manufactured and agricultural goods and is otherwise outside the Community for the purposes of free movement of persons, free trade in services and fiscal harmonisation the Island is not unaffected generally by developments in Europe."[2]

The United Kingdom, being the formal signatory on the Treaty of Accession, is responsible for Jersey's compliance with Protocol 3. As Jersey is not a state, it cannot be regarded as a third party state to the Community or have formal associate status, despite its relationship often resembling this position. The European Union has no authority over Jersey other than the European Court of Justice's role in enforcing Protocol 3 and few decisions of the European Union impinge on the island directly. However, the Commission has the power to review the operation of the Protocol and refer its recommendation to the

Council to vote on by unanimity, although it has yet to use this power or show any signs of doing so. Also, Jersey must adopt many directives due to its high level of economic integration with the United Kingdom. Other EU measures are voluntarily adopted as best practice, as a small island does not have the resources to set all of its own standards.[3] Thus to a degree, Jersey can pick and choose what elements of Community law it chooses to adopt by using some EU legislation to overcome its own diseconomies of scale.

Although the EU does not exercise direct sovereign power over the island, it has many of the characteristics of a metropolitan power. The Union membership encompasses all of Jersey's sovereign neighbours, including its metropolitan power. The majority of the island's trade is with European Union nations and any instability in the nations involved would inevitably spill over into the island. Therefore in many ways, the relationship with the European Union duplicates that with the United Kingdom. Both the EU and the United Kingdom, even if the United Kingdom is treated as distinct from the European Union, have overwhelming political and economic power over the island, should they wish to use it. Moreover, as became clear when the United Kingdom joined the European Economic Community, Jersey's status exists by permission of the Community, a reflection of the fact that Jersey has little to offer the European Union in exchange for its tolerance. Thus, Europe appears willing to ignore Jersey as an anomaly on its periphery and concentrate on the core issues surrounding the building of the European Union. It is in this area that the present arrangement could fray as Jersey's operation as an offshore finance centre is perceived by some individuals within Europe as a threat to fiscal stability. However, at present Jersey's autonomy is not only tolerated, but guaranteed, by the Protocol.

Attitudes to the European Union within Jersey are not, and have not been, favourable. The European Union has influence over the island, but unlike Westminster the island has no direct channels of communication to it and its arbitrary power is resented by a significant element of the population. The relationship with the European Union became another dependency relationship to be managed and in this, it seemed Jersey gained little. The European Union may have helped to produce general economic stability in Western Europe and has been the means to increase economic growth. On the other hand, it removed the tariff advantage which Jersey's produce enjoyed against continental European products which often reached British markets ahead of Jersey goods. The EEC has further considered harmonising duties across Europe. This would remove the attraction of duty free shopping, which has always been considered a major incentive for tourists visiting Jersey. Moreover, moves towards tax harmonisation threaten Jersey's role as an offshore finance centre.

Membership of Europe was seen as a threat to the Commonwealth, a body with which Jersey has always had close links, and perhaps a closer affinity to, as an association of former British dependencies. A further reason for the island's hostility to the Community was the failure to believe early advice that

"No one pretends that joining the Common Market means the immediate acceptance of all the existing regulations to the very letter."[4] In Jersey, the assumption from the beginning of the United Kingdom's negotiations was that Jersey would be forced to join the Community. Despite the fact that this has yet to happen, there is little local acknowledgement of the flexibility the Community has shown in its relations with Jersey.

Jersey's exact relationship with the European Community was defined in response to a parliamentary question to the Secretary of State for Foreign and Commonwealth affairs on 14 June 1993 as:

> The relationship of the Channel Islands and the Isle of Man with the European Community is governed by article 227(5)(c) of the Treaty of Rome - and the equivalent provisions in the ECSC and Euroatom treaties - and by Protocol 3 to the Act signed on 15 January 1972 concerning the conditions of the United Kingdom's accession to the Community. The islands chose in 1972 to remain essentially outside the Community. The broad effect of the Treaty of Accession is that the Islands are included in the Community solely for customs purposes and for certain aspects of the common agricultural policy and free movement of goods. The islands neither contribute to nor are eligible to benefit from Community funds.[5]

Article 227 of the Treaty of Rome (as amended by Article 5(c) of the Treaty of Accession) states that "this Treaty shall apply to the Channel Islands and the Isle of Man only to the extent necessary to ensure the implementation of the arrangements for those Islands set out in the Treaty concerning the accession of new Member States to the European Community".[6] The fact that this settlement is almost exactly what Jersey requested should be emphasised. Much of the discussion that follows will highlight potential problems or irritants in the relationship, but overall the Protocol has been a great success. This is illustrated by the fact that Jersey's aims with respect to the relationship were defined by the Policy and Resources Committee as seeking "no change in the present relationship."[7]

Britain is not the only member of the European Community to have dependencies. France, Portugal, Spain, Finland, Denmark and the Netherlands all have autonomous political units which enjoy a special relationship with the Community. The European Union has similar arrangements in place with the independent microstates of Andorra, Monaco, San Marino and Liechtenstein. Thus the Community has acquired a group of peripheral microstates with links to the Community.

The European Commission itself divides its relationships with the small autonomous regions into three categories: the French overseas departments, which now form part of France; the European or nearby regions of the Member States which enjoy autonomous or semi-autonomous status; and the overseas countries and territories referred to in Part IV of the Treaty of Rome.[8] Due to the fact that the French Overseas Departments of Reunion, Guadeloupe, Guyana and Martinique are legally regions of the French Republic, they are fully included in the European Union as if they were European Territories covered by Article 227(4). Included in the large number of European Dependencies covered by Part IV are the French Overseas Territories of Mayotte and Saint Pierre and Miquelon, the non-European countries of the Kingdom of the Netherlands and the United Kingdom Overseas Territories. The Part IV territories are eligible for EU aid while being able to trade with the EU on the same conditions as a member state.

Britain's problem with its dependencies and their position with respect to the Community are thus not unique within Europe. In fact, at the time of the accession negotiations the problem was shared by Denmark with its dependencies of Greenland and the Faeroes. The United Kingdom's dependencies can be divided into three groups as far as their relationship with Europe is concerned: the United Kingdom Overseas Territories except Gibraltar; Gibraltar as the only United Kingdom Overseas Territory in Western Europe; and the Crown Dependencies. The United Kingdom Overseas Territories are covered by Part IV of the Treaty of Rome which has given them access to EU aid as well as a wider export market.

Gibraltar was included in the Community under Article 227(4) of the Treaty of Rome as a European Territory for whose external relations a member state is responsible. The settlement between Gibraltar and the European Union in many ways mirrors the image provided for in Protocol 3. Gibraltar is part of the European Union but with certain exemptions, while the Protocol 3 dependencies are outside but enjoy certain rights as if they were included in the Community. Gibraltar is excluded from the Common Customs Tariff, the Common Agricultural Policy and does not need to apply value added taxes. The United Kingdom is, therefore, obliged to impose levies on the export of agricultural goods to the territory. Gibraltarians have the right of free movement and establishment in the Community, but are unable to vote in European Union elections. In the past, the constituency-based system used in the United Kingdom has made the inclusion of Gibraltar problematic. The proposed regional list system could have alleviated this problem. However, Gibraltar has not been included in the new system. This led the Chief Minister of Gibraltar to comment that "The people of Gibraltar cannot comprehend how a British territory that is part of the EU by virtue of the UK's membership is disenfranchised by the UK from this most fundamental of democratic exercises."[9] The lack of representation is perceived as being one of a number of problems deriving from Spanish claims to the territory, a claim which also stalled attempts at an air liberalisation package throughout the Community.

The arrangements between the European Union and its peripheral microstates tend to follow the pattern of excluding the territories from the Community's fiscal rules and political integration, but including them within the customs union as far as external goods are concerned, hence gaining the advantage of being able to sell their goods to the huge neighbouring markets. The fiscal independence has been a factor in attracting business to offshore finance centres. The political autonomy of such communities has avoided the problem of how such small communities could have political representation within the European Union. These arrangements are a concession by the member states of the European Union to ensure the continuing prosperity of these communities and suggests a tolerance similar to that shown by the United Kingdom towards dependent communities.

The Implications of United Kingdom Membership for Jersey

The main concern faced by the agricultural industry if Jersey joined the EEC was the loss of its tariff advantage over other European farmers which had helped to counter the seasonal advantage they had in exporting goods to the United Kingdom. As long as the United Kingdom remained outside the Community, Jersey grew the first tariff free produce to reach United Kingdom markets. However, if the United Kingdom became a member state and Jersey did not, not only would it have to compete with earlier tariff free produce but it would also find itself facing a tariff barrier to import into the United Kingdom. If Jersey were outside the common external tariff and Guernsey and the United Kingdom within it, estimated exports would attract rates of duty of between 17% and 20%.[10] The option of not exporting agricultural produce and instead attempting import substitution was considered, but this was felt to have the potential to lead to large increases in food prices. Nevertheless, this alternative was attractive because membership of the common exclusion zone would result in free access for all EEC goods to Jersey. However, even at this time the political power of the farmers was larger than their economic significance and it was noted that:

> In fact, in general economic terms in Jersey, as opposed to social considerations, the most severe effect that the cessation within a short period of time of exports to the United Kingdom of agricultural produce could have, might be only equivalent to the increase in revenue and expenditure and incomes in the Island brought about by a 10% increase in the number of tourist visitors.[11]

Diversifying exports to new markets was not an option, due to both geography and to the fact that the island historically has focused on exporting agricultural goods to the United Kingdom. Moreover, exclusion from the Community would deny farmers access to the Common Agricultural Fund.

The finance industry was not emphasised in the discussions surrounding Protocol 3. Despite its embryonic state, it was noted in reports from Brussels that "The few people in Brussels to have studied the peculiar position of the Channel Islands are unanimously agreed that they could not be allowed into the EEC as they are presently constituted, or with their current tax advantages."[12] However, this did not present an obstacle as finance only represented about

10% of GDP in 1970. [13] Nevertheless, Colin Powell claims that "We saw clearly that it [the island] was going to develop as an international finance centre - not as a centre for manufacturing, for instance."[14] The fiscal independence resulting from the Protocol ensured the large expansion of the industry.[15] The Community's long term plans for tax harmonisation which dated from 1961 did cause concern at the time and still do. The report commissioned at the time noted that "However, it might be recognised that in the event of United Kingdom membership, there might be indirect pressure on the United Kingdom to alter its taxation structure, and in certain respects this might not be to the advantage of Jersey in attracting wealthy residents."[16] It was also noted that if Jersey remained outside the Community, the existence of such harmonisation in the Community would be to the advantage of Jersey's finance sector.[17]

The introduction of value added taxation as required by membership of the EEC was also felt to be harmful to Jersey's interests. Jersey did not need the extra revenue as it already operated budget surpluses and it was felt the tax would harm its largest industry at the time, tourism, as the low rate of local duties on alcohol and tobacco formed a major part of the attraction of Jersey as a destination. It was also felt that if Jersey were to introduce VAT this would act as a deterrent to tourists as import costs tend to result in the cost of goods in Jersey being slightly higher than on the mainland. The effect of this is masked by the island not charging VAT which makes Jersey prices appear lower. At the time of the negotiations, the United Kingdom seems to have not understood Jersey's position, as it offered a common purse agreement in 1971 to offset the heavy administrative burden such a tax would impose on the island. The Constitutional and Common Market Committee rejected this offer which they felt would have infringed the island's fiscal autonomy.

The inclusion of the island in the European Customs area, if it could be achieved, offered opportunities for local light industry to export to the rest of Europe. In fact, by 1980 one Jersey company exported 25% of its output to West Germany alone.[18] This did not save local light industry from collapse. This was partly due to other European firms gaining not only reciprocal advantages on the island, but also access to the United Kingdom market on an equal footing. But neither of these factors was significant when compared with the inability of light industry to compete with the finance industry in terms of salaries and rentals. This was compounded by the lack of government support for light industry compared with elsewhere in Europe.

A Right of Establishment as provided for in the Treaty of Rome could lead to a large population increase if applied to the island. It was feared that membership would mean the end of current housing policy. There was concern that Jersey would have to provide welfare benefits at a level comparable to Europe for Community nationals. Reciprocal social security payments could impose a considerable burden on the island as small states have less ability to adapt to rapid inflows or outflows of money. Articles 117 and 188 of the Treaty of Rome did not require harmonisation of the social security system but implied the desirability of some approximation. Such an approximation could have forced Jersey to introduce some form of statutory unemployment benefit. At the time of entry, the Italian government was putting pressure on the Swiss government to improve the rights of foreign workers in Switzerland and this was seen as a potential threat to Jersey with its large immigrant community. The application of equal pay was also seen as an added burden by the authors of the report.[19]

Jersey and the United Kingdom's Application for Membership

Prior to 1961, at the time of the United Kingdom's first application to the EEC, there was neither a States debate nor consideration by the United Kingdom of what would happen to Jersey. The issue of what to do if the United Kingdom joined the EEC was not debated by the States until 1966.[20] At the time the Home Office felt the chance of securing a distinct relationship with the EEC was remote, although the then Home Secretary, Roy Jenkins, had promised Jersey the option to decide what was in its best interest.[21] However, whatever choice Jersey made, the United Kingdom's entry would impinge on Jersey due to the large degree of integration between the two economies.

The response of the States of Jersey was to appoint a Special Committee of the States of Jersey to consult with Her Majesty's Government in the United Kingdom on all matters relating to the Government's application to join the European Economic Community on 17 January 1967. Its brief was to produce a report listing the options available to the island and their consequences. In 1968 the Committee was renamed the Constitution and Common Market Committee so that it could also prepare the report to the Kilbrandon Commission. In 1970 the Committee's terms were extended to cover all matters to do with the Protocol 3 negotiations. The United Kingdom confirmed its constitutional sovereignty over the island by not inviting the President of the Constitutional and Common Market Committee to visit Brussels as part of the United Kingdom delegation for the negotiations. The lack of representation by the Crown Dependencies was apparently used by Geoffrey Rippon to gain sympathy from, in particular, France.[22]

The Committee engaged the services of Dr Hugh Thurston, a specialist in Common Market affairs, who wrote a report on the implications of the United Kingdom's accession for the island. He was recruited without a formal interview process after meeting Senator Krichefski. This emphasises the *ad hoc* and personalised way in which Jersey and other microstates operate in policy development.[23] Professors Robert Jennings and Stanley De Smith were recruited to advise on legal matters. The report of the Committee was presented to the States on October 10, 1967 and its recommendations were accepted by the States on November 14. The Report's conclusions were that:

If the Island remained out, without its historic right to import freely into the United Kingdom being preserved, the consequences for agriculture and horticulture would be disastrous. This essential right could be ideally maintained by the Island being within the Common External Tariff, as it is within E.F.T.A., and, in the opinion of the Committee, this would be the most desirable solution. If, however, this were found to be impracticable, the ancient right to export freely into the United Kingdom should at least be secured. If the Island followed the United Kingdom in, it can be foreseen that our right of self-government in many domestic matters would disappear.[24]

The negotiating tactic adopted by Jersey has been described by Senator Vibert as "why not ask for exactly what we want."[25] This tactic was later accepted by the other Crown Dependencies, the United Kingdom and ultimately the EEC. The policy was unanimously endorsed by the States in November 1967, adopted by Guernsey and the Isle of Man and formed the basis of the United Kingdom's negotiating position. The Committee further resolved that "The power of H.M. Government itself will be limited once entry into the E.E.C. is achieved, and the Island should do everything possible to anticipate the problems which may arise and to deal with them *before* entry. It may be too late afterwards."[26] The Committee therefore attempted to persuade the United Kingdom to make arrangements satisfactory to Jersey a requirement for United Kingdom membership, just like the Danish government had done in the case of the Faeroes.

Exclusion from the customs zone, if Jersey rejected membership of the EEC, was felt to destroy Jersey's ancient rights with respect to trade with the United Kingdom. The strategy recommended by the Report was, however, not a conclusion as to whether Jersey should be inside or outside the Community, with all the drawbacks of these options, but rather a list of Jersey's requirements. One proposed response was to let the experts at the Home Office sort out the arrangements. However, these officials had not inspired confidence with the response given to an insular delegation when the United Kingdom first applied for membership in 1961. The delegation was assured "that while it was not then contemplated that the Island would in fact wish to remain outside should the United Kingdom decide to enter the Community, it would be free to make its own decision in the matter."[27] Instead the insular authorities, via the Report, sought to convince the United Kingdom to adopt their preferred solution rather than the Home Office line that Article 227(4) could not be altered. This was done using the English legal practice of establishing a precedent by documenting the special arrangement the EEC had in operation with respect to other small communities in Europe.

The position of the United Kingdom was summed up by the Committee's report in the following terms:

It is clear that, whatever may be the strict legal position, the Island would have freedom of choice as to entry if H.M. Government made it a condition of its application that this was to be so. It is however appreciated the H.M. Government have considerably larger considerations to bear in mind than the interests of Jersey. At the same time, the Island is entitled to expect, in view of its long, close and honourable relationship with the United Kingdom, the H.M. Government will not wish to take any unilateral action which is contrary to Jersey's interest, nor to depart from long established constitutional practice, but rather will wish first to understand and then to try and relieve the difficulties facing the Island.[28]

The report's conclusions must, however, be regarded as representing what the island wished the United Kingdom's position to be, as the freedom to decide its position independently from the United Kingdom was only publicly confirmed in 1970. Moreover, the evidence of the Home Office's actions in 1961 do not suggest much knowledge of, let alone respect for, Jersey's relationship with the United Kingdom, but rather the overwhelming dominance of larger considerations in the United Kingdom's calculations on membership.

The Law Officers in their advice to the Committee argued that, even though Parliament can legislate for Jersey without the consent of the States, this is only under strict law which is limited by constitutional usage in domestic and fiscal areas. The Law Officers proceeded to argue that any enabling legislation required to implement the Treaty of Rome would fall into the areas of domestic and fiscal matters, and thus be the province of the States to legislate.[29] They concluded that "It is therefore considered that if the Crown were to bind Jersey to the Treaty of Rome without the consent of the States, or without modification of the Treaty, the Crown would assume in respect of the Island international obligations which could not, by reason of the constitutional position of the Island, be fully implemented without the consent of the States."[30] It must be noted, however, that this view of the Constitution contradicts the reading of Article 227(4) given by the Home Office at the beginning of the negotiations.[31]

The formal statement of the United Kingdom's position was given in the 1971 White Paper on the Common Market and consisted of two paragraphs out of one hundred and eighty nine. At its core was the statement that:

[The inclusion of the Channel Islands and the Isle of Man] in the Community would present constitutional, administrative and economic difficulties. Accordingly, after full consultation with them, we are seeking for the Islands arrangements short of full membership which would provide for an exchange of reciprocal rights and obligations between the Community and the Islands.[32]

The White Paper also noted the special constitutional position of the Crown Dependencies and proposed adopting a form of association under Article 238 of the Treaty of Rome.

Independence was considered as an option for the island at the time of the United Kingdom's application, should Jersey be forced to join the EEC against its will. However, even Jersey's own assessment of the consequences of independence did not look promising. The Home Office would have been aware of this and therefore any offer of independence by the United Kingdom was more of a threat than a gift.[33] The most dangerous element was, however, the threat that an independent Jersey would be excluded from the EEC's Common External Tariff. The lack of a defence guarantee and external representation by the United Kingdom would also cast doubt on the island's long term stability. As a result the finance industry would have been less eager to locate in an independent Jersey operating without United Kingdom supervision and entirely outside the EEC. Geoffrey Rippon emphasised the situation with respect to custom's duties by making it clear that "If any of the Channel Islands reject the E.E.C.'s offer this will, in effect, be opting for independence and will create "a new situation" between the islands and the United Kingdom in which Britain will have to impose E.E.C. levies on all goods."[34]

The Jersey Constitutional Association was established to campaign against the island's membership of the Community as a reaction to the perceived pressure on the island to join. The Association was a fierce defender of its vision of the constitutional *status quo* fearing that as a result of the negotiations under way "our constitution will become a matter of bargain."[35] The Association also doubted, with justification, that Jersey's requirements would be allowed to threaten the United Kingdom's entry. Its solution to the problems created by the United Kingdom being Jersey's sovereign power was that "Her Majesty's Government should declare it is not responsible for Jersey's external relations, other than at the request of the States",[36] a solution the United Kingdom was not prepared to contemplate.[37] The Association sought a reassurance that was not given that should suitable arrangements for Jersey not prove possible, the United Kingdom would not join the EEC.[38] This demand was seen as unrealistic, as Senator Vibert sensibly pointed out in retrospect "We couldn't expect England to say if we can't get what we want for the Channel Islands, we won't go in".[39]

Special Arrangements in Relation to the EEC which existed in 1967

As part of their brief, the Constitutional and Common Market Committee analysed the special arrangements already existing in Europe to seek out precedents to support Jersey's case. The most relevant cases considered included the Italian territories of Campione and Livigno. Campione is a one square mile piece of Italian territory surrounded by Switzerland on three sides and Lake Lugano on the fourth. Livigno is a small township on the Swiss border which has traditionally been excluded from the Italian customs territory. Both Livigno and Campione, although integral parts of the Italian state and not covered by Article 227(4), were at the time treated as outside the customs territory.

The report further identified two German cases. Helgoland had some autonomy in levying taxes and was not technically a part of the Federal Republic. This was in recognition of the lack of resources available on the island. Busingen, under a Treaty of 1965, had Swiss Federal and Cantonal regulations applied to it while preserving free trade with the German Federal Republic. Swiss immigration controls were also extended to Busingen in parallel to those of the German Federal Republic. In both cases, no reference was made by the German government to the EEC.

The report stated that:

> The conclusion that must be drawn from this review of special cases in relation to the E.E.C. is that at least in relation to Helgoland, Campione and Busingen, there is clear evidence that the practice within the Community by individual members has brought into being exceptional or unusual procedures which, if applied in Jersey, would go a long way to relieving the Island from the adverse consequences that membership of the E.E.C. might impose.[40]

The Report of the Special Committee on the EEC paid particular attention to the Faeroes' application. The significance of the arrangement was that:

> The Danish Government Memorandum on the situation of the Faeroes makes it entirely clear that no E.E.C. regulation or legal provision consequent on membership can be applied to the Islands without the concurrence of the Parliament and Government of the Faroes, although under the terms of the constitution it is clear that the Danish Government is responsible for the foreign affairs and defence of these Islands. If the Danish Government is obliged to ask for special provisions, as apparently it considers it is from its various memoranda, it must be questioned whether - (a) it is reasonable to expect that Jersey should agree to less consideration; and (b) whether the argument that special provisions for Jersey are likely to result in delay or special difficulty to Common Market negotiations, is tenable if the same questions arise from the Faroes, since it is inconceivable that the procedures of amendment to the Treaty of Rome in constitutional law of the various member countries will be conducted on other than a package basis.[41]

The Danish Government had listed Greenland and the Faeroe Islands on its application to join the EEC as specific problems to be overcome. The Faeroes' government requested consideration under a provision other than Article 227(4).

The Faeroe Islands had not been members of E.F.T.A. and both the Danish Government and the Faeroes' Parliament requested a status similar to that of Algeria under Article 227(2). In response to this, Article 227(5)(a) was drawn up allowing the Faeroes to opt out of membership. This was done in 1974 when the Faeroes Parliament, the Løg, voted against integration. The Faeroes are, therefore, not included in the Community; however, a fishing agreement has been signed. This was considered very significant in Jersey as it signalled both to the insular authorities and the Home Office that such a solution might be open to them as well. Moreover, it meant the island could apply for equality of treatment with the Faeroe Islands.

The Report's Conclusion

The Report of the Special Committee on the EEC came to a number of conclusions about the options available to the island. It highlighted the enormous body of Community Law and argued its implication for the island in both administrative and constitutional terms; the sheer bulk of Community legislation would present practical problems for a small jurisdiction.[42] The concern about how far Community legislation would impinge on matters previously viewed as domestic was also raised.[43] It was also noted that "It is of course the case that the United Kingdom itself, in joining the Community, would surrender its sovereignty to some degree. But in so doing the United Kingdom would retain an important voice in making all decisions, which Jersey would not; and the United Kingdom would be gaining a voice in the affairs of Europe, which again Jersey would not."[44] The Home Office responded to the island's anxieties about lack of representation by suggesting Jersey could send a representative as part of the United Kingdom delegation when issues affecting Jersey were discussed.[45] However, the Committee stated that it did not

> consider that the maintenance at Brussels, even on a permanent basis, of a Jersey representative having access to the United Kingdom delegation but having otherwise no voice, would be any substitute for the serious loss of the right of self-government which membership of the Community would entail unless the Island's constitutional position was expressly reserved.[46]

Therefore then, as now, there were concerns that such a small territory would be unable to influence events in the Community and thus be prevented from attempting to manage the relationship in any way.

The Negotiations

On May 3, 1967, Sir Philip Allen, Permanent Under Secretary of State at the Home Office, sent a letter to the Lieutenant Governor informing him that the Government's position was determined by Article 227(4) of the Treaty of Rome. This stated that the Treaty shall apply "to the European territories for whose external relations a Member State is responsible."[47] It must be noted that this commitment, when drafted for the original six members of the EEC, did not envisage the existence of European Dependencies analogous to the Crown Dependencies. However, it was believed that Jersey would automatically be included in the United Kingdom's accession as an European Territory for whose external relations a member state is responsible. This brought home the scale of the threat to Jersey's autonomy which United Kingdom membership of the EEC posed and also galvanised opposition to membership, which included that of the Jersey Constitutional Association. The Home Office in October 1970 assured Jersey representatives, in confidence, that the UK government would not impose accession to the Community. This represented a reversal of public policy from that laid down in the letter from Sir Philip Allen. It was, however, this flexibility which allowed the successful conclusion of the negotiations to occur although the insular authorities were asked to treat the Community negotiations as absolutely confidential. Consequently, the public perception of the difficulties the island was facing seemed more dire than they were in reality. In addition, the Committee would have been better able to counter the criticism from the Jersey Constitutional Association and others had they been allowed to give more details on how the negotiations were progressing.

The search for an appropriate settlement dragged on past the final settlement of the Treaty in June 1971 with an agreement to resolve the problem by means of a Protocol. This arrangement was criticised in Jersey as removing the United Kingdom's power to block the rest of the agreement if it did not get its way on the Crown Dependencies. However, there is no evidence the United Kingdom negotiators ever contemplated doing this. In many ways, the relative lack of importance given to the issue by both sides may have ensured a better deal for the island than if the issue had been deemed more important.

The United Kingdom began the negotiations by suggesting that a settlement should be reached under the auspices of Article 238. However, it was felt by the existing members that this Article was more appropriate for colonial territories than European dependencies closely integrated with a member state. Thus Jersey, due to its rare status, failed to fit into the existing models of political dependencies available in the Treaty of Rome, that of colonial territory or province with devolved powers. The Commission suggested Article 227(4) instead, but stressed that the United Kingdom must put forward details of the settlement it desired within these parameters.

The Home Office informed the Crown Dependencies in October 1970 that they would have the option of rejecting any terms agreed for Britain and the Community. This right was only revealed to the public in October 1971. The position of the Home Office is significant as, on this issue, it was willing to suspend the United Kingdom's position of sovereignty over the islands although it was never clarified what deal would have been made available to the islands if they had rejected the Protocol.

When the United Kingdom voted to accept the terms of membership on October 28, 1971, it became a priority to tie up the loose ends of the agreement.

By November 9, the special arrangements in form of Protocol 3 and Article 227(5)(c) were announced. A story widely believed in Jersey, and perhaps with some credence, is that the Protocol was the last item on a long agenda and thus perhaps not subject to the most detailed scrutiny by tired diplomats. The next day, the Constitutional and Common Market Committee expressed satisfaction with the terms.

The United Kingdom was also eager for the Protocol to be accepted. On November 19, Geoffrey Rippon, the Minister in charge of the overall negotiations, addressed the States to allay any doubts the island might have had. In his speech he emphasised that the Crown Dependencies would be in the Common External Tariff and had even gained new rights, which still exist, even though they have not been over-utilised since the agreement was signed:

> If you accept these proposals it will mean that your present trading relationship with the United Kingdom is guaranteed and you will, in addition, have opened to yourselves new markets in the member states of the existing Community. You will not only have preserved your charter rights but, in practical terms, you will have extended their field of operation.[48]

The speech attempted to reassure the island that the existing administrative burden would be light, mainly involving creating legislation to ensure free trade. Most importantly he emphasised that "Under the proposals, your fiscal autonomy has been guaranteed. I can say that quite categorically that there will be no question of your having to apply a Value Added Tax or any part of the Community policy on taxation."[49] Furthermore, even though there was no right of establishment in the EEC, this right had been preserved with respect to the United Kingdom. Moreover, implicit in the non-discrimination clause was the fact that the United Kingdom had given up its traditional right of access to jobs on the island as any regulation imposed by the island on access to work would apply to all EEC nationals equally.[50] Geoffrey Rippon emphasised the importance of this concession made by the United Kingdom to secure the terms; however, other political considerations were likely to prevent Jersey antagonising its metropolitan power by imposing any controls on immigration beyond those already implicit in the housing laws.

The speech also emphasised that the safeguard clause was not a threat to the island or the agreement. He went on to emphasise that:

> Some people say "Well this is almost too good to be true, there must be a snag in the small print." Well there really is not. I really think what the Community have done once they were satisfied and understood what the special Charter and constitutional rights were, what they have done in effect is to make a unique arrangement to meet a unique situation and they have said it is no part of a great Community to impose burdens on a small Community.[51]

He summarised the agreement as "I do not think better terms could have been negotiated. I think really you have terms which some people in the United Kingdom would like to have had. You have got all the benefits and avoided some of the obligations and difficulties."[52] The States debated Protocol 3 on the December 15, 1971 and voted to accept it by fifty-one votes to one.

The Protocol negotiated assuaged almost all the concerns expressed by the Special Committee. As far as agriculture was concerned the island could export as if it were a member state, however, as far as taxation and the finance industry were concerned the island was outside Europe. Moreover, the Protocol did not require Jersey to adopt social legislation or remove its housing controls. Therefore, the agreement ensured that Jersey's economy would continue to expand unhindered by the United Kingdom's membership of the EEC.

The Protocol must be seen as a triumph for Jersey's politicians as it created an acceptable structure to manage a new dependency relationship, and reasons must be given for this success. One reason is that while the relationship was of paramount importance to the island, this was not true of the Community or the United Kingdom. This can be seen in the Home Office's management of the issue. After beginning with the assumption that nothing could be done, an assumption based on a literal reading of the Treaty, it had to be shown by the Report prepared in 1967 that alternatives were available. Nevertheless, the Home Office was unwilling to develop alternatives of its own but eagerly accepted a solution developed by the island. This provides a good example of the benefits of the current United Kingdom relationship based largely on neglect. Jersey was able to secure the solution it wanted by merely asking for it. However, if it had not done so it would have been included in the EEC, regardless of what was in the best interests of the island. The position taken by the United Kingdom is understandable in that it was preparing for one of the most significant political events since the war. Under these circumstances, Jersey's needs must have been seen as at best a distraction, at worst an irritation. Jersey was also able to put together a talented team of advisers and politicians who were willing to take the initiative and propose a solution supported by considerable research. This represented a considerable achievement given the resources at their disposal.

The Jersey Constitutional Association rejected Protocol 3 as merely a 'diplomatic' solution and argued that "By removing some immediate difficulties, it made the Treaty acceptable to the Islanders but, in fact, it by-passed the constitutional issue the Treaty had raised and left the basic problem unresolved."[53] This view can be disputed and it would be possible to argue that the Protocol was an excellent example of the constitutional relationship in action in that the United Kingdom's absolute sovereignty to take the Crown Dependencies into the Community, if no other option could be found, was confirmed. However, within the arrangement an accommodation was found to give the island autonomy within the overall British position. As a result, Jersey gained a position which gave it the benefits, but none of the disadvantages, of being inside the Community.

The insular authorities were successful in negotiating the Protocol because Jersey could be portrayed as peripheral and of little importance and few people were aware of how much potential for expansion the finance industry had on the island. Moreover, time pressure meant that discussing the status of the Crown Dependencies was not a priority and was dealt with at the last moment. Given the pressure, a ready made solution was favoured. If the European Commission had been more aware of the potential strength of Jersey's finance industry, it might have treated the concerns expressed at the time about the island's fiscal autonomy more seriously. Consequently, Jersey's management of the crises was very successful as, unlike in the past when the island was of strategic importance, it could offer very little in exchange for any privileges guaranteed by the Protocol. Jersey also benefited from the dynamic political leadership provided by Senator Vibert. He not only organised a strong team of internal and external advisors, but also correctly analysed that what the United Kingdom preferred was a settlement defined by Jersey as the Home Office was more concerned about the time it would have to commit in determining the settlement, than about the content of the agreement itself. This set of negotiations must be seen as the most successful example of managed dependency undertaken by the insular authorities in the period under consideration. The significance of the Protocol cannot be underestimated as it has been a fundamental factor in shaping the island's current economic position. It created the political space for an offshore finance centre to develop and illustrated the extent to which Jersey has been able to protect its interests.

The Operation of Protocol 3 Today

While the Protocol has been successful in that it has allowed the island's economy to expand and the influence of the European Union has been minimised, it has nevertheless thrown up certain difficulties. Although these must be seen as an acceptable price to pay for the Protocol itself, they represent issues which have to be managed within the relationship. The problems can arise either directly or indirectly from the Protocol. In the field of environmental protection, the issue arises indirectly. The island is not required under Protocol 3 to follow EC directives concerning the environment but in this field, perhaps more than any other, it faces severe informal pressure to match environmental protection norms as its pollution will often directly affect the environment of the Community. Additionally, there is strong internal pressure from powerful local environmentalist movements. Currently, EU standards tend to be adopted as benchmarks for debate as it would be too onerous for the insular authorities to prepare, debate and justify its own environmental standards, internally and externally, across all areas.

The nature of the Crown Dependencies' representation with respect to the European Union represents another problem. They have no access to a MEP as they are not part of the Union. Even if they were, the experience of Gibraltar suggests that the provision of representation for such a small community may be problematic. Jersey is not a sovereign state and cannot therefore formally represent itself, but must rely on the good offices of the United Kingdom's representatives. Not only is representing Jersey not among the high priorities of the United Kingdom's representatives in Brussels, but they must also be approached along the official channels via the Home Office, which slows the transmission of information. Jersey's solution has been to rely formally on the United Kingdom to represent its interest while employing a legal advisor in Brussels and Dr Richard Plender as a specialist legal advisor on specific constitutional affairs. Both Philip Bentley and Graham Mather have argued that Jersey should use more assertive lobbying tactics in its relations with the European Union.[54] The drawback with such an approach is that it could offend the United Kingdom delegation as it may be seen as undermining their representative role. Such an approach could, however, be useful when issues directly relating to Jersey arise in order to clarify the island's constitutional position and present a defence of offshore finance, although it is unclear how effective such lobbying would be.[55]

Article 5 of Protocol 3 of the United Kingdom Treaty of Accession states that: "If, during the application of the arrangements defined in this Protocol, difficulties appear on either side in relations between the Community and these territories, the Commission shall without delay propose to the Council such safeguard measures as it believes necessary, specifying their terms and conditions of application." This provision appears to be one-sided as it only gives rights to the Commission. However, the Commission has yet to exercise its rights under this provision. This would appear to be another example of a facet of Jersey's relationship with a more powerful body. Although the external body would appear to have absolute power, the reality is that Jersey is free to pursue its own policy ends provided the other side has the theoretical, even if never exercised, power to veto such action. Therefore, unless Jersey seeks a direct confrontation in this area, concerns over the article seem misplaced.

Agriculture and Fisheries

Protocol 3 ensures that, even though the Common Agricultural Policy does not apply to the island, it indirectly determines the approximate level of agricultural subsidies. This is because local industry would be unable to compete with European Union products, if Jersey granted less than the Common Agricultural Policy levels of support.

The island's position with respect to the Common Agricultural policy reflects the rest of the Protocol in that no financial support is given to Jersey farmers by the Community, although all import measures apply between the island and third countries. The Community rules also apply to agricultural goods to the extent necessary to allow for the free movement of agricultural products.[56] The regulation not only forbids the granting of aid by the Community to the island, but also provides for the extension of the Treaty provisions governing state aid to the agricultural sector. This is to allow the Community to ensure that Jersey does not seek to gain an unfair market advantage in this sector through the mechanism of granting more state aid than the Community itself. Furthermore, the island is required to submit all systems of aid for examination and allow sufficient time for the Commission to submit its comments or modify any grants of aid. Colin Powell is of the opinion that some derogations are needed in the areas of the importation of live animals and liquid milk.[57] These are needed to maintain the tradition that no cattle can be imported, thereby preserving a pedigree breeding stock. Colin Powell feels that the Community should be sympathetic to Jersey's position.[58]

The issue of fishing rights around the Channel Islands was complicated by the agreement with the EEC. The status of the surrounding waters is unusual as their sovereignty has always been British, with Channel Island administration. It is unclear how far the Protocol applies to the waters surrounding the Crown Dependencies. Deemster Cain argues that Community rules only apply such "as are necessary to allow free movement and observance of normal conditions of competition in trade".[59] Thus, the Community rules with respect to net size and fishery log books apply to the Isle of Man because they are so closely bound with trade. Richard Plender cites the European Court of Justice which ruled in respect of Manx waters in 1980.[60] The United Kingdom's position was based on the special constitutional position of the Isle of Man and asserted that only the free movement of goods provisions of Community Law applied to the island's fisheries. The Commission argued that conservation measures must also apply to Manx waters. The European Court of Justice found that the United Kingdom, as the sovereign power of the Isle of Man, had acted in breach of the non-discrimination rules by unilaterally adopting rules on fish stocks. Plender argues, however, that this does not mean that the Common Fisheries Policy applies to Crown Dependencies' waters as "Had it been the intention of the draftsman to apply to the islands the whole of the Common Fisheries Policy (or the Common Agricultural Policy) other than the rules concerning financial aid, Protocol 3 could have been drafted much more simply."[61] In the end the issue was resolved when a new agreement on fisheries was concluded between the Isle of Man and the United Kingdom in 1991 under which the Manx authorities agreed to keep its rules broadly in line with those in force in the United Kingdom. This would seem to be an acceptable compromise where the island accepts rules similar to those in force in the Community, without necessarily accepting its authority in the matter.

Right of Establishment and Free Movement of Persons

Articles 2 and 6 of Protocol 3 means that the free movement provisions of the Treaty of Rome do not apply to those people deemed to be Channel Islanders or Manxmen. The application of the Right of Establishment was felt to be unacceptable in the island as such a ruling would undermine the island's *de facto* immigration control via Housing Laws. However, there could be no discrimination between European Union nationals and consequently any EU national enjoys the same privileges as United Kingdom citizens to live and work on the island, subject to the Housing Law. Furthermore, as full freedom of movement and establishment are denied to EU citizens a *quid pro quo* exists in Article 6 of the Protocol where those citizens deemed to have no links with the United Kingdom, denoted Channel Islanders or Manxmen, are excluded from the rights of establishment and free movement within the Community. Since this provision only applies to those who have not spent five years being ordinarily resident in the United Kingdom or who do not have a parent or grandparent who was born, adopted, registered or naturalised in the United Kingdom, this represents a decreasing minority, estimated informally at twenty five per cent of Jersey's population.[62] Additionally, this provision appears not to be enforced by the EU authorities. Despite this, its existence is the most unpopular aspect of Protocol 3 as it is felt to discriminate against those persons who are British citizens because of a connection with the Channel Islands or the Isle of Man. It should be noted that those described in the Protocol as Channel Islanders or Manxmen may be excluded from the Right of Establishment in the Community, but the United Kingdom itself is exempted from the provision. This would thus allow these Channel Islanders and Manxmen, if they so wish, to undertake five years residence in the United Kingdom to become entitled to the right of establishment in the rest of the Community. Therefore the lack of right of establishment for Channel Islanders must be regarded as a necessary *quid pro quo* for maintaining the Jersey's housing controls. Moreover, Channel Islanders and Manxmen are allowed to carry European Union standard British passports, albeit in a modified form.[63] The Community has given the island the right to apply immigration controls provided there is no discrimination between natural and legal persons of the Community.[64] Deemster Cain argues that the absence of the right of establishment has allowed the Isle of Man to retain its work permit legislation as well as Jersey and Guernsey their legislation controlling housing rights.[65]

Non-Discrimination Clause

Article 4 of Protocol 3 of the United Kingdom Treaty of Accession states that "The authorities of these territories shall apply the same treatment to all nationals and legal persons of the Community." One effect of this provision was to grant equal status to the Portuguese, Irish and French minorities in Jersey, including the right to vote. This move was significant as it granted rights to minorities who had traditionally done the worst paid jobs on the island and created a legal means to ensure equality of legal treatment with the residents on the island.

The problem with Article 4 is the lack of qualifying phrases to determine the extent of its application. The provision was considered by the European Court of Justice in 1991 in the case of <u>DHSS v Barr and Montrose Holding Limited</u>.[66] The case was derived from a challenge to the Manx legislation requiring all employees on the island to have a work permit. The work permit legislation in the Isle of Man functions as a form of immigration control in a way analogous to the use of housing legislation in Jersey and Guernsey. The difference is that rather than limiting immigration by preventing those not born on the island from having normal residency rights, the Isle of Man controls the right to work. The appellant argued that the Manx work permit legislation was invalidated by Article 4 of Protocol 3. The judgement of the European Court of Justice confirmed that Manx Courts, and by extension Courts in Jersey and Guernsey, have the power to refer questions to the European Court of Justice although they are not Courts of a Member State. The Court also ruled that the provisions of Article 4 were not limited to those matters covered by Article 1 of Protocol 3, but all situations governed by Community Law in the Member States. Consequently, any new aspect or development in Treaty Law apply to the Crown Dependencies. However, the Court qualified its position by ruling that Article 4 cannot be used as an indirect means of applying any provision of Community Law, other than those included in Article 1 of the Protocol, to the Isle of Man and by implication all the Crown Dependencies. This statement counters a perception amongst some in the Crown Dependencies that Article 4 could be used as a means to expand the ambit of community legislation without amending the provisions of Protocol 3.

The somewhat confused situation which arose from the Court's ruling in Barr v. Montrose was clarified by a ruling made in July 1998. The case involved a Portugese national, Pereira Rui Rocque, who arrived in Jersey following Portugal's accession to the Community. Following a conviction for larceny, Rocque was given a written warning by the Immigration Service that a recommendation for deportation would be made if he were convicted of a further offence within the Bailiwick's jurisdiction. As a result of a second conviction the following year, the Lieutenant Governor made a deportation order. Rocque began proceedings to challenge the order on the grounds that it was inconsistent with Article 4 as British citizens, under the Immigration Act 1971, can only be bound over to leave the island, not deported. A further complication was that Jersey's inclusion in the Common Travel Area would result in the plaintiff being prohibited from establishment in the United Kingdom, the Irish Republic and the other Crown Dependencies. The Royal Court referred the question to the European Court of Justice. Rocque's lawyer cited the ruling in Barr v. Montrose that non-discrimination was not limited to those areas covered by Article 1 of the Protocol. The contention of the insular authorities was that such an interpretation would grant citizens of the European Union greater rights in Jersey than they had in the United Kingdom, which along with other member states reserve the right to deport for public health, public order and security reasons.[67] The Court ruled that Article 4 does not prevent Jersey from deporting citizens of the European Union, except those of Britain. Additionally, any deportation orders made by Jersey would be restricted to that area alone and not include the rest of the Common Travel Area. Thus it appears that in the case of citizens of the European Union, Crown Dependencies' procedures and orders will have to operate so as not to infringe the free movement provisions which apply elsewhere. The social effect of this ruling has been to confirm the restrictions on the rights of a minority of the population which already feels it is exploited. The most significant aspect of the cases was the confirmation that Article 4 cannot be used as an indirect means of extending European Union legislation not covered by the Protocol to Jersey.

The Single Market

The introduction of the single market provisions did not alter the Protocol, but has had considerable indirect effects by complicating the problem of determining which directives on the movement of goods apply to the island. Prior to the Single European Act, the basic rule was that any legislation adopted with respect to Article 30 of the Treaty regarding standards imposed on products imported from third countries applied to Jersey, while those based on Article 100 on approximating the laws of member states did not. As a result of the Single European Act, the practice developed of enacting uniform standards for both domestic and imported production, thus combining the legislation derived from both Articles. This procedure has also been adopted with respect to agricultural goods. The unintended side-effect of removing the divide between traded goods and those for internal consumption was to complicate the operation of Jersey's relationship with the Community. The Single European Act has therefore caused problems because it has blurred the divide between external and internal policy areas and hence was seen as further infringing on the island's domestic autonomy. This development can be seen as undermining the core compromise at the heart of the island's autonomy, where external affairs are the responsibility of the United Kingdom and domestic affairs the responsibility of the insular authorities.

The Treaties of Maastricht and Amsterdam

Neither the Maastricht Treaty nor the Amsterdam Treaty was used to change any aspect of the formal operation of Protocol 3. The Home Office's assurance to the Manx government stated that the Treaty on European Union "applies to dependent territories only to the extent that the Community Treaties apply to them."[68] However, most effects of the Community on Jersey are indirect. As such it is the change in the political and economic environment engendered by a Treaty, rather than the Treaty itself, which was the significant worry to Jersey. A more unified political direction undertaken by Europe at Maastricht and an "ever closer union"[69] means that policy increasingly is made in Brussels and thus this indirect relationship gains importance at the expense of the more tested direct relationship with London.

The Maastricht Treaty had some indirect effects which led to legislative changes in Jersey. As it was felt that elections in Jersey were municipal, under the Treaty's terms, Jersey law was amended to extend the franchise in Jersey to cover all European Union nationals. The Treaty of European Union created a common citizenship. Under these proposals, citizens of Crown Dependencies will have the right of diplomatic and consular protection from other member states in any third country where the United Kingdom is not represented. Crown Dependencies' residents will also have the right to petition the European Parliament or complain to the Ombudsman if the matter is governed by Protocol 3. However, if the scope of the rights of citizenship of the Community continues to expand, the potential danger exists that this would create a form of European parliamentary sovereignty over the island.

The Social Chapter in the Treaty rekindled fears that the European Community would directly, or indirectly, impose changes in social policy on the island.[70] Until the election of the Labour government in 1997, Jersey was unable to implement the Social Chapter, even if it had so desired, due to the United Kingdom's opting out. The new administration's adoption of the Chapter has removed that defence. However, Jersey will not be required to implement the entire Social Chapter, although large portions will be adopted to maintain equivalence with the United Kingdom and pre-empt any adverse publicity which would occur if Jersey maintains too discordant a position. Jersey is also vulnerable to pressures to harmonise policy in this area as it avoided providing reciprocal arrangements for social services with most European states by relying on most individuals' links with the United Kingdom to ensure the provision is met. Instead, Jersey has negotiated separate bilateral agreements with states on social security matters. Unfortunately, a small number of individuals do suffer under this arrangement by, for example, being unable to benefit from free health care in the European countries to which they may wish to retire. Although this is another example of the United Kingdom allowing Jersey political space to develop external policies to suit its own scale and political preferences, it does mean that Jersey must take responsibility for policies developed on its own initiative.

The effects of the introduction of the Euro on the island have been the subject of considerable debate.[71] Jersey issues its own notes and coins which are accepted as legal tender in Guernsey, while banks will exchange them for sterling at parity in the United Kingdom. Under the Currency Note (Jersey) Law 1959, the Finance and Economics Committee can issue notes of any denomination it sees fit for circulation on the island. It is argued by Colin Powell that under this legislation Jersey could issue notes denominated as Euros.[72] He further argues that it is within the powers of the insular authorities to determine that notes issued by the European Central Bank are legal tender. As a consequence, Jersey could switch currencies without changing its relationship with the United Kingdom or the European Union. Such a statement is correct in so far as no constitutional modifications would have to occur for the island to adopt the Euro in the way it has adopted sterling. Fiscal realities would, however, change in that the European Central Bank, rather than the Bank of England, would define the fiscal environment in which Jersey operated by determining interest and exchange rates. It is also possible that the nations already operating the Euro could create a fiscal environment hostile to offshore finance and the United Kingdom, being outside the EMU, would be unable to prevent this development. Under these circumstances, the United Kingdom could be presented with a situation where, if it wished to join the Euro, it would have to accept the fiscal measures already taken regardless of how they affected the interests of its dependencies. However, this may well turn out to be an issue like membership itself where the island is effectively left without choice in the matter due to the actions taken by the United Kingdom. If the United Kingdom joins the Euro, there will be no sterling rate for the island to follow. Some consideration has been given to launching a separate island currency which could, for instance, shadow the dollar. It must, however, be regarded as highly unlikely that Jersey would possess the financial resources to defend such a currency given that even the United Kingdom has been unable to defend sterling in times of currency turmoil. It is also unlikely that the United Kingdom would wish Jersey to join the Euro ahead of its own membership. Although the United Kingdom would not seek to veto such a use of the island's fiscal independence, the European Union would act to discourage such an action which would be viewed as complicating the larger aim of ensuring United Kingdom's membership of the currency.

Finance and the European Union

The effect of Protocol 3 is to place the Crown Dependencies within the Common External Tariff as regards physical products. Consequently, to maintain the integrity of the boundary Jersey must impose custom duties on products emanating from third countries at levels laid down by the European Union. However, for all other products the Channel Islands are effectively third countries. Therefore Jersey is within the Community as far as physical movement of goods is concerned, but outside for fiscal purposes which covers value-added tax and excise duties, exactly the settlement which the insular authorities desired. The Community rules on custom matters, qualitative restrictions and free movement of industrial, agricultural and horticultural goods apply to Jersey in the same way as to United Kingdom. This creates a situation where, as far as these issues, and only these issues are concerned, Jersey is inside the Single Market. The removal of duty free within the Community will boost the local tourist industry as the island will be one of the few places within easy reach of the United Kingdom where duty free goods can be purchased. Therefore, thirty years on from negotiating this concession, its benefits will prove even greater than before.

The most important aspect of the relationship in financial terms is the debate about fiscal harmonisation. Under Protocol 3, proposals for fiscal harmonisation, fiscal directives and other proposals do not extend to the island. Institutions on the island are treated as if they were in third countries outside the Community. They are therefore excluded from taking advantage of the Community's 'single passport' for free movement of services; instead each member must be approached separately to arrange access to their markets. Indeed, the introduction of the Undertaking on Collective Investments and Transferable Securities directive in 1989 led to a limited outflow of funds from Jersey to the Community's two 'offshore finance centres', Luxembourg and Dublin.[73] The Protocol therefore denies the island free access to a huge financial market, but provides a degree of protection from intervention in Jersey's fiscal policies by the Community. On paper this protection seems absolute. The Protocol guarantees formal fiscal independence and cannot be modified without unanimity; however, Jersey's position may well be undermined by indirect measures towards fiscal harmonisation. These will be more difficult for the island to oppose as it cannot argue it is the direct target of the policy. Moreover, the island is vulnerable to indirect political pressure to change its fiscal policies.

The issue of tax harmonisation has recently resurfaced, in particular with respect to the debate as to what financial regulation is necessary for a single currency to function. The Community's only formal fiscal competencies under Protocol 3 are in relation to agricultural levies and duties and import duties; thus tax harmonisation could not be imposed directly on the Crown Dependencies. This does not, however, stop indirect pressure being exerted on the United Kingdom to implement such a measure. It could be argued that the imposition of such measure by the United Kingdom is possible under the good government provisions whereas imposition under Protocol 3 might not be possible. A precedent for the United Kingdom's intervention in Jersey's fiscal affairs that might be cited is the United Kingdom's unilateral announcement of a review of Jersey's finance industry in the form of the Edwards' report.

Mario Monti, when European Union Commissioner, proposed moves to harmonise certain features of taxation law throughout the European Union and the introduction of a common withholding tax idea was mooted in June 1998. This work is to be co-ordinated with the OECD review of tax havens. Protocol 3 would prevent the Community from imposing such a tax directly, but as these proposals are specifically targeted at offshore finance centres it is likely that the Community would try to extend such a tax to Jersey. Graham Mather, MEP is of the opinion that "the core feeling in the European Commission and in key member states is that "tax havens" must be eliminated. The chief current attack on so-called tax havens is the withholding tax, and they want to apply it to the whole of Europe."[74] In the same article, Mather cites the former French Finance Minister, Dominic Strauss-Kahn, on the subject of whether codes of practice on tax matters were sufficient or legislation should be used to achieve fiscal harmonisation "And equally, if member states are being difficult about accepting these directives, we must decide whether we shouldn't abolish the unanimity rule and move to a qualified majority voting system for tax harmonisation."[75] Strauss-Kahn also refused to rule out a change to the Treaty to achieve this end. Thus there is a very real danger that the impetus created by the need to make the single currency succeed will result in more general fiscal harmonisation within the Community and attempts to restrict the operation of European offshore finance centres.

In 1997 the Commission issued a communication on harmful tax competition which was debated at the Ecofin meeting. On December 1, 1997, two resolutions were taken by the Council of Ministers: the first was to adopt a Code of Conduct on business taxation and the second called upon the Commission to present proposals on the taxation of savings. Both of the proposals could affect Jersey; however, it is the code of conduct which may impinge on Jersey's autonomy more directly. Philip Bentley, while acknowledging that these measures "do use language which appears, at first sight, to impose obligations on the United Kingdom to promote certain principles in its dependent and associated territories",[76] observes that these measures are not legally binding. Instead "By the Code of Conduct, the Member States commit themselves, in the political sense, to a standstill on the introduction of all new harmful tax measures, and agree to abide by a review process for the assessment of existing measures."[77] The Code does include a commitment for "Member States with dependent or associated territories or which have special responsibilities or taxation prerogatives in respect of other territories commit themselves, within the framework of their constitutional arrangements, to ensuring that the principles of the Code are applied to these territories."[78] The Code, while giving what appears to be legal protection to Jersey, would seem to preclude any tax harmonisation measures; moreover, it is not legally binding. However, it is unclear how far the United Kingdom's prerogative in external affairs would allow pressure to be exerted on the island to comply with such a Code of Conduct.

The Code of Conduct seeks to prevent business being attracted by the provision of benefits not available to local firms or individuals as well as preventing businesses already operating from being granted tax benefits for operations which include no real economic activity, lack transparency or infringe OECD principles in this area.[79] It is unclear at present how far these principles will be deemed to apply to Jersey. It also must be remembered that the Code remains as Code and therefore has no legal force.

The Bailiff, Sir Philip Bailhache, has sought to reassure the finance industry on the island by arguing that European Union has no legal power to enforce its will on tax harmonisation on the island. Indeed, he stated that "We have built our house not upon the sand, but upon the rock of our ancient privileges and constitutional status".[80] This statement would appear to reflect the general analysis of the situation in Jersey and is an interesting illustration of the Bailiff fulfilling two of his functions at the same time, both acting as an independent constitutional adviser, whilst, as a spokesman for the insular authorities, seeking to reassure the island and the offshore finance industry about their future. The statement from the Bailiff was part of a new strategy towards Europe in response to the move within the Community towards tax harmonisation. The policy was defined by Senator Frank Walker as being "proactive with a new approach so that we can establish our right to determine our own tax affairs while still being considered good neighbours by the rest of Europe."[81] This policy is very ambitious as it is Jersey's determination of its own tax levels that promotes the operation of an offshore finance centre and results in Jersey being viewed as a bad neighbour by the European Union. It would also seem to overlook the fact that the United Kingdom and the Commission are unlikely to use the law, but rather political or economic pressure, to force a change in policy by Jersey.

It might seem logical to argue that Jersey's role as an offshore finance centre will not be challenged by the Community as long as the Community has effectively two offshore finance centres, Luxembourg and the Dublin International Financial Services Centre, as members. According to Graham Mather, "Luxembourg was complaining that it didn't see why its banking secrecy and Belgium flow of money should be given up just for it to go to the Channel Islands instead."[82] Therefore instead of protecting other offshore finance centres, Dublin and Luxembourg could seek to use their position inside the European Union to protect their finance industries, if necessary, at the expense of Jersey which lacks a voice in the development of Community policy. The need to include other offshore finance centres in the scope of the tax harmonisation measures was illustrated when "the Times" reported that, if the Council of Ministers had adopted a directive imposing a twenty percent withholding tax, one of the results would have been a £100 billion net outflow of funds from the Community to the Channel Islands.[83] The danger is that Jersey is now considered important enough to pose a threat in terms of tax leakage to the Community. The challenge to the insular authorities is how to defend Jersey's position against the overwhelming size of the Community.

In the past the island has sought to maintain a somewhat contradictory, if advantageous, position with respect to its relations as an offshore finance centre with the European Community. According to Colin Powell "The Island will need to continue to work to ensure it is not shut out of markets in Europe, particularly with the extension of the Single Market for financial services to the European Economic Area. However, the Island's position "offshore Europe" is still considered to remain in the best interests of the Island as a finance centre."[84] This strategy of seeking to try and preserve the best of both worlds by maintaining access to the market, while avoiding its regulation, may not be tolerated indefinitely by the Community as Jersey, at least in this sphere, is nowadays a major offshore finance centre. The long term problem for the insular authorities remains that, even if they are successful in preventing intervention in their fiscal affairs by the Community, the finance industry may decline anyway as the political instability generated by the controversy will make institutions wary of investing in the island. Thus even the hint of conflict could destroy one of the key attractions of the island as an offshore finance centre, namely its political stability.

Modification of the Protocol

Protocol 3 has yet to be challenged, as thus far it has served both sides well. However, the glory and flaw of Protocol 3 have been its brevity and the lack of case law interpreting the Protocol. As case law develops, the Protocol will lose some of its flexibility, which may prove to be the main problem in the relationship in the future. The case law has already confirmed the right to appeal to the European Court of Justice from Jersey Courts. This has opened up a significant, if circumscribed, area of appeal from the island and has made the European Community an actor in shaping policy in Jersey. Another area of concern is how far the Protocol is open to change as the result of political pressure and whether Jersey should seek to amend the Protocol.

Philip Bentley is of the opinion that "there is no express provision in the Treaty of UK Accession which would allow the UK, or the Channel Islands to repudiate Protocol No. 3."[85] Therefore, unless the United Kingdom is prepared to repudiate the whole European Union Treaty system, change must be achieved by amendment. It should be noted that the opportunity to amend the Protocol was not taken when the Treaty of Rome was amended at either Maastricht or Amsterdam. As such an amendment to the Treaty requires unanimity, the insular authorities have assumed the United Kingdom would use its veto to block any change in the Protocol not in the island's interest. This theory does, however, assume that there will not be a stronger countervailing interest for the United Kingdom to support such changes.

The Protocol has survived unchanged hitherto, mainly because there has been no conflict between Jersey and the European Union which has required the Protocol to face a serious political challenge. It should be borne in mind that it would not be without risk to reopen negotiations on the Protocol. Jersey would have most to lose as it has an agreement providing almost exactly the situation it requires. The United Kingdom and the European Union, on the other hand, would risk creating an issue which would fuel hostility to the European Union in the United Kingdom and take up a disproportionate amount of time relative to its importance to reach a satisfactory conclusion. The problem is that both the European Union and the Crown Dependencies have changed since the agreement was originally signed. This has created some tension in the relationship, in particular as the Crown Dependencies are no longer entirely irrelevant peripheral communities, but significant finance centres. Colin Powell certainly believes that "The view continues to be held that the present arrangements between the Island and the European Community remains of advantage to the Island."[86]

Options to the Protocol

Jersey had three options when the United Kingdom joined the EEC. It could adopt Protocol 3, seek full membership or seek independence. If Jersey had sought accession, it would have benefited from membership of the Common Agricultural Policy. On the other hand, its tourism industry would have lost the attraction of duty free shopping, and the lack of fiscal autonomy would have been a hindrance to the expansion of the offshore finance centre. It is also likely that the island would have become a net contributor to the European Union due to its relative affluence and small agricultural sector. The alternative of independence would have deprived Jersey of representation overseas, defence and perhaps, most importantly, the perception of stability that the finance industry believes is inherent in a British dependency. Therefore, the Protocol, even though it has never been tested by a political crisis, must be regarded as the best option open to the island, both at the time and at present, particularly as the agreement represented the EEC meeting all of Jersey's demands presented during the negotiations.

Independence might be seen as an advantage because the current criticism of offshore finance centre is focusing on non-sovereign territories. However, this situation may not persist as it rests on the direct influence which nations such as Liechtenstein, Luxembourg and Switzerland exercise on international bodies, including the OECD and European Union. This means their votes are always used directly to support their interests. This has led to the conclusion that dependencies are weaker than independent microstates because their metropolitan powers might accept concessions at international forums in exchange for ending the fiscal privileges the dependencies enjoy. However, if long term security is considered, the dependencies have at least one large ally with a degree of obligation to them, which includes the maintenance of an acceptable standard of living. In the event of the European Union deciding to make it impossible for offshore finance centres to operate, the dependencies will have a source of aid to mitigate the distress caused by the destruction of their economies which the independent states will not. The implied cost entailed is perhaps the strongest argument for the dependencies' metropolitan powers to preserve their viable economies and not create new economic burdens for themselves. It could also be argued that the sovereign offshore finance centres would be ill advised to allow the larger states to attack the non-sovereign centres in the hope of creating more business for themselves. As the larger states are unlikely to distinguish between the two, any attacks are likely to affect both sets of offshore finance centres and thus they would be better advised to try and create some solidarity themselves to promote their cause to international organisations; currently this is lacking.

The core of Jersey's problem in managing its relationship with the European Union derives from its position as a dependency. As a dependency it can rarely, if ever, hope to be at the top of the United Kingdom's agenda. It is therefore vulnerable to political deals where its interests are sacrificed to meet other aims of the United Kingdom. Indeed, the United Kingdom is responsible for protecting Jersey's interest within the European Union and Jersey remains dependent on the United Kingdom's willingness to use its veto to defend the island's interests if necessary. However, being a dependency has its advantages as, unlike independent microstates, Jersey has indirect access to the corridors of power which produced the desired result at the time of the United Kingdom's accession. Nonetheless, the relationship with the EU has complicated Jersey's external policies as it offers a further indirect relationship to manage. On the other hand, Jersey has, via its relationship with the United Kingdom, more access to the means to manage that relationship than if it were independent. The lack of direct power over the relationship explains much of local hostility to the European Union. Furthermore, Jersey had to accept that it could not prevent the United Kingdom from seeking membership, but only seek the best arrangement for itself within British membership. This is the reality of being a dependency. If Jersey wants to influence United Kingdom policy directly in this area it must seek incorporation in the United Kingdom. Alternatively, if it seeks to avoid the consequences of any United Kingdom decisions which it dislikes, independence is the only option. As a dependency, it must accept that the metropolitan power will act in its own perceived best interest regardless of the feelings of its dependencies.

Conclusion

Protocol 3 is both legally secure and has, so far, been successful in allowing the island's economy to grow whilst protecting Jersey from excessive interference in its domestic affairs. However, if a threat to the Protocol occurs it will not be in the form of a legal challenge, but rather in the shape of political pressure. This pressure, either from the Commission itself or via the United Kingdom, is likely to be used to erode Jersey's autonomy with the island's enforced consent. Moreover, Jersey's relationship with the United Kingdom has subtly changed, both by the influence of European legal and constitutional practice which membership of the European Union entails and by the need for the United Kingdom to consider its broader interests in the Union while representing Jersey's interests. Change in the Protocol, however, remains unlikely as it has been very successful. Further, the European Union has been very tolerant of microstates, both in Europe and globally. It has even been prepared to risk sanctions from the United States to protect the banana-dependent microstates of the Caribbean. It should be remembered that Jersey would always need some form of relationship with the European Union, as it could not survive economically if it were excluded from Europe. The current Protocol, despite its flaws, meets Jersey's needs very successfully.

Jersey has, therefore, become a dependency of the European Union to the extent that its current relationship is dependent on the tolerance of the member states of the European Union. The alternative of casting itself adrift from Europe by seeking independence and then having to re-negotiate its relationship with both the United Kingdom and the European Union would seem ill-advised, as Jersey is unlikely to be able to negotiate as good a deal as it already has. As the island is no longer viewed by other European states as peripheral, a new agreement would require financial concessions from Jersey in exchange for its privileged position. Moreover, the discussion would create instability on the island as its outcome would affect the future of the insular economy while creating the danger of damaging discord with the United Kingdom and the European Union.

146

References

[1] See Appendix 1.

[2] Powell, G. C., <u>Annual Report to the Chief Adviser to the States</u>, States of Jersey, Jersey, November 1993, 34, hereafter, Powell 1993.

[3] This was achieved by the European Communities Legislation (Implementation) (Jersey) Law 1996.

[4] op. cit., EEC Report 1967, 144.

[5] <u>Hansard Parliamentary Debates, Commons</u>, vol.226, column 421.

[6] Article 227 Treaty of Rome.

[7] Policy and Resources Committee, <u>Strategic Policy Review and Action Plan</u>, States of Jersey, Jersey, 1996, 54.

[8] <u>The European Community's Relations to French Overseas Departments, European Autonomous Regions, Overseas Countries and Territories and Independent Countries within EC Boundaries</u>, Background Report issued by the Commission of the European Communities, London, 10/12/92, 1.

[9] Text of a Speech by the Hon. Peter Caruana, Chief Minister of Gibraltar, to the European - Atlantic Group, 24/11/97, 11.

[10] op. cit., EEC Report 1967, 181.

[11] ibid., 183.

[12] Williams, H., "The Channel Isles and the Common Market: A view from Brussels", <u>Jersey Evening Post</u>, 27/5/68, 7.

[13] Herbert, C., "Staying out: It suits them and it suits us", <u>Jersey Evening Post</u>, 12/7/96, 20.

[14] ibid.

[15] Owen, E., "Battle for Special Terms Jersey and the Common Market", <u>The Islander</u>, June 1980, 33-37, hereafter, Owen.

[16] op. cit., EEC Report, 1967, 55.

[17] ibid.

[18] op. cit., Owen, 33-37.

[19] op. cit., EEC Report 1967, 191.

[20] This was in anticipation of a second application for membership by the United Kingdom.

[21] op. cit., EEC Report 1967, 4.

[22] op. cit., Vibert interview.

[23] op. cit., Vibert, 137.

[24] op. cit., EEC Report 1967, 11.

[25] op. cit., Vibert, 1991, 138.

[26] op. cit., EEC Report, 1967, 4.

[27] ibid.

[28] ibid.

[29] ibid., 45

[30] ibid.

[31] op. cit., Allen letter.

[32] "Including C.I. in E.E.C. would mean constitutional, administrative and economic difficulties", <u>Jersey Evening Post</u>, 8/7/71, 1.

[33] "Concom recommend acceptance of terms", <u>Jersey Evening Post</u>, 23/11/71, 1.

[34] "Rejection of terms would constitute U.D.I. and make U.K. impose tariffs", Jersey Evening Post, 19/11/71, 1.

[35] "Common Market: Misunderstandings placed the Island in Jeopardy", Jersey Evening Post, 11/11/70, 1.

[36] ibid.

[37] op. cit., Kilbrandon 1973, 447, para 1477.

[38] "Assurance from Mr. Rippon prompts a question for the Home Secretary", Jersey Evening Post, 29/9/71, 1.

[39] op. cit., Owen, 33-37.

[40] op. cit., EEC Report, 1967, 78.

[41] ibid., 79.

[42] ibid., 6.

[43] ibid.

[44] ibid.

[45] ibid.

[46] ibid.

[47] op cit., Allen letter.

[48] "Mr Rippon's C.I. visit" Jersey Evening Post, 19/11/71, 2.

[49] ibid.

[50] ibid.

[51] Speech to the States of Jersey by Geoffrey Rippon, QC, Chancellor of the Duchy of Lancaster, 19 November 1971. See States Minutes of this date

[52] ibid.

[53] Owen, E., "How Self - Governing Are We?", The Islander, October 1980, 18-22.

[54] Interview with Philip Bentley, 15/2/99 and "Tax: Are we dancing on the slippery slope?", Jersey Evening Post, 9/11/98, 8, hereafter, Tax.

[55] Mitchell and Sikka have published an article casting doubt on the effectiveness of lobbying by the island in the United Kingdom. It would seem logical that if such lobbying is ineffective in the United Kingdom where some knowledge and sympathy exist towards the island, such lobbying would be even less effective in Europe. The article is Mitchell, A. & Sikka, P. "Jersey: Auditor's Liabilities versus People's Rights", Political Quarterly, 1999, vol. 70, no.1, 3-15.

[56] European Economic Community Regulation 706/73.

[57] Powell, G. C., Jersey and the European Community An update 1992, Office of the Economic Adviser to the States, Jersey, 9, hereafter, Powell 1992.

[58] ibid.

[59] Address by Deemster T.W. Cain, "The Isle of Man and the European Union", 24 November 1995, 12,hereafter, Cain.

[60] Case 32/79 Commission v United Kingdom, [1980] E.C.R., 2403 at 2444, paragraphs 41 to 43.

[61] Plender R., "The Channel Islands' Position in International Law", IPC conference, Jersey, 1998, 17.

[62] Interview with Martyn Furzer, Chief Officer, Immigration and Nationality Department, 1/4/97.

[63] A stamp is inserted indicating the restricted rights of those termed Channel Islanders by the Protocol.

[64] op. cit., Powell 1992, 14.

[65] op. cit., Cain, 13.

[66] Manx Law Reports, 1990 - 92, 243.

[67] Plender, R., "The Rights of European Citizens in Jersey," <u>Jersey Law Review</u>, vol. 2 no. 3. October 1998, 220 - 242.

[68] <u>The Treaty on European Union and the European Economic Area Agreement</u>, A Report by the Council of Ministers, Isle of Man, November 1993, 19.

[69] Prologue to The Treaty on European Union.

[70] <u>Jersey Evening Post Europe Review</u>, 10/7/96.

[71] For example, the "Jersey in or out of Europe Conference" held in Jersey on 11/9/97.

[72] "Jersey need not fear the Euro", <u>Jersey Evening Post</u>, 21/10/98, 10.

[73] op. cit., The Offshore Interface, 142.

[74] op. cit., Tax, 8.

[75] ibid.

[76] Bentley, P., "Channel Islands and the UK: Their relationship: The Law: The Future?" IPC conference, 1998, 5, hereafter, Bentley 1998.

[77] ibid.

[78] ibid., 6.

[79] ibid.

[80] "Our status is safe, Bailiff tells Europe" <u>Jersey Evening Post</u>, 19/8/98, 1.

[81] ibid.

[82] op. cit., Tax, 8.

[83] Miles, R., "Channel islands to get EU tax boost.", <u>The Times</u>, 2/6/98.

[84] op. cit., Powell 1992, 7.

[85] op. cit., Bentley 1998, 4.

[86] op. cit., Powell 1993, 37.

Chapter 7 - France: A Neighbour of Little Consequence

Introduction

Jersey's geographical proximity to France might be thought to imply that the relationship would be of considerable importance, but in fact it has become increasingly irrelevant. Nevertheless, Jersey must maintain some form of relationship with France, which is not only its closest neighbour, but also an influential country in its own right. The distinguishing feature of the relationship, however, is its weakness; France is not relevant as a counterbalance to the United Kingdom's power and influence. Moreover, management of the relationship is not a priority for the insular authorities and policy towards France has therefore tended to be reactive. The relationship is characterised by a series of relatively minor disputes resulting from the island's proximity to France. Jersey puts far less effort into maintaining its economic relationship with France, than with the United Kingdom, thereby making it almost inconsequential. If a stronger economic relationship existed, it would prevent the relationship from being dominated by confrontations on airspace, fishing and nuclear issues.

Jersey's relationship with France is complicated by the very different approach France takes to its overseas territories when compared with Britain.[1] The French attitude is based on the Republic's precept that it is one and indivisible and therefore all parts of the Republic, as far as possible, regardless of their position on the globe, should be administered in the same way. This approach means that the French overseas territories do not enjoy the extensive autonomy that British Dependencies and United Kingdom Overseas Territories are allowed.

There is no desire in Jersey to accept French rule. Indeed, such a development is not even considered an option. At the time of the negotiations surrounding the United Kingdom's admission to the EEC a study of the relative underdevelopment and declining population of Belle Île, an island off the south coast of Brittany, was used to illustrate the dangers of membership of the European Union.[2] The study was used to suggest that Jersey's autonomy as a British dependency has produced more economic growth and a larger population than would have been achieved if it had been part of France.

Some residual French influence is apparent in the persistence of historic, cultural and legal links and has led to the view summed up by the Bailiff's statement that "I think they see us as being hybrids. They recognise that we are not English but on the other hand we are clearly not French."[3] This statement highlights the importance of the perception of a strong link to France to differentiate between Jersey and

English identities. Nevertheless, the relationship has been in decline throughout the period under consideration, a fact emphasised by the closure of the French consulate in Jersey in 1993.

Historically Jersey's relationship with France was assumed to be bolstered by a large French population living on the island. In 1891, French nationals made up ten per cent of the population, whereas those born in other parts of the British Islands made up sixteen per cent. In 1996, the equivalent figures were one per cent and thirty nine per cent.[4] The influence of the French minority, however, was limited by the majority of those of French nationality on the island being Bretons. As such they did not share the Norman cultural heritage of the island and saw themselves as Breton, not French. In addition, before the twentieth century, they would have spoken Breton as a first language. The Bretons tended to be farm labourers, or later owners of small farms, making the French minority on the island neither powerful nor respected.

Constitutional, Legal and Linguistic links

The link with France is perhaps most strongly demonstrated by the residual Norman law contained in Jersey's constitutional and housing laws. It should be remembered, however, that the link is primarily to pre-revolutionary, not modern French law. Thus Jersey law is of less interest as a direct comparison to French law than as an interesting medieval survival. Until 1946, all local legislation was drafted in French. As a law written in French can only be amended in French there is still a residual need for local lawyers to be able to read French. The tradition of Guernsey lawyers reading Norman law at the University of Caen was temporarily introduced to Jersey by Sir Peter Crill during his tenure as Bailiff with the requirement to study at the University of Caen for six months.[5] The Caen training requirement was in addition to courses on Jersey law examined on the island. However, following opposition from the legal profession, the practice ended in 1995 as a mandatory requirement to qualification in Jersey law. Jersey lawyers generally resented the Caen training requirements and questioned its relevance to a modern offshore finance centre. David Moon, a retired senior partner of Jersey's largest law firm, believes the Caen training for local lawyers was a waste of time and an expensive way to teach lawyers French and legal history. He further believes that the teaching of pre-Revolutionary Norman law confused lawyers as Jersey law has changed so much since then and bears little relevance to contemporary economic and social conditions.[6] Some attempts are being made to preserve the link between the island and Caen University, in particular through research projects and making the Caen course optional. The fact that few local lawyers have chosen to attend the course suggests that the attempt to strengthen the link with Caen University will not be successful.

The linguistic links between Jersey and France are not as close as it would seem at first glance. Two languages are spoken which are claimed to make Jersey a francophone society: Jersey Norman French or *Jersiaise* and modern French. *Jersiaise* as a language evolved from medieval French. This means that it is not immediately comprehensible to a speaker of 'modern' French. The two languages are often seen as competing with each other, rather than representing two aspects of Jersey's French heritage. In particular, it was felt in the past that if a form of French was to be taught in local schools it should be modern French, which is of use outside the island and has more social prestige. *Jersiaise* was viewed as the language of the peasantry.[7] This social divide was reinforced by the fact that States debates and laws used modern French whereas *Jersiaise*, until the nineteenth century, was largely unwritten.[8]

The teaching of modern French is theoretically compulsory for one hour a day from the age of seven. This provision is not enforced and little more French is taught in Jersey schools than in United Kingdom schools. Part of the problem is that many teachers are born and trained outside the island. The number of people on the island fluent in modern French is currently not more than 7%.[9] *Jersiaise* is spoken by half that number[10] and was introduced for the first time in 1998 as an option in Jersey schools.[11] The number of speakers will decline as the majority of them are now elderly.

Economic Aspects of the Relationship

The most powerful explanation of the state of Jersey's relationship with France is the impact of the dominant offshore finance centre on the local economy. The finance industry focuses on the City of London. This results in a preference for trading in English with English speaking clients. French investors prefer French speaking banking centres such as Luxembourg or Switzerland. Moreover, the French authorities tend to be hostile to the hosting of offshore finance centres.[12] Consideration was undertaken about outsourcing work from Jersey, in particular, from the finance industry to *Basse Normandie* which has high levels of unemployment. Such employment of French nationals might reduce French hostility to Jersey's activities as an offshore finance centre. However, one of the major obstacles which exists for such a project is the lack of a double taxation agreement between Jersey and France. Sympathetic French regions lack the authority to change this situation as the French state will not sign double taxation treaties with territories it regards as tax havens operating outside the EU.[13] This illustrates a major advantage of Jersey's autonomy in that, while Jersey as a microstate could adapt its law to surmount this problem, it is doubtful that the French National Assembly would see such modification on behalf of *Basse Normandie* as a high enough priority, even if it were deemed desirable. Outside the finance industry, wages in Jersey are not significantly higher than the levels of unemployment benefits in France, therefore it is unlikely that many French nationals would be tempted to work in Jersey. It is thus not feasible for Jersey to exploit the high levels of unemployment in *Basse Normandie* by either moving large amounts of work to Normandy or importing significant numbers of workers.

Tourism, Jersey's second industry, would seem ideally placed to benefit from its close proximity to such a large neighbour, although in 1996 only 5,700 people out of 1.4 million based in the Normandy region stayed in Jersey more than one night.[14] Most travel is in the opposite direction. France offers good marinas and golf courses

152

and there is a shortage of both in Jersey. Islanders also own a large number of second homes in France. Jersey's attraction to French visitors would seem to be duty free and VAT free shopping; however, this is limited by customs allowances and the cost of importing goods to Jersey would seem to nullify most of the cost reductions. Furthermore, this trade is very dependent on currency fluctuations to flourish. Improvements in tourism from France would require better transport links but attempts to expand links, in particular to *Basse Normandie*, have failed.[15]

Trade with France has declined to a mere shadow of former levels.[16] Expansion is hindered by the majority of produce still being imported from the United Kingdom. This is, in part, because of a tendency by the United Kingdom based chains on the island to harmonise product packing throughout their stores and therefore to process at a central location in the United Kingdom. Importation of goods is also constrained by the small size of the car ferry to France. Two areas where trade is strong are the supply of building materials and electricity. Due to the constraints of scale on the island, Jersey has been reliant on French supplies for the large reclamation scheme under construction around St Helier.[17] Jersey is also attached to the French national grid. France, therefore, supplies fifty per cent of Jersey's electricity.[18] Additionally, a second and larger electricity cable is to be installed with the possibility of some electricity being exported onwards to Guernsey, which is not currently part of the French national grid.

Strengthening the trading links with France is problematic as Jersey's main trading links are with St Malo in Brittany, the nearest deep water port, whilst most of the efforts to improve relationships are between the insular authorities and local authorities in *Basse Normandie*.[19] Additionally, Brittany is a richer region and therefore it would also seem natural for trade to focus on St Malo. However, for political and cultural reasons, rather than economic, the effort to expand trade has focused on the relatively impoverished Norman coast which lacks an adequate deep water harbour.

Maritime Disputes

Jersey's relationship with France over the post-war period has been dominated by the need to define the limits of fishing rights and the question of who has sovereignty over two reefs situated between Jersey and France: Les Écréhous, located six miles from the north-east coast of Jersey and eight miles from Normandy and Les Minquiers which are nine miles south of Jersey and thirteen from the French mainland. Both reefs are only inhabited in the summer. The issues of the fishing rights and sovereignty over the reefs, while intertwined, are not identical and the sovereignty issue has been resolved. The issues are intertwined because many in Jersey feel sovereignty should imply fishing rights. The French state has accepted Jersey's sovereignty over the small land area of the reef, but it does not accept the exercise of the same sovereignty over the large sea area where the only important resource at stake is fish. Jersey is prevented from exercising sovereignty over the waters surrounding the reefs because the extent of the island's territorial waters has not been resolved in talks between the United Kingdom and France.

Jersey fishing boats have traditionally unloaded their catches in France and this trade is estimated to be worth 35 million francs a year.[20] Fishing is not a major element in Jersey's economy. Indeed, it could be argued that if France represented a major trading partner of Jersey, for instance through the local finance industry, the fishing dispute would be regarded as little more than a minor irritation to an otherwise successful relationship. The fishing disputes also create tension as reflected by the earlier sovereignty dispute. Jersey feels its autonomy is threatened by the unrestrained actions of fishermen supported by a far bigger and more powerful nation, while the French fishermen perceive that an already rich community progressively excludes them from their historic fishing grounds. The major reason for trying to resolve the issue is the need to preserve the fishing stocks themselves. Given that the Bay of St Malo is one biological entity, national fishing limits are of limited use. It is, therefore, vital that an agreement is reached between the Channel Islands and France as regards the fishing limits which should apply to each.

It should be noted that Jersey is not covered by the Common Fisheries Policy. Richard Plender argues, even though the evidence is contradictory, that "the tendency suggests that the institutions have not hitherto considered Channel Island and Manx waters as covered by European Community access and conservation measures."[21] The current status seems to be that the waters are not European Union waters, but French and British fishermen are allowed to fish in them under the *mer commune* provisions. This is important because, if the Common Fisheries Policy applied to local waters, all previous Conventions would be superseded. As a consequence, the conflict over fishing rights in local waters would be of a different character and under the jurisdiction of the European Union, rather than the national governments involved. Membership of the Common Fisheries Policy would offer the island adjudication of disputes by a third party, but would allow access to the waters to fishing boats of all European Union nations, thus depleting the stocks still further. Moreover, the Common Fisheries Policy allows each State exclusive rights within a six mile limit, the implementation of which would heighten tension in the area.

A Convention signed in 1839 is still the most important fishing convention with respect to Franco-Jersey fishing rights.[22] The Convention defined the extent of French and Jersey fishing rights within the Bay of St. Malo, the latter being set at three miles distant from Jersey's shoreline. Any water lying between these two zones, the *mer commune*, was to be shared. Unfortunately, the 1839 Convention ignored the issues of fishing rights around Les Écréhous and Les Minquiers, thereby losing the opportunity to solve what would become a long-running dispute.

Throughout the nineteenth and the early twentieth century, the issues of fishing rights and sovereignty over the reefs remained sources of controversy.[23] Incidents implying French sovereignty included a French citizen being granted a deed to land in Les Minquers by the Land registry at Coutances. Nonetheless, attempts by that citizen to build on the island were halted by the French Ministry of Foreign Affairs. The disputes intensified as the fishing industry recovered after the war as French fishermen took the opportunity of taking over former Jersey fishing grounds while Jersey was still occupied. In the immediate post-war years, diplomatic efforts were made by the United Kingdom government on behalf of the authorities in Jersey "to obtain from the French Government an unequivocal acknowledgement of His Majesty's sovereignty over Les Écréhous and Minquiers Islands."[24] When these efforts failed, the United Kingdom government, with the support of the States of Jersey, sought a ruling from the International Court of Justice.[25] The joint submission made by France and the United Kingdom requested the Court "to determine whether the sovereignty over the islets and rocks (so far as they are capable of appropriation) of the Minquiers and Écréhous groups respectively belongs to the United Kingdom or the French Republic."[26]

The International Court of Justice

A temporary agreement was reached in 1951 pending the ruling on sovereignty by the International Court of Justice (ICJ). Its main objective was to prepare the ground for the ICJ ruling by defining the exact areas which would be granted to the nation awarded sovereignty over the reefs. These zones were a third of a mile circle round the beacon on La Maître Île, the largest isle of Les Écréhous, and a circle of one half mile around La Maîtresse Île, Les Pipettes rocks and La Maison rocks in Les Minquers. The area included above consists mostly of dry land and does not even cover the whole reef, in either case.

The decision in 1953 to allow the International Court of Justice to determine sovereignty over the reefs was an illustration of the peace and stability which existed in the relationship between the United Kingdom and France, albeit not always between Jersey and *Basse Normandie*. Moreover, the decision illustrated that the French state had long ago renounced any claims to the Channel Islands and further was willing to let a third party adjudicate the boundary.[27]

The case illustrated the complex nature of Jersey's autonomy as its preparation involved the Home Office, the Foreign and Commonwealth Office, the Ministry of Agriculture, Fisheries and Food and the Ministry of Defence in the United Kingdom and the Finance Committee and Economics Committee, the Harbours and Airport Committee and the Law Officers Department in Jersey. As in all negotiations, Jersey was represented by the United Kingdom. The evidence itself was largely prepared by the authorities in Jersey, however, the relevant United Kingdom departments were required to give their approval to each step in the development of the case. Jersey's Attorney General was part of the team which represented the United Kingdom alongside the Attorney General of England, Wales and Northern Ireland and Professor E. C. S. Wade. The final judgement was twenty-five pages long with an additional thirty-six pages for the individual opinions of two of the judges. The written pleading and oral arguments involved in the case was published in two volumes at a total of 1,260 pages. While this amount of documentation may not be abnormal, it gives some indication of the considerable burden the preparation of a case of this nature places on a small administration.

The United Kingdom's formal claim was based on "having established the existence of an ancient title supported throughout by effective possession evidenced by acts which manifest a continuous display over the groups."[28] The French submission, on the other hand, consisted of two separate claims. Firstly, the French government argued that the critical date on which sovereignty crystallised was 2 August 1839, the date on which the 1839 Convention was signed.[29] Consequently, all subsequent acts should be excluded from consideration. The French based their claim on the phrase in the Convention that the area of the oyster fisheries between the two defined lines, the *mer commune*, was common to subjects of both countries. The Court rejected this submission as in their opinion, the Convention dealt solely with fishing rights, not sovereignty over land areas.[30] In addition, the French contention that no events subsequent to 1839 were relevant was incompatible with the behaviour of the French government during that period.[31]

The second argument put forward by the French was based on the fact that the Duchy of Normandy had only been granted as a fief by the King of France and under the ruling of the Court of France of 1202, the King of England was to forfeit the Duchy.[32] Following this argument, France would have been granted sovereignty over, not only the reefs, but by implication the whole of the Channel Islands, an outcome the French government had not sought. The French Government also argued the Minquiers were a dependency of the Chausey Islands.[33]

Both nations also presented evidence of feudal ties and diplomatic and administrative links to the reefs. Jersey's submission included States of Jersey Committee Acts and the administration of inquests into deaths on the reefs while the French side pointed to the provision of buoys and lighting for the reef. The Court also noted that since at least 1820 and 1815 Jerseymen had built habitable dwellings on Les Écréhous and Les Minquiers respectively.

The final ruling of the ICJ, which was accepted by the French authorities, was that "The Court, unanimously finds that the sovereignty over the islets and rocks of the Ecrehos and Minquiers groups, in so far as these islets and rocks are capable of appropriation, belongs to the United Kingdom."[34] As a consequence, the States of Jersey extended its limits to a two mile zone around the Écréhoues and Minquiers.

Fishing Rights

Although the International Court of Justice ruling was not about fishing rights, its emphatic confirmation of British sovereignty over the strategically placed reefs was bound to affect the talks about fishing rights. The difficulties of the delimitation of fishing rights around Jersey and the complications created by the fact that Jersey is a dependency are illustrated by the history of fisheries legislation on the island.[35] In 1962, the States passed legislation to regulate fishing within a three mile limit of Jersey itself, a three mile limit around Les Minquiers and a two mile limit around Les Écréhous.[36] The Home Office, however, has recommended caution in this area and requested that the insular authorities would not use the powers of the Act in relation to Les Minquiers and Les Écréhous. It should be noted that the United Kingdom has never explicitly stated that Jersey's autonomy extends to the waters surrounding the island, but only the reefs themselves. The Law with respect to Jersey's own three mile limit did not come into force until 1974 while the Law relating to the reefs came into effect in 1989.[37]

French fishermen have invaded Les Écréhous on two occasions. The more serious one was undertaken in 1994 and involved fishermen as well as right-wing French nationalists who threatened both to damage Jersey owned properties and to breach the rabies quarantine law. In response, the Bailiff summoned Jersey's Emergency Council to muster what limited resources Jersey had to police what could become a violent event. The insular authorities contacted the Home Office to request assistance and brief the United Kingdom authorities. In response, a fisheries protection vessel was sent to the Channel Islands. This was, however, not dispatched to the reef, perhaps for fear of exacerbating the situation. Jersey's Attorney General was also summoned to London to attend a meeting with officials from the Home Office, the Foreign and Commonwealth Office and the French Embassy. The island, meanwhile, deployed a large proportion of its police force to the reef.[38] French vessels landed one hundred and fifty protesters, the bulk of whom were fishermen, though some far-right activists were also present. The demonstration was peaceful, although several unsuccessful attempts were made to remove the Union Jacks present on the reefs. Similar demonstrations have affected Les Minquiers and are periodically exploited by minority political groups to gain attention in the British and French media.[39]

While this invasion, like all other invasions of the reefs, contained an element of farce, there were serious implications both for Jersey and its relations with France. The first and simplest is that of the cost and strain on the island's resources of policing such events, which not only require a considerable number of the island's police, but special expenditure including the hiring of a spotter aircraft. Such operations, if repeated frequently, could rapidly create ill will towards the French authorities who, it can be argued, often choose not to control the more militant elements in their fishing communities. The dispute emphasises Jersey's difficulties as a microstate in policing large demonstrations and challenging the French warships periodically sent to travel alongside French fishing boats in disputed waters. The island's metropolitan power has, however, ensured that Jersey's sovereignty over its dependencies is recognised and will support the island *in extremis* by dispatching fisheries' protection vessels. Nevertheless, the main problem remains that, although the boundary of Jersey's sovereignty and its continental shelf are defined, the fishing boundaries are not and this is the source of much of the current conflict.

A series of temporary agreements and years of talks both at regional level and between the British and French foreign offices have yet to produce an agreement. The main hope for a resolution of the dispute lies in the development of talks at a sub sovereign state level. The insular authorities are facilitating direct talks between local fishermen and their French counterparts in an attempt to solve the dispute. This has been attempted via a joint fishermen's management committee for the Bay of Granville. The group consists of four representatives each from the Norman, Breton and Jersey fleets. However, as long as a mutually acceptable and enforceable solution to the problem of managing and delineating fishing rights around Jersey remains unresolved, the issue will continue to embitter and prejudice the relationship between the two communities.

It is not Jersey's policy to use local legislation to exclude French fishermen from the *mer commune*, in particular as Jersey would have limited means of enforcing such a policy. In addition, such overt claims of sovereignty, if exercised, have the potential to provoke sizeable protest from neighbouring French ports. The French fishermen resist any change and many still consider the 1839 Convention to be the only binding decision in this area. However, the Convention was drafted with small sail-driven fishing boats in mind. The use of modern large fishing boats travelling long distances to fish mean that provisions of the Convention places the existing fish stocks under threat.

The fishing dispute must be seen against the background of Europe-wide overfishing, in part caused by technological developments in fishing, the French government policy of supporting the industry with low interest loans, the French fishermen's claims over Channel Island waters and the activities of extreme right wing groups seeking to benefit from the crisis. On the Jersey side, local fishermen also suffer from the decline in stocks while the insular authorities have always made a point of asserting and, as far as possible, defending their sovereignty over the reefs.

The French claims over the reefs were irritants to both Jersey and the United Kingdom's relationship with France. Their successful resolution by the International Court of Justice showed the extent to which the relationship is stable and peaceful. Moreover, the French state has been careful not to support protests by French citizens on the reef. Problems still remain on the delimitation of broader fishing rights, but Jersey is secure in that, unlike Gibraltar, its nearest neighbour has no desire to challenge sovereignty over the territory.

Nuclear Issues

On the adjacent Cotentin peninsula, two French nuclear installations are situated: Flamanville, a conventional nuclear power station, and Cap de la Hague, a nuclear reprocessing plant, similar to the Sellafield plant in Cumbria. The insular authorities and the powerful local Green lobby have long held fears about the safety of these installations and the damage which even a minor leak could cause the local tourist industry if the media in the United Kingdom chose to publicise it. The force of the insular authorities' protest is somewhat weakened by the fact that the power station provides much of the island's electricity. Nevertheless, the worries about nuclear safety are sincerely held by a large number of islanders, many of whom can see Flamanville on a clear day. The insular authorities have objected to plans for further nuclear installations to be built on the Cotentin Peninsula.[40] Shipments of nuclear waste to and from Cap de La Hague for reprocessing also pass through Channel Island waters. The Channel Islands, although objecting to this practice, cannot invoke sovereignty over these waters to prevent transit through their waters. This could only be done by the United Kingdom, but it chooses not to do so.

The States of Jersey has taken a number of initiatives to highlight its concerns. It employs an independent nuclear adviser who co-operates with the Emergency Planning Officer and the States Environmental Adviser to assess the risk of nuclear accidents affecting the island. Jersey has also set up an early warning system to warn the island of problems with the French reactors and has instructions on what to do in such an emergency in all telephone books. Jersey has also had extended to it a number of international conventions relating to nuclear installation safety, not because it intends to build any reactors, but to place some moral pressure on the French authorities. The Channel Island authorities have further requested meetings with the United Kingdom at ministerial level to express their concerns about the French nuclear programme. The aim of these meetings was to express to the United Kingdom the strength of feelings on the island so that these could be passed on to the French authorities. The United Kingdom authorities have done so and have also arranged briefings on issues of concern.[41] As the United Kingdom government's stance is more or less identical to that of France as regards this area, it is vulnerable to French allegations of hypocrisy unless it takes the position that the United Kingdom supports French policies, but will pass on Jersey's protest. It could be argued that this strategy further weakens Jersey's already small influence over French policy. Therefore, the States have also sought to make direct protests. In June 1998 the States voted by a margin of thirty-five to thirteen to make a formal complaint via official channels about the discharging of nuclear waste from the Cap de La Hague reprocessing plant into the marine environment.

The French authorities have sought to calm local fears about the safety of the installations by arranging a series of tours and local receptions for islanders. A visit in October 1997 led by the Bailiff included twenty States members and six senior civil servants. The visit was effective in that most of the visitors from the island were impressed by how the plant was operated.[42] The States of Jersey is the only foreign member of the Flamanville and Cap de la Hague *Commission d'Information* which meets two to four times a year. Under the auspices of the group, any observer may question the officials present and the presence of a prominent Normandy Green politician on the Commission would appear to guarantee that the meetings are not just public relations stunts for the French nuclear industry. The French authorities would seem by these actions to have assuaged some of the doubts in Jersey. It also suggests that Jersey's fears are being acknowledged by the French authorities despite the fact that Jersey can, in reality, do little to hinder the French nuclear programme.

Perhaps it is in the area of nuclear politics that Jersey would benefit most from independence. Its metropolitan power has the same policies as France and, on this issue, disagrees with the position taken by Jersey. The United Kingdom acts as a conduit for Jersey's complaints and these protests may have been one influence on the French decision not to build any more nuclear installations on the Cotentin peninsula. It is, however, debatable how much more Jersey could achieve if it had sovereignty. It would still be open to the French authorities to ignore the island's protests. Moreover, such protests would not be routed via a country with which France has a considerable interest in maintaining a good relationship. The French authorities have granted the island the right to be given all the information they give neighbouring French local authorities. In this, the French have gone as far as they are prepared to. Jersey's ideal of having all the installations closed is unachievable, but it has probably achieved all it can reasonably hope to short of fulfilling that aim.

Control of Airspace

In 1947 Jersey was given technical control over the Channel Islands Air Traffic Control Zone, an area between 49 and 50 degrees north and 2 and 3 degrees west and airspace up to 19,500 feet. As Jersey is not a sovereign state, the airspace is divided between the United Kingdom having 11 percent and France 89 percent. All aircraft requiring use of this airspace pay a fee to Eurocontrol, which divides its revenue between the states involved. These states then make payments to Jersey airport. Jersey renewed the agreement for ten years in 1990, however, in 1998 the Home Office was notified of the French authorities' desire to abrogate the agreement.

The arrangement brings in between £3.5 and £4 million in revenue for the airport and provides employment for about forty people. The end of the agreement would mean giving France direct control over all flights to the island. The loss of control over the airspace would be not only be symbolically important, but would result in airlines requiring access to Jersey airport having to compete for priority with those requiring access to French airports. This could limit the number of flights to the island at the height of the tourist season. The issue has parallels with the disputes about fishing rights in that the French stance is perceived by the insular authorities as intransigent. The French authorities, however, defend their desire to control Channel Island airspace as it is part of a reorganisation of the French air traffic control system which involves giving responsibility to regional centres for airspace up to 11,500 feet and it would seem logical to include the Channel Islands in such an arrangement as they are largely in the French zone.[43] Additionally, while the money the French authorities pay Jersey airport for air traffic control services is a significant amount in terms of the airport's budget, Guernsey airport operates successfully without revenue from air traffic control operations.

The source of some of the tension in the dispute was the fact that the insular authorities failed to anticipate the change in French policy.[44] The insular authorities value the air traffic control operation, but seem to have failed to anticipate that the French would wish Jersey to fall into line with practice in other French area control centres. The French policy allowed Jersey to operate as, in effect, a French traffic control centre, but the autonomy did not extend to operating in a way different to the other French centres. The failure in the management of the relationship was that the insular authorities also failed to develop any contingency plans to cope with a French refusal to renew the deal.

The French Law on Privacy and the Media

The proximity of Jersey to France has created a potential problem for the media in the island. Laws on privacy in France are more developed than in the island or the United Kingdom and the Barclay brothers who own the island of Brecqhou have sought, with some success, to use this fact in the French courts to challenge articles in "The Observer" newspaper and reports on BBC Radio Guernsey about their business activities and the construction of their large estate on the island of Brecqhou.[45]

The Barclay brother's lawyers argued that, as the newspaper was available in France and the news broadcast from the Channel Islands can be picked up in France, they were entitled to challenge these articles using French privacy laws. The partial success of this action threatens to undermine Jersey's judicial autonomy as individuals could seek redress under French law in cases where insular legislation is less stringent. This is also an example of a more general problem as broadcasts cannot be restricted to a single nation. The problem then arises of who should have jurisdiction over this output. Sovereignty might help the island seek a solution to the problem of whether it is possible to have jurisdiction over another nation's media output purely because it can be accessed in that territory. As Jersey as a dependency cannot initiate such discussions, the United Kingdom must. As the United Kingdom is less vulnerable to this problem it has less of an incentive to seek a solution. However, it would be difficult to justify the risks of seeking independence to solve, what is at present, a unique case.

Political Links

The French consulate was shut on October 15, 1993. The consulate in Jersey covered the whole of the Channel Islands with a vice-consul stationed in Guernsey. The French foreign minister justified the action by citing the need to re-deploy staff to new posts in the former communist block.[46] After a reassessment of the future of all its consulates it was decided that retention of a full-time consul in Jersey could no longer be justified. Further reasons for the action were the small and declining number of islanders registering to vote in French elections and the feeling that Jersey did not value its links with France.[47] To replace the consulate, Robin Pallot, a French-speaking Jerseyman and local businessman, was appointed French consul with one full time employee. Before it was closed the French consulate employed a consul, a vice-consul and three staff.[48]

The closure of the French consulate after 150 years confirmed the perception that Jersey's relationship with France was withering on the vine. The last French consul, Marie-Claire San Quirce, accused "Jersey people of being 'as rich as they are indifferent' about their links with France."[49] A delegation led by the Bailiff and the President of Policy and Resources went to France but failed to get the decision reversed. Representations through official channels via the Foreign and Commonwealth Office met with a similar fate. Unfortunately, the insular authorities failed to appreciate how angry their perceived lack of interest had made commentators in France. The editor of the bilingual magazine "La Normandie" commented that "The closure will be compensated by sending new diplomats to eastern countries. At the end of the day, it is better to be present in countries with strong potential for development than in those of children too spoilt even to be interested in their neighbours."[50] In Jersey's defence, Senator Horsfall argued that "it was probably more useful to Jersey to have a French consul than to the French, who had to pay for it despite a fall in recent years in the number of French people living and working in the Island."[51] It was therefore perhaps optimistic to expect the French government to support a consulate which was of more of benefit to Jersey than France. One could argue that if such a link is considered useful to Jersey, then Jersey should fund it.

The powerful blow to the relationship caused by the closure of the French consulate in Jersey revitalised attempts to maintain the relationship. The efforts were led by the neighbouring French region of *Basse Normandie* and some of the responses by the insular authorities have appeared half-hearted. The Lower Normandy Regional and Economic Council commissioned a report into "the possibilities of furthering relations between Lower Normandy and the Channel Islands."[52] One of the results of the report was the creation of the *Maison de la Normandie et de la Manche à Jersey*. It employs French local government officials and costs one million francs a year to run. It consists of an information centre in one of the premium shopping sites in St Helier which promotes tourism, economic, social and cultural links to La Manche. However, all official contacts are handled by the honorary consul who has an office in the same building.

The *Basse Normandie* initiative also resulted in a bilingual senior Jersey civil servant being seconded to Caen for the first six months of 1997. The secondment was the result of an offer of a loan of office space by the President of the *Conseil Régional de Basse Normandie*. The civil servant was "to examine the best long term option for furthering links with France."[53] The civil servant drafted a report for the Policy and Resources Committee in which he recommended the establishment of a permanent office in Caen. The role of the office would be to support tourism, educational exchanges and to act as a business advice centre. He was also to investigate the provision of back office services for the finance sector in France. The cost of such an office was estimated as £40,000-50,000 a year. The Policy and Resources Committee, however, "were not convinced"[54] that the expenditure was justified. This position highlights the lack of importance of the relationship to the insular authorities and the limits this imposes on the amount of support they will give such initiatives. The office was, however, opened with funding of £15,000 from the Finance and Economics Committee and an equal amount from the Jersey Electricity Company.

Jersey is a member of the *Assemblée Parliamentaire de la Francophonie*, an inter-government French-speaking institution. It works to promote the French language and the cultural pluralism of French nations.[55] It operates as a democratic forum for French speaking nations, a forum for exchange of information and to promote law and develop democracy. Thus the role of the *Assemblée Parliamentaire de la Francophonie* can be seen as equivalent to that of the Commonwealth Parliamentary Association and the benefits of membership must be viewed as similar, although membership is much less expensive.[56] The membership of the *Assemblée Parliamentaire de la Francophonie* was in 1992 thirty seven Parliaments from a mixture of states and communities. Some membership is overlapping in that both Canada and Quebec, Nova Scotia, New Brunswick and Ontario are represented. Jersey is the only part of the British Islands represented and has been a member since the organisation was founded. A number of members are microstates or small provinces of larger nations including Monaco, Vanutu and Jura. The main benefit which could be claimed to derive from membership of this organisation is the largely informal exchange of information. It may also give the island influence with the French government which has been keen to promote the size and activities of francophone organisations. Membership also promotes Jersey's position as a bilingual community, a claim which may increasingly be disputable. The main problem Jersey would appear to have with its membership is finding States members and civil servants with adequate language skills to represent it. Nevertheless, it should be noted that despite all these advantages, Guernsey has decided that the benefits of membership do not outweigh the costs.

The *Commission Amicale* was set up in September 1994 in response to the closure of the consulate. It consists of seven Jersey and seven French members and its joint *ex-officio* Chairmen are the Bailiff and the President of the *Conseil Régional de Basse Normandie*. The delegations meet every six to nine months. Senator Jeune, then President of the Policy and Resources Committee, justified its creation on the grounds that "It is extremely important for us to have friends other than the UK in Europe."[57] Whilst this may be true with respect to relations with the European Union, French goodwill may be of limited value to Jersey in a crisis in its relations with the European Union. First as Jersey's policy requirements will be even less of a priority to France than to the United Kingdom, and secondly, if Jersey were to take a too pro-French position on some issues it would not only offend the United Kingdom, but France would seem to usurp the United Kingdom's role as Jersey's sovereign power.

Another response to the consulates closure was the establishment of a local branch of the *Alliance Française* in 1996. The *Alliance Française* is the largest teaching organisation in the world and was introduced to the island as part of the drive to revitalise links between Jersey and France. In Jersey it will concentrate on language teaching in the business community. This is likely to promote some business but will not overcome the fundamental problem that the finance industry does little business in French or with France. Other links with France include five island Parishes which are twinned with French communities as well as some research links being maintained between the *Société Jersiaise* and the *Société Linnéenne de Normandie*. However, neither of these links, like the relationship more generally, is remotely on the scale of that which Jersey has with the United Kingdom.

Conclusion

Jersey's relationship with France is strongly regional in its basis. This point was perhaps exemplified by the fact that when the French government closed the full time consulate it was the *Conseil Régional de Basse Normandie* which, at least symbolically, stepped into the void. Indeed the closure of the consulate could be argued to have produced a minor renaissance in the relationship. There are, however, limits to this renaissance as the relationship is of limited importance to Jersey in both economic and political terms. Nonetheless, France retains a significant influence, albeit indirectly, as a member of the European Union. In this arena, France's support for tax harmonisation proposals could seriously affect the island's finance industry.

Therefore, Jersey's direct relationship with France may now be of less importance than its indirect one via the European Union.

An option for Jersey to manage its dependency on the United Kingdom would be to attempt to use France as a form of counterbalance to the United Kingdom's power in the relationship in the way that Malta attempted to use closer links with Libya to express its displeasure with actions by the United States or European countries. The relationship has, however, been allowed to become far too weak for this to be a realistic option and, in addition, the United Kingdom would not perceive such a move to be a threat. The island's economy is dependent on the United Kingdom and the majority of the population was either born in or have spent considerable time in the United Kingdom. Thus the adoption of French culture would be unthinkable to many people and unworkable in economic terms. Further, it is highly unlikely that France would risk a serious conflict with the United Kingdom over any of the issues Jersey is concerned about. Jersey has to accept that the United Kingdom has much wider interests in its relationship with France than Jersey.

The success of the existing formal arrangements with France, channelled as they are via the Home Office and the Foreign and Commonwealth Office, is patchy, although more successful sub-sovereign links are tolerated in the fields of fishing and nuclear issues. It is possible to question how forceful the United Kingdom has been in representing the island's hostility to French nuclear installations. However, rapid support was offered at the time of the Les Écréhous invasion and a meeting was arranged with the French Embassy. In addition, the expert advice available from the United Kingdom together with its greater diplomatic weight remains an advantage.

The most important issues in the relationship remain the nuclear and fishing disputes, where some progress has been made due to the United Kingdom's willingness to allow informal contacts at a regional level. Without these, little progress would have been made in resolving the issue of fishing rights, and the closure of the consulate would not have been followed by a renaissance in the relationship at a regional level. Nonetheless, it must be noted that these issues, and all other aspects of Jersey's relationship with France, pale in significance compared to Jersey's relationship with the United Kingdom. Finance, tourism and agriculture are all dependent on access to United Kingdom markets. English and French may be the official languages in Jersey, but French is rarely used for States business and is spoken fluently by a decreasing minority of the population. Shared historical trading and cultural links are also in decline. Jersey will seek to preserve at least the historical memory of the French link, if only to help differentiate the island from the United Kingdom. However, the relationship will not strengthen significantly because Jersey is economically integrated into the City of London and politically dependent on the United Kingdom.

References

[1] Drower, G., Britain's Dependent Territories A fistful of islands, Dartmouth, Aldershot, 1992, 32.

[2] op. cit., EEC Report 1967, 78.

[3] Petters, L., "A piece of Jersey in France", Jersey Evening Post, 20/7/98, 8.

[4] Etat Civil Committee, Report on the Census for 1996, States of Jersey, Jersey, 32.

[5] Jersey Advocates were required to sit a Certificate of Norman and French Law Studies between 1992-95.

[6] Interview with David Moon, 10/9/97, formerly Senior Partner, Mourant Du Feu & Jeune.

[7] op. cit., Kelleher, 121.

[8] It is still permissible to make a speech in French in the States, although such an event is exceptionally rare.

[9] Cartel, A., Basse Normandie Report: Lower Normandy and the Channel Islands, Conseil Economique et Social Régional, Caen, December 1994, 16, hereafter, Basse Normandie Report.

[10] Etat Civil Committee, Report on 1991, Etat Civil Committee, Jersey, 1991.

[11] Crosby, A., "Thoroughly modern Jèrriais", Jersey Evening Post, 8/10/98, 7.

[12] op. cit., The Offshore Interface, 102.

[13] op. cit., Basse Normandie Report, 117.

[14] Crosby, A., "Our man in Caen", Jersey Evening Post, 17/7/97, 8, hereafter, Caen.

[15] op. cit., Basse Normandie Report, 113.

[16] Exact figures for trade are not available as neither the United Kingdom, nor the French government, include trade between Jersey and France in the overall United Kingdom figures. However, Cartel and Droulin give a best guess. See Cartel, A., Basse Normandie Recommendation: Lower Normandy and the Channel Islands, Conseil Economique et Social Régional, Caen, December 1994, 6, hereafter, Basse Normandie Recommendation.

[17] This scheme was in 1994 the biggest harbour development project in Europe with a final cost of £51 million.

[18] op. cit., Basse Normandie Report, 89.

[19] op. cit., Basse Normandie Recommendation, 12.

[20] op. cit., Basse Normandie Report, 84.

[21] Plender, R., "The Channel Islands position in International Law", paper presented to the IPC conference in Jersey entitled "The Channel Islands and the U.K. Their Relationship: The Law: The Future?", 13/11/98, 20.

[22] Convention between Great Britain and France for Defining and Regulating the Limits of the Exclusive Rights of the Oyster and Other Fisheries on the Coasts of Great Britain and of France, Paris, B.S.P., No 27/983, 1839, hereafter, Fisheries Convention.

[23] op. cit., Rodwell, 328-331.

[24] Resolution of the States of Jersey 14th September 1948, cited in ibid., 335.

[25] ibid.

[26] The Special Agreement concluded between the Governments of the United Kingdom of Great Britain and Northern Ireland and the Government of the French Republic signed on 29th December 1950, ratified Paris 24th September 1951, cited in ibid., 333.

[27] International Court of Justice Ruling of 17 XI 53, 10, hereafter, ICJ Ruling 17.

[28] ibid., 7.

[29] op. cit., Fisheries Convention.

[30] op. cit., ICJ Ruling 17, 15.

[31] ibid., 16.

[32] ibid., 13.

[33] ibid., 27.

[34] ibid., 29.

[35] The French Republic and the United Kingdom both extended their territorial waters from three to twelve miles in 1971 and 1987 respectively, but these extensions did not cover the Channel Island area - see op. cit., Rodwell, 346.

[36] The Sea Fisheries (Jersey) Law 1962.

[37] This Law was superseded by The Sea Fisheries (Jersey) Law 1994.

[38] op.cit., Rodwell, 348, gives figures of at least thirty paid police, plus five honoraries, out of a paid police force of about two hundred.

[39] Askill, J., "Hey hey we're the Minkes!", The Sun, 10 & 11, 2/9/98; Mactintyne, B., "Channel Islet seized by King of Patagonia", The Times, 1/9/98, 1; Macintyne, B. & Jeune, P., "British bobby retakes Channel Isle", The Times, 2/9/98, 1&2; Tanner, M., "Husband and wife interrupt day trip to reconquer Channel isle for Britain", The Independent, 2/9/98, 6 & Harion, N., "Silly season brings touch of old Minquier business", Jersey Evening Post, 2/9/98, 5.

[40] Foley, S., "French spell it out: No nuclear plant", Jersey Evening Post, 18/4/96, 1.

[41] op. cit., Morris interview.

[42] Crosby, A., "Fact finding on the nuclear front", Jersey Evening Post, 6/11/97, 8.

[43] "McRandle, H., "Meeting of minds over air traffic control issue", Jersey Evening Post, 7/7/98, 5.

[44] ibid.

[45] Sweeney, J., "Privacy rules the French air waves", The Observer, 26/1/97, 1.

[46] op. cit., Basse Normandie Report, 103.

[47] Scriven, S., "The honorary consul", Jersey Evening Post, 1/10/94,7.

[48] op. cit., Basse Normandie Report, 1994, 103.

[49] Scriven, S., "Sir Peter criticises former consul", Jersey Evening Post, 1, 15/12/93.

[50] ibid.

[51] Scriven, S., "French government asked to reconsider closing consulate", Jersey Evening Post, 7/6/93, 5.

[52] op. cit., Basse Normandie Recommendation, 3.

[53] op. cit., Caen, 8.

[54] Herbert, C., "JEC help funds office in Caen", Jersey Evening Post, 4/4/98, 5.

[55] Assemblée Internationale des Parliamentaires de Langue Française, pamphlet issued by Secretariat General in Paris 1996.

[56] The budgets in 1999 was £8,500 p.a. for the Assemblée Parlementaire de la Francophonie and £40,000 p.a. for the Commonwealth Parliamentary Association.

[57] Falle, P., "States seek closer ties with French", Jersey Evening Post, 19/9/94.

Chapter 8 - Guernsey and the Isle of Man: Two Cases for Comparison

Introduction

This book aims to offer a case study of a single microstate. If a comparative study were to be made, the most relevant candidates of comparison would seem to be the other Crown Dependencies. Since they are so often treated as one entity it is helpful to bring out their similarities and differences. To recapitulate, the Crown Dependencies consist of the Bailiwicks of Jersey and Guernsey and the Isle of Man. The Bailiwick of Guernsey uniquely consists of three political units: Guernsey itself, Sark and Alderney. I do not intend to consider the islands of Alderney and Sark separately as their small sizes makes such a comparison of limited value.

Physical size is the fundamental difference between the Channel Islands and the Isle of Man. The Isle of Man has an area of 221 square miles and a resident population in 1996 of 71,714 whereas equivalent numbers for Guernsey, excluding Sark and Alderney, are 25 square miles and 58,681 and Jersey 45 square miles and 85,150. This means that problems of resource limitation and scale are more relevant to the Channel Islands than to the Isle of Man which has a population density of about half that of the United Kingdom.

All the islands can be seen as feudal survivals and in the medieval period control over the islands changed. Mann passed from Norse to Scottish to English control and the Channel Islands from Norman to English suzerainty. The Isle of Man experience was different in that it was in the direct control of a feudal overlord as a personal fief of the Stanley family between 1333 and 1765, whereas the Channel Islands for a period were granted to a succession of lords of the Isles as a fee for life and were more directly a peculiarity of the Crown. Uniquely the Isle of Man was also the subject of the Revestment, where the legal rights to the island were transferred directly to the Crown by Parliamentary intervention in 1765. This was to end endemic smuggling in the island and was the most direct exercise of parliamentary sovereignty over the Crown Dependencies in their history.

If language is used as a measure, the Manx community identity is stronger than either Jersey's or Guernsey's. The Manx language, despite declining to near extinction, has undergone a revival since 1992 and Manx Gaelic has been an option under the National Curriculum. Further evidence of a revival in Manx culture has been the establishment of a centre for Manx studies in the University of Liverpool. Moreover, the Isle of Man uniquely has a national anthem.

All the Crown Dependencies are in a situation where about half the population are not locally born. In 1991 Manx-born people were for the first time a minority on the island comprising 49.6% of the population compared to the Jersey figure of 52% for people born on the island.[1] The latest available figure for Guernsey born people as a proportion of the Guernsey population is 65%.[2] Each island has tried to control population growth by different methods.

The difference between the Channel Islands and the Isle of Man is that, although all seek to limit population growth, the Isle of Man does not face a population density problem. Indeed, if the Isle of Man's population density equalled Jersey's, the Manx population would be over 400,000. The Isle of Man has from 1975 chosen to limit population growth mainly by the use of work permits. This was the result of the island's immediate post war experience of a decline in population and fears of increasing unemployment with all of its resulting problems. Therefore, the need to avoid a declining population is an aim of Manx policy makers. As a result of the reversal of the decline in population, and more lately population growth, in the Isle of Man some housing regulations aimed at population control were introduced during the 1994-95 session of the Tynwald. The Manx work permit legislation requires employers to employ those defined as Isle of Man workers unless a special permit is issued by the Department of Industry. To qualify as an Manx worker you must either have been born on the island; been resident for ten or five years with certain qualifications; have married a person who qualifies or have parents who qualify.

Economic Comparisons

A comparison of the Crown Dependencies' economies is difficult because the three islands use different scales of measurement. Moreover, the compilation of economic statistics for small communities is notoriously difficult. This is exacerbated by the islands not producing statistics for identical time periods.[3] However, bearing these provisos in mind some general conclusions can be drawn. All three islands have enjoyed expanding economies. Jersey and Guernsey are currently richer than the Isle of Man, although the Isle of Man is catching up with both the Channel Islands and the United Kingdom. In 1995, the Bailiwick of Guernsey's estimated GDP per capita was £14,859 or 117% of the United Kingdom figure[4] while Jersey's amounted to £15,095 or 125% of the United Kingdom figure[5]. Equivalent figures for the Isle of Man in 1995-96 was estimated at £9,540 or 79% of the United Kingdom. As a comparison, the Manx figure in 1985-86 was 57%.[6]

The economies of the Crown Dependencies are similar, being based on offshore finance and prior to that a mixture of low cost tourism, agriculture and light industry. The similar development patterns in the Crown Dependencies are the result of the limited development options available to small island communities. Some light industry remains, the most significant examples being avionics in the Isle of Man and pharmaceuticals in Guernsey. Each island is committed, in principle, to maintaining a diversified economy and this has been achieved with varying degrees of success. The statistics available, with the provisos discussed above regarding the difficulties of using them, confirm the preceding general points. Guernsey's statistics for the contribution for what they define as primary export sectors to total net export receipts in 1995 divides up the economy as follows: finance 57%, the rentier sector[7] 15%, tourism 15%, manufacturing industry 9% and horticulture 4%.[8] The Manx statistics, at first glance, are quite different, but this is the result of the inclusion of the public sector in the figures. The 1993-94 Manx figures for national income reveal finance as providing 35%, manufacturing 11%, tourism 6%, construction 7%, retail 6%, public administration 6%, agriculture and fisheries less than 2%, professional services 15% and other 20%.[9] It must also be noted that the Isle of Man includes services provided by lawyers and accountants within the category of professional services, whilst the majority of this item is included in financial services for Jersey's and Guernsey's statistics. Jersey's figures for 1994, for comparative purposes, are financial services 54%, tourism 25%, agriculture 5%. The rest of the contribution to Jersey's GDP is investment holding. The relatively large light industry element in the Manx figures arises because the Isle of Man has, due to its size, lower land costs than the other islands and, therefore, increases in land cost have not driven this sector from the island as has happened in Jersey.

A hierarchy between the islands exists in the perception of the quality of their respective offshore finance centres. This is emphasised by the nature of the financial business they have been able to attract with Jersey, on the whole, being the most profitable and Mann the least. Jersey concentrates on international private banking and fund management. It admits only the top five hundred banks in terms of size whilst Guernsey hosts more insurance companies and grants bank licences to less highly capitalised banks. The Isle of Man has insurance, private bank operations, a shipping register and a free port at the airport. Jersey's leading position in the development of the finance industry is illustrated by the fact that it can exclude from consideration any business beyond the five hundred largest banks. Indeed, Jersey has gone through periods when it has been accepting no new business which has then had to go to Guernsey or the Isle of Man. This is despite all three islands having similar advantages in the form of political stability, fiscal independence, low taxation, good communications and being located in the same time zone as London. However a hierarchy seems to exist at present, with Jersey as the most favoured and the Isle of Man as the least. The hierarchy is reflected by the fact that the Isle of Man maintains a lower rate of income tax than Jersey or Guernsey and therefore to a degree competes on price rather than quality. This can be put down to Jersey's lead in successful development of an offshore finance centre, which has created both stronger support services for the finance industry and a degree of inertia, since there are cost implications of moving site, even in such a mobile industry as banking.

Direct taxation rates in the Channel Islands were by historical accident already attractive to investors and therefore, initially at least, did not need to be changed. In contrast, the creation of an offshore finance centre in the Isle of Man was a deliberate act brought about by changes in taxation in 1961 and again in 1979-81. This formed part of a government initiative to arrest population decline in the Isle of Man by attracting new business to the island. The Isle of Man embarked on a dash for growth which resulted in the finance industry being the biggest industry on the island by 1972. As part of this policy, the Tynwald passed the ill-considered Companies Act of 1974 as a result of which "a rash of companies with no banking parentage, inadequate capital and indifferent management were licensed to carry on banking business in the Isle of Man."[10] Consequently, the development of the Isle of Man finance industry was hindered by a bank failure in 1982. The Manx response was to set up the Financial Supervisory Commission in 1983 and the Insurance Authority in 1986. These became role models for developments in the other Crown Dependencies.

Jersey is the most extreme example of what might be regarded as the Crown Dependency economic model, with finance being the dominant industry, agriculture and tourism being in rapid decline and light industry destroyed. As Jersey was the most successful, at first, in developing a prospering finance industry, the other islands have had the advantage of studying Jersey's experience before embarking on developing their own offshore centres. The reason for Jersey's success in attracting the most desirable financial investors could also be analysed by the other Crown Dependencies. Key factors were an image of financial probity and good communications. The other two islands sought to improve both these elements in an attempt to remove Jersey's competitive advantage in these areas. In the field of regulation this was achieved by the mid 1990s. Jersey, as the leading offshore centre, also suffered from teething troubles first and the most external criticism due to its higher international visibility.

Relationship with the UK

The three islands share many aspects of their relationship with the United Kingdom, notably the Home Office being responsible for administration and the United Kingdom maintaining its powers of good government and parliamentary sovereignty over the islands. The metropolitan power, however, allows each of the Crown Dependencies a high level of autonomy and each island believes the United Kingdom will not intervene in its domestic and fiscal affairs. In political terms Guernsey has taken a conservative stand on both internal developments and its relationship with the United Kingdom in contrast to the Isle of Man's dynamic and proactive approach. Thus the Isle of Man has actively considered the option of independence. This aspiration has resulted in concrete actions such as the removal of all United Kingdom statutes from its statute book to achieve "more complete self government".[11] Guernsey, on the other hand, has, as it argued in its evidence to the Kilbrandon Commission, accepted the uncodified *status quo*. Jersey, while maintaining a position close to that of the Guernsey, has taken a more dynamic approach reflecting a longer history as an offshore finance centre, an experience which, in this area, has forced the island to operate in a global economy.

All three Crown Dependencies are ruled by the Crown in Council, although the Isle of Man has a separate committee. The Isle of Man appealed to this Committee in 1967 over the Broadcasting Dispute. The other islands have not been in such open conflict with the United Kingdom government. The issue illustrated the interchangeability between the Privy Council and the government of the day as the issue was dealt with by a committee consisting entirely of United Kingdom ministers, one of the parties in the dispute. Calls for a separate Privy Council were rejected by the Home Office, *inter alia* on the ground that it raised broader constitutional issues regarding "the power of Her Majesty to appoint freely to Committees of Her Privy Council".[12]

The broadcasting dispute began in 1962 when Tynwald sought to legislate to create a commercial radio station to broadcast to the United Kingdom to promote tourism. The Royal Assent was withheld and the United Kingdom refused to revoke two Orders in Council relating to Broadcasting. The United Kingdom justified its actions on the grounds that the area concerned was covered by an international convention. The real reason was the government's hostility to commercial radio. In an attempt to circumvent the ban, the Manx authorities allowed the pirate radio ship Radio Caroline North to broadcast from its waters. The United Kingdom imposed an order in Council on the Isle of Man to prevent the ship receiving supplies from the island. This Order was also derived from an international convention. The Manx authorities' response was to threaten to lodge a complaint with the United Nations. This was a dangerous path to tread as it could have resulted in full independence. An attempt was also made to request arbitration from the Commonwealth Secretariat, but the Home Office refused to forward the request. As a result of the controversy the Isle of Man was allowed a low powered commercial transmitter, which can only be received on the island, and a joint working party on the constitutional relationship was set up under Lord Stonham. Two further Manx Bills were refused the Royal Assent in 1974 and 1993.

The Home Office's neglect of its relationship with the Crown Dependencies attracts more hostility in the Isle of Man than elsewhere. T. St. J. N. Bates, the Clerk of Tynwald, Secretary to the House of Keys and Counsel to the Speaker, highlights the "plethora of errors" contained in a Home Office briefing paper on the constitutional position of the Isle of Man.[13] These mistakes can be harmful to any Crown Dependency's reputation. As an example, the Home Office forgot to extend a United Nations' sanction order to the Isle of Man in 1996 thus allowing a Manx-based firm to export arms to Rwanda legally. The Home Office acknowledged its mistake, but it was the Isle of Man's and not the Home Office's image which was tarnished. The Isle of Man has, however, like the other islands benefited from the *laissez faire* attitude of the Home Office. The legislation permitting the Isle of Man TT race was given the Royal Assent in

1904 despite the Home Office view that such legislation was foolish.[14] The other Crown Dependencies are less worried about the levels of interest shown by the Home Office. While all the insular authorities express dissatisfaction from time to time with individual Home Office actions, with the exception of the Isle of Man, there is little evidence of a desire to change the *status quo*. The Isle of Man has also opted for a different approach to its relationship with individual members of the United Kingdom Parliament. While the Channel Islands have sought to distance themselves from Parliament, for fear of the implicit acknowledgement of Parliament's powers over the island this would constitute, the Isle of Man has developed close links via the British Manx Parliamentary Group. The group was formed in 1977 with representatives from the three main political parties.

Each island has a different means of contributing to services shared with the United Kingdom. The Isle of Man has opted for a more formal contribution agreement which sets a limit on the island's fiscal autonomy. This arose out of the Common Purse agreement of 1894 where custom duties were shared between the United Kingdom and the Isle of Man. The agreement has been subject to periodic revision, the last being in 1994 where a formula based on payment of £1.75 million a year with an inflation element was agreed. The agreement covers the provision of common services, including diplomatic representation, advice to Manx departments and defence, but excludes health and social security costs which are the subject of separate arrangements. The contribution agreement is opposed by the local tourism industry as it prevents the Manx authorities from lowering duties on alcohol and tobacco which might increase the number of visitors to the island. The finance industry also dislikes the agreement as it is felt to create the false impression that the United Kingdom has direct influence over direct taxation on the island. However, the agreement does benefit manufacturing industry as it means the Isle of Man is within the EU VAT area.

Guernsey's contributions to defence and foreign affairs costs as agreed in 1985 was to take over from the Ministry of Defence the cost of maintaining a large breakwater in Alderney and to make a voluntary contribution to maintaining of a Royal Naval Port Headquarters in Guernsey. The authorities in Guernsey also agreed to pay the United Kingdom authorities all fees derived from issuing passports in the island and finally to pay identifiable expenses incurred by the United Kingdom in representing the island. The different element is that unlike Jersey's military contribution and the Isle of Man's cash contribution, Guernsey, in part because of the presence of these installations, offered to take over the running costs. It was felt at the time that Guernsey had achieved a beneficial settlement, however, the cost of maintaining a large and ageing breakwater in the stormy seas off Alderney has been substantially more than expected. The settlement also removed a charge from the United Kingdom defence budget for a harbour of no military value. The cost of the breakwater had been borne by the United Kingdom since 1945 due to the damage Alderney suffered in the occupation which meant that the island could not afford to maintain its own harbour. The Guernsey contribution was projected at about £600,000 in 1985.[15]

Jersey's contribution takes the form of a Territorial Field Squadron of the Royal Engineers together with payments of foreign representation and passports. Of the three islands' contributions, Jersey's has been the least expensive per capita. The Manx contribution, linked as it is to taxation, tends to rise over the long term as the economy expands while the breakwater has proved more expensive to maintain than expected. Jersey, however, even though its solution would seem the least innovative, has seen the cost of its unit fall in real terms since it was created.[16]

Independence

The most radical change in any Crown Dependencies relationship with the United Kingdom would be a declaration of independence. The States of Jersey's consideration of independence was restricted to the period around the United Kingdom's accession to the European Economic Community while the States of Guernsey have never considered independence as a viable option. The Isle of Man is thus unique in having undertaken a detailed consideration of independence as an option.[17] The conclusion of the Manx report on future constitutional objectives issued in 1993 was summed up as:

> The pursuit of independence should be a response to some widely-felt serious political, social and economic disadvantage which would be overcome by the achievement of independence. A clear understanding of the benefits to be secured must exist because to launch into the unknown for some ill-defined or speculative gain would be grossly irresponsible.[18]

At present, the constitutional aims of the Isle of Man are defined as being:

> to promote and continue the evolution of the constitutional relationship between the Isle of Man and the United Kingdom towards 'more complete self-government' in accordance with the declared and accepted policy of the United Nations for the self-determination of the peoples of dependent territories. This objective thus includes not only the right and the principle of self-determination, but also, in application of them, assured autonomy in respect of the Island's internal affairs.[19]

A reflection of this desire for more complete self government, not articulated in the other islands, can be seen in the policy of substituting Manx legislation for Orders in Council. However, this drive for more autonomy is not absolute since the Isle of Man has retained its contribution agreement with the United Kingdom.

Further evidence of pressure for independence from within the Tynwald is illustrated by efforts to include the Isle of Man in the list of territories with which the United Nations Special Committee on Decolonisation is concerned.[20] Such a move is at present resisted by the Chief Minister of the Isle of Man and the Home Office.[21] Manx politicians have argued that the United Kingdom is obliged under international law to promote the realisation of the right to self determination in the Isle of Man.[22] The desire to move towards greater self determination in the Isle of Man differentiates it from Jersey and Guernsey where no long term support has existed for independence. Instead the issue has emerged only at times of crises between the Crown Dependencies and the United Kingdom, such as the latter's accession to the European Economic Community; only to dissipate as soon as the crisis has passed.

The Home Office would appear to be open to any of the Crown Dependencies opting for independence providing that it represented the settled will of the islanders. It is also aware of the stronger desire for independence in the Isle of Man which is partly due to the relative poverty of the island, until recently.[23] The desire for independence as expressed in all three islands focuses, as it has done since the 1960s, on perceived threats from the European Union to their constitutional privileges. This approach challenges that adopted in the Channel Islands of seeking a low profile and not challenging actions by the United Kingdom. However, the mature consideration of such an issue and its rejection would seem not to have destabilised the Manx relationship with the United Kingdom.

Uniquely, therefore, nationalism is a significant political force in the Isle of Man. The Manx nationalists' wish is to establish an independent constitutional monarchy under the Queen.[24] The core of their case is that independence is the only way to protect the island's cultural identity, create fiscal independence and prevent depopulation. In the 1960s the Manx nationalist revival began responding to the perceived absolute rule of the Lieutenant Governor and the moves to develop an offshore finance centre. The nationalist revival included the political party *Mec Vanin* and the underground direct action group *Foo Halloo*. The anti-offshore finance position of the Manx nationalists is distinctive. The desire for independence in the other two islands is linked to the objective to preserve, rather than destroy, the local offshore finance centre.[25]

Other External Relationships

The idea of a federal, or at least more integrated, relationship between the Crown Dependencies or just the Channel Islands has been mooted periodically. The most developed of these ideas was the proposal for a Council of the Islands made in Kilbrandon. The Council would have consisted of a chairman, two independent members appointed by the Crown together with six representatives of the United Kingdom and six representatives from the islands. The primary role of this body was envisaged as keeping "relationships between the United Kingdom and the Islands under review and to seek to find solutions to the more difficult questions referred to it."[26] However, the Council failed to materialise due to lack of interest in Jersey and Guernsey. The Isle of Man supported the idea of the Council and resented the disinterest shown by Jersey and Guernsey.

A Federation of the Channel Islands or the Crown Dependencies, no matter how logical it seems to those outside the islands, is not in the process of evolving. There is very little desire for close formal links, in particular between the Channel Islands. Instead long lasting informal links exist. Indeed formal co-operation is the exception rather than the rule even in the Channel Islands where the main fields in which it occurs, such as that of air route licensing, are defined by geographical necessity. Formal six monthly and annual meetings occur between the United Kingdom and the Crown Dependencies and between the Crown Dependencies themselves. The meetings have been successful on specific issues, but such meetings are consultative in nature and have no formal constitutional status. There are also strong links between the Channel Islands through shared BBC and ITV network coverage. However, this experience has enjoyed limited success as many people in Guernsey feel that the ITV company, in particular, which is based in Jersey, does not give sufficient coverage to events in Guernsey.

A major problem for the image of offshore finance in the Channel Islands is the so called Sark Lark. The issue is, in part, a result of the fact that Sark and Alderney have a high degree of autonomy within the Bailiwick of Guernsey. Sark allows its residents to be directors of companies operating elsewhere. As a result, it is estimated that 50 of the 400 odd adults in Sark hold directorships.[27] One Sark resident, Philip Croshaw, holds the world record of 2,400 directorships, 2,035 of them British. However, he admitted that "in 90 per cent of the cases he does not know the real owners."[28] Real doubt exists as to whether it is possible to be a director of that many companies and the Department of Trade and Industry in the United Kingdom is seeking to ban Philip Croshaw from being a director of British companies. The Sark Lark represents one of the least reputable forms of offshore activity. Maurice Fitzpatrick, of chartered accountants Chantrey Vellacott, observed that "There is no tax advantage in having Sark directors with a British registered company. This is all to do with masking ownership. It is evasion, not legal avoidance."[29] The relevance of the Sark Lark is that Sark is a Channel Island and in the past the operation was organised from Jersey or Guernsey.[30] It is therefore felt that the activities on Sark reflect badly on the other Channel Islands. However, neither Jersey nor Guernsey has been able to persuade Sark to refrain from this activity. United Kingdom action is, however, more likely to succeed.

In addition, Sark is also in conflict with Barclay brothers over the ownership of the island Brechquo. As Sark is part of the Bailiwick of Guernsey, the Barclay brothers' action in the European Court of Human Rights is against the Crown and the Bailiwick of Guernsey. As the estimated wealth of the Barclays is twice the annual budget of the Bailiwick, the Bailiwick of Guernsey has been forced to involve the Crown in an issue which could be seen as domestic to Sark.[31] This legal action illustrates the vulnerability of small communities to action by the wealthy individuals or companies they seek to attract.

175

The Crown Dependencies do not have a close relationship with the nearest states to them. Historical links to Ireland and France respectively exist, but little modern cultural or economic interaction. The relationships are dominated by minor irritations caused by geographical proximity. The Isle of Man's links to the Irish Republic may be strengthening due to the emergence of Dublin as, what is in effect, an offshore finance centre and the Irish seat on the British-Irish Council. In contrast, Guernsey's links with *Basse Normandie* are weaker. France, and later *Basse Normandie*, have concentrated diplomatic efforts on Jersey as the bigger and nearer island. This ignores the fact that Guernsey objects to the assumption that an office in Jersey automatically covers the Channel Islands.

Jersey and Guernsey share the same waters and have similar views on the presence of nuclear installations on the French coast as does the Isle of Man towards the British installation at Sellafield. However, their attitudes to French fishing rights have been different. Jersey seems to have taken a more accommodating approach to the French claims. This is assisted by Jersey having an agreement with France on fishing rights. A further factor is that Jersey, being geographically closer to France, is limited in claiming extensive waters as France's proximity would make a twelve mile limit off the east cost impossible to justify. The difference in attitude has the potential to cause conflicts between the Jersey and Guernsey authorities because they negotiate separately with the French on access to their own waters. Disputes have flared up between Guernsey and French fishermen over an agreement between the Guernsey and French authorities over access to the Schole Bank. These disputes mirror those between Jersey and France and cause the same problems for jurisdictions with limited resources to police such incidents.

The Imposition of Overseas Norms

All three Crown Dependencies have experienced pressure from governments, courts and the media to adopt European norms of behaviour. The hostility of elements of the United Kingdom media to all of the islands is due to a mixture of their roles as offshore finance centres and their more conservative social stance. These fears are reciprocated in the islands by a long held fear of European tax harmonisation and social values imposed from outside. The most controversial matters in relation to which these pressures have been exerted are capital punishment, homosexuality and corporal punishment. Each island was successfully pressurised by the United Kingdom to remove any anomalies within their local legislation. However, the extent to which each island resisted this pressure differed. The Isle of Man faced not only formal pressure by the Home Office, but was taken to the European Court of Human Rights over the issue of corporal punishment.[32] In this case, the Home Office, in effect, allowed the European Court of Human Rights to impose the change via legal action. Homosexuality was legalised in the Isle of Man in 1992 after intense pressure from the Home Office, which culminated in the Home Office making it clear in public that it would legislate if Tynwald did not.[33] Jersey had enacted legislation two years previously. Guernsey acted earlier, although the vote in 1983 was imposed against the States members' "better judgement."[34]

The islands each seek to develop an independent voice by membership of international bodies, such as the Commonwealth Parliamentary Association. Beyond this, the organisations which the islands choose to join vary. Jersey is a member of the *Assemblée Parlaimentaire de la Francophonie* while Guernsey is not and the Isle of Man is a member of the Conference of Peripheral Member States of the European Union. In the case of Jersey and the Isle of Man, their membership of the separate organisations is an assertion of an aspect of their identity they consider important. Jersey feels that membership of a Francophone organisation forms part of a policy of preserving a bilingual heritage and the Isle of Man, despite recent economic growth, has a long experience of the economic damage suffered by peripheral communities.

The extension of international agreements to small territories is a concern in all the islands. The President of Advisory and Finance in Guernsey, Conseiller Roydon Falla, told a 1986 Commonwealth forum "that the time had come to refuse any more conventions unless they were of direct relevance to the Channel Islands." He justified this position by reference to the workload which the agreements created.[35] The Manx delegate supported this view. The issue arose because the States in Guernsey were debating the renewal of the individual right of petition to the European Court of Human Rights. The right was extended to the island on the basis of the British government's view that a refusal to renew the right of petition would be greeted unfavourably by other member states, which include Britain.[36]

The islands' relationship with the European Union is identical. The Manx authorities adopted Jersey's position in the Protocol negotiations. This was in part because both islands employed Dr Hugh Thurston to advise them on the matter. This illustrates the high levels of co-ordination that developed between the Crown Dependencies on the issue. The Isle of Man authorities argued, as they still do, that independence from the United Kingdom was a better option than full membership of the European Union. The Isle of Man was specifically worried about exclusion from access for Manxmen to the United Kingdom labour market, a worry symptomatic of the parlous state of the Manx economy at the time. The other distinctive concern related to the possible development of a common shipping policy and the effects this might have on the Manx shipping register. In the final analysis the Isle of Man was willing to go independent rather than be incorporated. The Isle of Man felt particularly threatened by the United Kingdom's accession to the EEC as it had just managed to reverse its population decline, in part by changing its tax structure to become an offshore finance centre. In contrast, Guernsey was willing to accept membership, whilst Jersey avoided taking a stance on this issue by allowing Senator Vibert to finesse a compromise which developed into Protocol 3.

The more recent approaches of the islands to the European Union have varied and different means of monitoring the European Union have been adopted. Jersey and Guernsey tend to favour the use of a legal adviser to monitor events whereas the Manx authorities have sent delegations to Brussels, despite the potential this action has for damaging relations with the Home Office, who may be bypassed by the procedure. Guernsey also sought unsuccessfully to have Article 2 of the protocol revoked in 1992 at the time of the negotiation of the admission of Sweden, Finland and Austria. Article 2 of the Protocol which denies Channel Islanders and Manxmen the right of freedom of movement in the European Union is resented in all the islands. The islands have adopted different stances on what to do if the United Kingdom adopts the Euro. The Isle of Man favours independence; Guernsey was in the mid-nineties considering launching its own currency pegged to another currency, possibly the Swiss franc, however, it later moved to the same position as Jersey, which will adopt the Euro.[37] The main influence of the Crown Dependencies on each other is the fact that a ruling in the European Court of Justice originating from a case with respect to one island will apply to all the others.

In all the islands the public is wary of the European Union in that all, to varying degrees, feel threatened by it. Protocol 3 is the most invasive international agreement which has ever been extended to the islands, and its aim is to require the Crown Dependencies to adopt a minimum of European norms in return for their special status. These norms, however, will be determined by the needs and environment of the member states. The member states of the European Union cannot be expected to bear in mind the special situations in each associated political community when passing legislation and, if they did, they might seek to impose legislation designed to limit some activities in these communities. Therefore the Crown Dependencies accept some irrelevant or objectionable laws in exchange for the current relationship and the tolerant lack of interest shown by the Community towards them.

Constitutional Reform

The structure of government differs in each island. Each Bailiwick executive is committee-based whilst the Isle of Man operates a ministerial system. In addition, the Bailiwicks operate a unicameral legislature whilst the Isle of Man has a tricameral system. The Legislative Council and the House of Keys sit separately for legislative issues, but together for financial and general policy purposes, forming the Tynwald. A formal separation of powers is more apparent in the Isle of Man than in the Channel Islands. The Deemsters are the head of the judiciary in the Isle of Man, but no longer sit in the Legislative Council. Moreover, the ministerial system of government means that not all members of the legislature are also in the executive. In both Bailiwicks the Bailiff presides over the Assembly and heads the judiciary, as well as having considerable executive powers.

Manx autonomy was a later development than autonomy in the Channel Islands. D.G. Kermode dates the achievement of Manx self-government to the post war years.[38] Its evolution occurred through a series of Commissions, the first being in 1944. In 1959 the MacDermott Commission followed and finally the Stonham Report in 1969. The Manx authorities at this stage requested both membership of the United Nations and that no Orders in Council would apply to the island unless Tynwald had given prior consent. This was rejected by the Home Office which regarded the demands as producing a situation which was tantamount to independence. During this period the Channel Islands undertook major post war reforms in parallel with each other and were included with the Isle of Man in the Kilbrandon Commission report. Differences in the islands' constitutional positions were revealed in their evidence to that Commission. The Isle of Man, like Jersey, sought to codify the constitutional relationship with the United Kingdom via a United Kingdom statute. The Commission and Guernsey opposed this option.[39] Jersey and the Isle of Man also sought to attain the association status then being considered for the West Indies.[40] Guernsey opposed this proposal as did the Royal Commission. Guernsey wished to preserve the *status quo* and believed accurately that the Kilbrandon Commission was not going to accede to any requests to change the relationship fundamentally. The Manx and Jersey attitudes can be seen to reflect worries about the impeding negotiations with the European Union. Once this issue was settled, Jersey's interest in major constitutional reform waned.

An example of the later development of real autonomy in the Isle of Man is the evolution of the Manx government's fiscal powers. Unlike the budgets in Jersey and Guernsey, the Isle of Man budget was under direct and detailed control by the United Kingdom Treasury until 1958 and the Lieutenant Governor remained, in effect, the finance minister until 1976.[41] Moreover, the Isle of Man is prevented by statute from running a budget deficit. This was in addition to the exchange controls imposed by the Bank of England, which existed in all the islands until 1979.

The role of the Manx Lieutenant Governor was distinctive in that he was far more involved in the island's executive for a longer period than his counterparts in the Channel Islands. The Lieutenant Governor presided over the legislative council until 1980 and could thereby dominate politics in the island.[42] The Manx Lieutenant Governor still performs some roles in Council acting on the advice of the Council of Ministers. However, the importance of the post is declining. In this, the Isle of Man can be seen as moving away from a model common in the United Kingdom Overseas Territories to a Channel Island model. In fact, it could be argued that the Isle of Man has leapfrogged the Channel Islands in this area as the Isle of Man Lieutenant Governor has the devolved power to give the Royal Assent to Manx legislation.[43] This distinction must not be exaggerated as the Home Office retains the right to withhold the assent. In addition, it is likely that the Home Office would now allow the Channel Islands such a concession since it has been granted to the Isle of Man. The Isle of Man is also the first Crown Dependency to have a non-military Lieutenant Governor appointed.[44]

The Isle of Man has a desire for constitutional change. Manx government policy is "To promote and continue the evolution of the constitutional relationship between the Isle of Man and the United Kingdom towards more complete self-government and to ensure appropriate recognition of the Island's interests internationally." In more detail, the aims are:

> To take responsibility wherever possible for the extension of international obligations to the Isle of Man.
> To defend the Island's autonomy in relation to its internal affairs.
> To retain a link to the Crown.
> To maintain a constructive relationship with the European Community which ensures the Island's continued right to trade with Member States and protects established rights and safeguards.[45]

The Isle of Man, thanks to recent reforms, has adopted a more dynamic and streamlined system of government. As this difference is recent, it raises the question of whether the economic growth and stability in the other Crown Dependencies has led them to be complacent and thus not keen on reform. The lack of constitutional reform in Jersey and Guernsey reflects their relative success and a fear that change might inhibit that success. This is reverse of the situation in the Isle of Man. An example of this active consideration of the direction which its constitution could take was the 1993 IoM Second Interim Report on the Future Constitutional Objectives prepared by the Constitutional and External Affairs Committee. It requested that the functions of the Lieutenant Governor be transferred to the Isle of Man - "On 5th November 1992, the Council of Ministers noted the possibility of the Crown being advised by Tynwald rather than the Privy Council on matters relating to the Island had been raised by a number of Members of Tynwald."[46] It must be noted that this request was also put to the Kilbrandon Commission and rejected.[47] The power to give Royal Assent was delegated from the Crown to the Lieutenant Governor by Royal Assent to Legislation (Isle of Man) Order 1981. However, the Order provides that the Secretary of State has the power to give directions to the Lieutenant Governor in granting the assent which preserves the United Kingdom's power to withhold the Royal Assent. The Channel Islands' statements on the Constitution are far more conservative. Guernsey's Government Statement of Principles is "to protect the international constitutional status of the Island" and " to secure the representation of the Island's interests on international matters."[48] Jersey's mission statement is even less dynamic containing phrases such as "equality of opportunity," "freedom from discrimination" and "the retention of the Island's existing relationship with the United Kingdom and the European Union."[49]

The Isle of Man has taken a position shared by Guernsey, but not Jersey, of emphasising its autonomy by refusing to use United Kingdom Orders in Council as a means of implementing local legislation. Instead it enacts legislation as local Manx Law. The Manx authorities feel so strongly on this issue that they have been passing Manx legislation to replace existing Orders in Council. St. J. N. Bates at the third Commonwealth Parliamentary Association Seminar held on the Isle of Man in 1991 argued that "I think this use of parallel Manx legislation rather than applying UK legislation is perhaps that the most significant example of the development of the Manx/UK constitutional relationship in the last few years."

The lack of separation of powers is the fundamental difference between the Manx and Channel Island constitutions. The issue makes the Channel Islands vulnerable to external pressure to change their constitutions. Channel Island constitutional development tends to be driven by external forces whilst in Mann change is driven internally. In this area the Isle of Man, by removing the First Deemster from the Legislative Council in 1975, may have provided a model for the future. Separation of powers was considered in Guernsey and Jersey in 1991 in response to the sacking by the Crown of Jersey's Deputy Bailiff, Vernon Tomes, but was rejected in both islands.[50] In 1998 an external challenge to the role of the Bailiff emerged when the Commission of the European Court of Human Rights upheld a claim that elements of the lack of separation of powers in the role of Bailiff make the Royal Court in Guernsey not an independent tribunal and thus contrary to Article 6 of the Convention.[51] This ruling, if confirmed by the Court, may force a separation of powers on both Bailiwicks which will bring them closer to the Manx Deemster model.

The High Court of Tynwald is different from the States of Jersey and Guernsey and consists of the Legislative Council and the House of Keys. They sit separately for legislative purposes and together for finance and general policy. The Legislative Council in the Isle of Man consists of the President of Tynwald, the Lord Bishop, the Attorney General and eight elected members from the House of Keys. The House of Keys includes 24 members elected for five year terms. The President and Deputy President of Tynwald are elected from amongst their number for a five year term. The Legislative Council serves as the revising chamber for the House of Keys. It can only delay, not veto, House of Keys Bills. This is an aspect where the Isle of Man more closely mirrors the arrangement in the former colonial possessions with the upper chamber in both cases evolving as the United Kingdom appointed officers who ran the island. The Isle of Man legislature with its use of a tricameral system has some attractions for a small community as it increases the time for reflection and acts as a check in a small system in which, by necessity, oversight tends to be limited by the small size of the civil service.

The States of Deliberation in Guernsey is closer to the Jersey model. It consists of the Bailiff, 12 Conseillers, 33 People's Deputies, 10 Douziane Representatives, Her Majesty's Controller and Her Majesty's Procureur. People's Deputies are elected by universal suffrage for constituencies. These are roughly by population but each of the ten parishes has at least one deputy. Douziane Representatives are nominated by Parish Councils or Douzaines for one year, unlike Jersey where the Constable of the Parish does not sit in the States. From

181

1994 Conseillers were elected by island wide vote for six year terms. Candidates must have served 30 months in the States of Deliberation. This removed a system of indirect election which could have made the island vulnerable to external pressure. Legislation is now in place to abolish the post of Conseiller and increase the number of People's Deputies to 45 and extend the term of office to four years from 1 May 2000.

The Isle of Man has adopted an executive headed by a Council of Ministers and Chief Minister. Prior to these reforms, it had a committee system akin to the other islands with boards ranging in size from 3 to 29, including 24 directly elected members. These boards were dissolved and replaced with nine ministries, nine departments and seven statutory boards. A Minister may be reinforced by 'non-Council of Minister' members and this practice could see the old committee system re-establish itself by stealth. The Council of Ministers was created in 1990 and the first Chief Minister was appointed in 1986. The Chief Minister must be a member of Tynwald and be appointed by the Lieutenant Governor on the nomination of Tynwald. Candidates hold office for an electoral term or until a vote of no confidence is passed by 17 members of Tynwald. The Chief Minister and Council of Ministers fall together, reflecting their nature as a cabinet. The Chief Minister deals with external relations. The Council of Ministers operates via five standing committees, including a constitutional and external relations committee.

Guernsey operates a committee system but, unlike Jersey, committee membership is not automatically limited to States members. A committee will consist of a President from the States and four States members. Two additional members may be drawn from outside. The Advisory and Finance Committee is the major exception to this rule as its membership must consist of only States members. The Advisory and Finance Committee is required to co-ordinate all projects laid before the States. In 1996 there were 45 committees or boards of the States in Guernsey creating 234 positions to be filled by 56 States members. This figure is lower than Jersey's as non-States members are used to fill some posts, but still creates the same problem of members of the legislature being distracted by a large number of executive tasks and thus unable to fulfil their legislative roles adequately. Both Jersey and Guernsey have considered the merits of Cabinet government.[52] While it is perhaps too early to come to any firm conclusions about the Manx experience, it has reduced the fragmentation apparent under the old committee system, clarified accountability within government and produced a situation where an opposition is beginning to develop within the Manx assembly. Each of these factors would correct flaws in the committee system in Jersey and Guernsey.

Even though the Manx ministerial system is more amenable to party operations, formal party politics has not developed, bar a small Manx Labour Party and the Manx nationalist party, *Mec Vanin*. However, due to the ministerial nature of the system a party system of sorts exists between those in power and those not in power. The fact that the Isle of Man has a general election, rather than staged elections for a multiple franchise assembly as in Jersey and Guernsey, also helps parties gather the political momentum to gain seats.

The Isle of Man lacks a powerful local government in the form of parishes which, in Jersey's case in particular, has created a quasi federal system. Guernsey, even though it has a parish system like Jersey, has a weaker local government. This is partly as the parish representative in the States of Guernsey is a delegate of the parish, rather than the Constable. The power of local government in such a small community tends to act as a force for conservatism as its origins are in tradition. The fact that its basis is defined by reference to land area, rather than size of population, empowers the rural community against the urban centres. Therefore, part of the reason why the Isle of Man can reform whilst Jersey finds such reforms difficult is that the parishes in Jersey via the Constables act as a conservative block on any reform perceived as a direct threat to their status as *ex-officio* members of the States.

In the area of constitutional reform the Channel Islands can be seen to be moving closer to a political model pioneered by the Isle of Man. The Manx model seems to offer certain advantages. Firstly, it reduces fragmentation both within the civil service and the political executive. This would not only improve the career structure for civil servants in the Channel Islands, but also clarify the accountability of the political executive by making it impossible to attribute decisions as in a ministerial system to an individual, rather than to committee members as a group. Secondly, the existence of too many committees may produce an impressive workload for all the assembly members, but it tends to result in many of the committee meetings being dominated by material which could, and would, be delegated to the civil service if the existence of fewer committees forced work to be prioritised. Fewer committees would also ease strategic policy planning as more planning would have to be done within departments rather than on the floor of the house and thus the outcome might be more coherent. Just as importantly, the fewer posts a committee or ministerial system requires to be filled, the more time is available to members to scrutinise the executive properly. The lack of scrutiny and an effective opposition are major problems in Jersey and Guernsey. Therefore it would seem to Jersey's and Guernsey's advantage to study some of the developments in the Isle of Man. The recent reforms, which in Guernsey replaced Conseillers with Peoples Deputies and in Jersey reduced the number of committees, would seem to illustrate a movement towards adopting elements of the Manx model.

Conclusion

Each of the Crown Dependencies is faced with the same problem of survival on the periphery of their sovereign power. They have all made a success of this, as shown by their expanding economies and political stability and are not dependent on the United Kingdom for any financial support. In achieving this they have followed a very similar economic model to that pioneered by Jersey by using their constitutional autonomy to provide the political space required to develop an offshore finance centre. Thus Guernsey and the Isle of Man have had the benefit of developing later and the opportunity of learning from Jersey's experience. To a degree this model was followed because of its success in Jersey, but it has also formed part of a global development as high net worth individuals and transnational corporations have sought to create an offshore network to manage their wealth. In this the Isle of Man's experience is different to that of the Channel Islands as more efforts were made to attract the finance industry as a result of a fear that the island would otherwise become as depopulated as the Western Isles of Scotland.

A general model of how the Crown Dependencies operate in constitutional terms is emerging. All three began with a form of committee government. However, there is evidence that Jersey and Guernsey are now adopting elements of the reformed constitution evolving in the Isle of Man. The Crown Dependencies' models of government have become more similar due to external pressures militating both for the adoption of certain international norms in the field of human rights and fiscal regulation and the need for more efficient government to administer the dynamic global finance industries on the islands.

The two most important relationships are those with the United Kingdom and with the European Union. The latter has been a recent development and, despite the fact that Protocol 3 guarantees the islands' current arrangements, all remain wary of the future attitude of the European Union and its member states. Each island has attempted to manage its relationship with the United Kingdom. However, the Isle of Man has the stormiest relationship with the United Kingdom, a result of the later development of high levels of autonomy in the island. The Channel Islands have not had to agitate for more autonomy which has created fewer irritants in their relationship with the United Kingdom. Once Mann had reached the same level of autonomy as the Channel Islands, the islands' fates became linked. The Home Office treats them as one unit and any right granted by the United Kingdom to one is regarded as available to all. This will bring the islands closer together as each can adopt any privilege gained by another. In short, none of the Crown Dependencies can gain a long term constitutional advantage over the others.

References

[1] op. cit., Census 1996, 32.

[2] Report on the 1996 Guernsey Census, Population and Migration Committee, Guernsey, 1996, 115.

[3] op. cit., Jersey's Offshore Finance Centre crisis.

[4] Home Office, Review of Financial Regulation in the Crown Dependencies, Cm 4109 - III, The Stationery Office, 1998, Part 3, 11.

[5] Home Office, Review of Financial Regulation in the Crown Dependencies, Cm 4109 - II, The Stationery Office, 1998, Part 2, 8.

[6] Annual Review of Policies & Programmes, Isle of Man Government, 1995, Appendix 4, 147,

hereafter, Isle of Man Annual Review, 1995.

[7] This sector of the Guernsey analysis represents the direct contribution to local taxation revenue of certain wealthy individuals allowed to settle on the island.

[8] States Advisory & Finance Committee, Policy Planning Economic & Financial Report 1996, States of Guernsey, 1996, 853, hereafter, Guernsey Policy Report, 1996.

[9] Isle of Man Official Year Book 1996, Executive Publications, Isle of Man, 1996, 70.

[10] Solly, M., Government and Law in the Isle of Man, Parallel Books, Isle of Man, 1994, 89, hereafter Solly.

[11] Council of Ministers, "Second Interim Report on Future Constitutional Objectives", Isle of Man Government, 1993, 7, hereafter, Second Constitutional Report.

[12] op. cit., Kilbrandon 1973, 11.

[13] Bates T. St. J. N., ""Après le Déluge: Where should Mann be paddling?", Presentation to the Euroclub, Palace Hotel, 1/11/92, 13.

[14] op. cit., Kermode, 146.

[15] Guernsey Evening Press and Star, 5/11/85, 1.

[16] Defence Committee, Defence Contribution: Territorial Army Unit (P. 124/97) - Report, States Greffe, Jersey, 1998, 5.

[17] op. cit., Kilbrandon 1973, 27, para 3.

[18] op. cit., Second Constitutional Report, 9.

[19] ibid., 7.

[20] Minute of the Court of Tynwald, 11/4/90, T1469-T1472.

[21] ibid.

[22] Minute of the Court of Tynwald, 21/2/84, T706-T711.

[23] op. cit., Morris interview.

[24] op. cit., Kilbrandon 1973, 87, para 3.

[25] Richards, J., "Politics in Small Independent Communities: Conflict of Consensus?", Journal of Commonwealth and Comparative Politics, 1982, Vol 20 (2), 168.

[26] op. cit., Kilbrandon 1973, 459, para 1520.

[27] Ingoldby, G., Out of Call or Cry The Island of Sark, Hieneman, London, 1990, 174.

[28] Johnston, L., Gillard, M. & Calvert, J., "'Sark lark' directors may lose bonanza", The Observer, 19/4/98, 3.

[29] ibid.

[30] Falle, P., "Call to tighten up financial controls." Jersey Evening Post, 24/11/97, 1.

[31] Parks, E., "Twins lose bid to exclude Crown", Guernsey Evening Press and Star, 15/8/96, 1.

[32] op. cit., Solly, 191. In Tyrer v United Kingdom, (1978-80) MLR 13, the European Court of Human Rights ruled 14-1 that the action was in breach of Article 3 of the European Convention of Human Rights.

[33] Bennetto, J., "Islanders take moral umbrage at criticism", The Independent, 11/6/97, 7.

[34] Horner, S. A., "The Isle of Man and the Channel Islands - A Study of their Status under Constitutional, International and European Law", EUI Working Paper No. 98, European University Institute, Florence, 1984, 67.

[35] "Islands disagree on rights convention", Guernsey Evening Press and Star, 28/6/86, 3

[36] "Deputy wants decision on right of islanders" Guernsey Evening Press and Star, 3/4/86, 1.

[37] Interview with John Dickson, 13/8/96; Ward, D., "Island haven fears EU tax disaster", The Guardian, 18/2/99, 10 & "Jersey need not fear the Euro", Jersey Evening Post, 21/10/98, 10.

[38] op. cit., Kermode, 53.

[39] op. cit., Kilbrandon 1973, para 1494.

[40] ibid., para 1395.

[41] ibid., 120.

[42] op. cit., Kermode, 35.

[43] op. cit., Solly, 299.

[44] Memorandum of discussions in Jersey on Judicial Reform and the Office of Lieutenant Governor between Home Office and Insular Officials. The document is undated but refers to discussions in 1957-58. PRO file HO 284/3.

[45] op. cit., Isle of Man Annual Review 1995, 144.

[46] op. cit., Second Constitutional Report, 9, para 3.1.

[47] op. cit., Kilbrandon 1973, 466, para 1539.

[48] op. cit., Guernsey Policy Report, 1996, 840.

[49] op. cit., Strategic Policy Report 1996, 3.

[50] Jackson, N., "'Split law, politics' idea are shelved", Guernsey Evening Press and Star, 27/5/93. In Jersey, despite Senator Tomes' election on a platform of reforming the role of Bailiff, no such reforms occurred.

[51] European Commission of Human Rights, Application No. 28488/95, Richard James Joseph McGonnell v the United Kingdom, 20/10/98.

[52] Ogier, M. "Cabinet Government needed", Guernsey Evening Press and Star, 21/11/91 and Falle, F., "Cabinet Government 'essential'", Jersey Evening Post, 25/4/98.

Chapter 9 - Conclusion

Introduction

Jersey is a distinctive community with highly developed autonomy, nevertheless its proximity to the United Kingdom permeates local politics and is fundamental to the island's prosperity. Jersey is much more than an interesting medieval survival. It has used its distinctive status to survive and prosper in the latter half of the twentieth century. It thereby offers an example of how small peripheral communities can use their constitutional independence or autonomy to ensure economic prosperity as well as illustrating that, contrary to established wisdom, small need not be primitive.

Jersey's political and economic structures are similar to those in the other Crown Dependencies. The other two Crown Dependencies have watched Jersey's economy grow and sought to emulate the more successful parts of it, moving closer to a common economic model. The Crown Dependencies have also moved closer to a common political model, but in this case the islands have not been emulating a successful Jersey model. Indeed, it could be argued instead that Jersey's very affluence has prevented reforms necessary to modernise government on the island. However, increasing contact between the governments of the islands and the realisation that the United Kingdom will allow any extension of autonomy it grants to one island to all the others have allowed each to copy reforms in the other islands, should they so wish. Therefore a form of informal interdependence has developed between the Crown Dependencies where the insular authorities meet frequently formally and informally and exchange ideas. More formal integration will not occur due to the fact that the islands are economic competitors and have a strong sense of independence.

Jersey has achieved its prosperity by hosting an offshore finance centre which has required the island to have a distinctive external policy, the key requirement of which is political stability. The dominance of the finance industry in Jersey is not only shown by the fact that it accounts for over half of the economy, but also through its effects on policy-making in the island. France, despite its importance as a foundation for much of the island's distinctiveness and as a source of a considerable part of Jersey's law and constitutional practice, is now largely irrelevant to the island because it is not an important market for the island's offshore finance centre. Thus, the major local impact of France derives from minor irritations due to its geographical proximity. France's main significance to the island in the future could well be the fact that it is one of the most hostile members of the European Union towards offshore finance.

The Parameters of Autonomy

The United Kingdom's authority is in theory all encompassing; it has the good government powers as well as full authority in defence and foreign affairs. However, the reality of the relationship is that Jersey has real autonomy. The key parameter of that autonomy is that Jersey must not embarrass the United Kingdom in international arenas or hinder its own policy aims. Beyond this, the insular authorities have virtually full discretion. Jersey's key survival strategy has therefore been to know where the parameters of its autonomy are set and operate within them, rather than to provoke confrontations with the United Kingdom it cannot win.

To help assess where these parameters lie the insular authorities have developed the strategy of seeking to keep communication informal and maintaining good personal contacts with those who administer the relationship for the United Kingdom. This serves to both warn the island of any potential disputes and help to keep them out of the public domain, should they emerge. Thus both sides in the relationship work to mollify any potential disputes before they occur. This is particularly important because, in many cases, the Home Office view and the views of the insular authorities are subtly different on important constitutional issues, such as the extent to which Parliament can legislate for the island. However, both sides seek to avoid disputes by finessing differences or not openly challenging the other's interpretations of the relationship. The most important aspect in managing the relationship is the formal nature of the links between Jersey and the United Kingdom. Even though most of the relationship is informal a structure exists in which to manage it. This identifies the individuals responsible for the relationship and therefore the individuals with whom to work. Moreover, it creates a bond whereby the larger, more powerful nation is bound to consider the interests of the smaller community.

Jersey could break the parameters of its autonomy by seeking independence. This option would seem to give Jersey the freedom to operate its own external relations, manage the offshore finance centre as it wished and disassociate itself from the European Union. However, despite the superficial attractiveness of this idea it is flawed as Jersey thrives on its position in the grey area between nationhood and absorption. If Jersey were to seek independence a new relationship would have to be negotiated with the European Union. This would not be as beneficial as that existing at present due to the member states' hostility towards offshore finance, a factor that was not a major issue in the initial negotiations. The finance industry is wary of investing in newly independent states and on the whole prefers the added security of dependency status. In addition, the island would lose defence and foreign representation which are provided at a cost considerably below that of the per capita cost of the United Kingdom and at a level Jersey could not sustain on its own.

Moreover, the United Kingdom allows Jersey almost total autonomy in domestic and fiscal matters together with a right of veto over the extension of most international agreements. Given this, it is difficult to see what else Jersey could gain by declaring independence. Its current position would seem to give it all the real independence it could hope for with the added bonus of having a tolerant and protective metropolitan power. In addition, an independent Jersey would still remain economically and politically dependent on the United Kingdom while lacking the advantage of having a formal link through which to manage its dependency.

The United Kingdom tolerates Jersey's autonomy because revoking the current asymmetric relationship would cost the United Kingdom more than keeping it. The relationship is long standing and has shown a high degree of stability and both of these factors can be used as arguments against change. The island also benefits from a metropolitan power with a tradition of tolerance to constitutional survivals. Therefore as long as Jersey is economically self sufficient and not corrupt, the United Kingdom will be loathe to intervene. However, the growth of the island's finance industry and the development of international law may change this calculation as the costs of maintaining the relationship will begin to include increasing tax leakage and international hostility towards the United Kingdom because of its tolerance of Jersey's offshore finance centre. This lack of intervention by the United Kingdom can be characterised as neglect. However, this neglect has given Jersey the space to manage and profit from its own autonomy. This is best exemplified by the most significant challenge faced by the island in the period under consideration, the United Kingdom's accession to the European Union. The United Kingdom's tolerance or neglect was illustrated by the fact that it was willing to accept any solution that Jersey proposed provided it did not hinder the fundamental objectives of British policy. Nonetheless, it appeared unwilling to devote any resources to assisting the Crown Dependencies to develop a satisfactory solution to their problems.

The Management of Dependency

Jersey's success is not entirely due to its own efforts. It has benefited from fortuitous external circumstances, the most significant being that there has been peace and stability in Western Europe in the period under consideration. Therefore Jersey's constitutional settlement has not been severely tested by a catastrophic event. Jersey was also lucky that the global economy developed in such a way as to provide opportunities for more offshore facilities. The island was selected not only due to its political stability and dependency relationship with the United Kingdom, but also due to its convenient location with respect to London and fears about instability in more established centres like the Bahamas.

Nevertheless, the insular authorities have shown ability to manage the island's position to its benefit. The main area in which Jersey's dependency has been managed is in overcoming the problems of small scale on the island. Despite the disadvantages of scale, the island possesses a dynamic, modern economy based on an industry, which is little disadvantaged by the island's scale. Therefore the promotion of the finance industry on the island was, in the beginning at least, an astute development policy pursued by the insular authorities. Jersey has also used its dependency status to share services with the United Kingdom to overcome some of the diseconomies of scale on the island. Although the benefits accruing to the island in this field have declined in recent years, Jersey's defence contribution is still a fraction of the United Kingdom's per capita spending and Jersey students, despite paying more than their United Kingdom counterparts, pay less than those from outside the European Union. Further, the relationship with the United Kingdom gives Jersey the ability to overcome one of the greatest handicaps of a small community: its people can train, study and work freely in the United Kingdom, thereby securing a host of opportunities not available on the island. This access to the United Kingdom has also been a way for those unhappy with opportunities on the island to escape and, since no unemployment benefit exists on the island, a way of exporting unemployment. It is possible to argue that a rich community like Jersey, if independent, could counter these problems of scale by purchasing all these services. However, such services would be more expensive than previously and such goods as air sea rescue would be less guaranteed if the emergency required resources in the United Kingdom as well. This also reduces Jersey's vulnerability to a major disaster it could not cope with using its own resources, a fundamental problem for all microstates. The link also provides Jersey with access to a tariff-free large market for goods and services, thereby overcoming a critical development hurdle for a small community by providing a market large enough to operate effective industries.

The downside to Jersey's economic success is that it has put a brake on the necessary reform of political institutions surviving from the medieval period as there has been no need for an efficient responsive public administration to develop. Moreover, while many of the medieval remnants of the constitution may appear harmless some, such as the lack of separation of powers apparent in the role of Bailiff, have made the island vulnerable to external intervention which might yet force a change in the constitution. Part of the reason why these medieval legacies retain their power lies in an attempt to preserve Jersey's distinct cultural identity in the face of the large scale immigration and economic transformation apparent over the past thirty years. The political stability required by the offshore finance centre has also reinforced a strongly conservative attitude on the island that is of the opinion that any reform reduces the island's distinctiveness and therefore threatens its autonomy. The little reform that has occurred in Jersey is on the whole driven by external factors, such as the occupation and the reforms that followed in the immediate post-war years. The chances of meaningful reforms are also reduced by the fact that more radical individuals on the island often choose to emigrate to the United Kingdom rather than staying and seeking to effect reforms on the island. While this acts as a safety valve for local dissent, as does the fact that islanders can appeal for redress to the United Kingdom, it serves to further dissipate demands for reform. The tendency of radicals to seek reform by appeal to outside bodies has also produced a distrust of international organisations reflected in a dislike of international agreements amongst a significant number of islanders.

A danger exists that the finance sector has been allowed to expand too far and Jersey's larger neighbours and elements of the United Kingdom government now perceive the finance centre as a threat. Jersey has allowed itself to become dependent on a politically controversial industry viewed as one of the more destructive elements of the global economy[1]. However, it could be argued that in becoming an offshore finance centre Jersey was adopting its only survival option. Indeed, it is difficult to see what would sustain Jersey's economy if the finance industry on the island were to decline. However, the conflict between states, transnational corporations and high net worth individuals inherent in the use of offshore finance centres to reduce the tax burden on individuals and corporations can be very dangerous for the microstates involved. They are the weakest party in the equation and are dependent on one or other of the parties to the relationship to protect them from threats, often derived from another party to the relationship. In the case of the Barclay brothers, Sark is dependent on the United Kingdom to protect it from high net worth individuals. In the case of tax harmonisation, the Crown Dependencies are reliant on the lobbying power of the City of London against many of the member states of the European Union. Moreover, individual microstates are in competition with one another to attract business and there is a danger that an attempt is made to attract business by lowering regulatory thresholds. This exposes the microstate to further criticism by those hostile to offshore finance. Offshore finance centres are also vulnerable to changes in legislation onshore which erode their business. Thus while the offshore finance centre's growth has been spectacular, it is essentially fragile as it is dependent on the ability of the insular authorities' continued success in managing the island's relationships with a series of more powerful economic entities. Despite the apparent attractions of independence in managing these relationships, being a British dependency is a definite advantage. The United Kingdom has acted as a guarantor for Jersey's stability and tolerates the operation of offshore finance centres. An independent Jersey would be far more vulnerable to external pressure and financial institutions would be more difficult to convince that internal stability was guaranteed.

It is possible to argue that offshore finance, as a global industry, reduces Jersey's reliance on the United Kingdom given that two thirds of deposits in Jersey are held in foreign currencies.[2] The existence of the finance industry also prevents the island from being financially dependent on the United Kingdom. However, Jersey's dependence on finance is now just as vital as its dependence on the United Kingdom and these two dependency relationships can come into conflict. The tension between the two was evident in the Limited Liabilities Partnership debate where one element, finance, wanted the law and another, the United Kingdom, was opposed. The exposure of this explosive and potentially irreconcilable conflict inherent in the operation of Jersey's economy damaged the political institutions on the island.

Conclusion

Over the past thirty years Jersey represents an example of a successful microstate. Part of this success has been due to good fortune, but the insular authorities have also been able to manage the island's dependency relationship with both the United Kingdom and indirectly the European Union to mitigate the threats that a small community faces. The insular authorities have chartered a third way between absorption by the United Kingdom and independence and Jersey has thrived under this status. The strategy has relied on managing the island to become economically dependent on offshore finance, an industry well suited to the needs of microstates. On the other hand, it is a politically controversial industry which is not tied to Jersey by bonds of national loyalty or resource demands. The insular authorities have also sought to maintain the high levels of autonomy the United Kingdom has granted the island and using this freedom of action to maintain a regulatory environment that is attractive to offshore finance. Crucially, the decision to allow the development of Jersey as an offshore finance centre has ensured that the island is financially independent of the Home Office and therefore free of the Treasury intervention in domestic policy which an impoverished island would face.

Jersey has survived, on the whole, by knowing where the parameters of its autonomy are set. This has combined with the United Kingdom's desire to avoid open crises that would necessitate a more proactive oversight of the island's government to allow Jersey a high degree of autonomy. The relationship is eased by the fact that both communities have uncodified constitutions and the flexibility in the arrangement allows differences in each side's interpretations of the constitutional relationship to be glossed over. The United Kingdom could exert absolute sovereign control over Jersey, if it so wished. If the insular authorities objected to this, independence would be offered as the only alternative as the Home Office believes that such a gift amounts to a poisoned chalice. In fact this issue rarely arises due to the Home Office's high level of tolerance and the fact that the current arrangements are mutually beneficial. The island's relationship with the United Kingdom is therefore predicated on the United Kingdom's policy of non-intervention in fiscal and domestic affairs. Jersey, therefore, derives from the relationship the protection of a larger sovereign power while retaining what is effectively *de facto* day to day independence. The relationship's stability and success is due to the fact that both sides have more to lose than to gain from its collapse and the insular authorities manage the dependency relationship to prevent the United Kingdom's views from changing on this matter.

References

[1] Hutton, W., The State We're In, Jonathan Cape, London, 1995.
[2] "Jersey banks deposits top £90 billion", Jersey Weekly Post, 16/5/96, 1.

Epilogue

In this epilogue I shall draw on the salient events of the period from November 1998 to July 2001 to elucidate elements contained in my doctoral thesis, which forms the basis of this book. The discussion which follows does not seek to be exhaustive, but merely illustrative of trends already noted in the preceding chapters, as the outcome of many of the events described below is not yet clear. For instance, at the time of writing it is unclear whether the Clothier report will be accepted and, if so, to what extent; if the OECD will avoid including Jersey on its definitive list of tax havens; and what, if any, will be the long term effect of the Lord Chancellor's Department taking over responsibility from the Home Office for the relationship between the United Kingdom and the Crown Dependencies.

The Offshore Finance Centre

The publication of the Review of Financial Regulation in the Crown Dependencies (the Edwards Report) and the possibility that the OECD would list Jersey as a tax haven have not only crystallised the debate about the role of offshore finance in Jersey, but has also been symptomatic of a wider intensification of the international debate on offshore finance and the effects of globalisation. Evidence of the international nature and increasing international interest in this debate can be seen by the fact that the pressure group ATTAC demonstrated against globalisation and its effects in both Jersey and at the EU summit in Gothenburg in 2001.

If Jersey is to remain largely economically dependent on its finance industry, recent international interest in offshore finance centres has increased the need to successfully manage external relationships. The expansion of the Financial Services Commission and the increased use of lobbyists by the States of Jersey exemplify the efforts devoted by the States of Jersey to managing its external relationships. The need to manage the island's relationship with the United Kingdom was illustrated by the fact that the Edwards report was a United Kingdom government initiative. Also, in the case of both the EU and the OECD, it is the United Kingdom government, not Jersey, which can directly influence events, given that Jersey cannot be a member state of either body. Even if an independent Jersey were accepted into either organisation, the island's influence would be minimal compared to the substantial influence which the United Kingdom can exercise over both organisations.

Protocol 3 remains the most desirable basis for the island's relationship with the European Union. The introduction of the Euro into circulation in 2002 represents a watershed in the development of the European Union and one which, if successful, could have a profound impact on Jersey. The United Kingdom could find it difficult to resist introducing the Euro if it proves to be a success, in which case Jersey would have to follow suit. The introduction of the Euro also marks a deeper integration of European Union economic policy. This integration, if focused on the erosion of the European Union tax base, could be used either to amend regulations onshore to make the operation of offshore finance centres more difficult or place directly co-ordinated political pressure on offshore finance centres to restrict their activities.

The Edwards Report

The newly elected Labour government announced a Review of Financial Regulations in the Crown Dependencies, the outcome of which became known as the Edwards Report. Such a review could have had dire consequences for both the island's finance industry and the relationship between the insular authorities and the newly-elected government. The commissioning of the Report, which signalled an apparent lack of confidence by Jersey's metropolitan power in the island's finance industry, could have driven away investors. In addition, the intervention by the new United Kingdom government could have provoked a constitutional crisis. The strength of Jersey's relationship with the United Kingdom was illustrated by the fact that the review was managed and reported in such a way that this did not happen. It was not in Jersey's economic interest to try to block the review, irrespective of how offended the insular authorities were at not being informed that such a review was about to be commissioned. The insular authorities were also aware that any resistance would have created the impression that Jersey had something to hide. Moreover, the positive manner in which the Edwards Report was phrased made it easier for the island to accept its recommendations and present its findings to the outside world. The website of the Jersey Financial Services Commission (FSC) quotes the following extract from the Edwards Report, "Jersey was in the top division of offshore centres; had a formidable arsenal of legislation and had money laundering legislation better than many countries in the FATF [Financial Action Task Force] or European Union."[1] However, as even the FSC website had to concede, the Report made a number of recommendations. The website goes on to list eleven significant responses, including two new laws, as a response to the Report's recommendations and conclusions.

Whether the Report causes long-term damage to the island's offshore finance centre depends, in part, on how it is viewed by three audiences: firstly, the electorate, who, on the whole, are not immersed in the details of offshore finance, and will be reassured by the positive wording of the Report; secondly, those working in the finance industry on the island who will be more interested in the details of the Report. Presentations of the Edwards Report to the finance industry were organised by the insular authorities at the time of publication. This audience may in private be the most difficult audience to convince as they

194

possess as much, if not more, information on the industry as the authors of the Report. However, they share with the insular authorities a strong interest in presenting the Report in a positive light; the final audience's reaction is the most difficult to judge, namely that of external investors. Whilst the positive statements in the Report will be used in promotional material and presented by the island as endorsing the offshore finance centre, external investors might be suspicious of the need for a report and may, after reading elements of it, be unhappy to place their funds in such a jurisdiction.

Whilst it is not possible at this early stage to analyse the long-term effects of the Edwards Report, it is nevertheless possible to draw some short-term conclusions. The Report is an excellent example of the kind of document which the United Kingdom writes when it requires significant change to take place in the island. Although phrased in a complimentary way and emphasising the positive aspects of Jersey's offshore finance industry, the Report has resulted in a substantial increase in the policing of the finance centre together with significant regulatory change.

OECD

In April 1998 the OECD approved a report entitled "Harmful Tax Competition: An emerging Global Issue", which developed an OECD criteria to identify tax havens. In June 2000, a second report was published identifying 35 'tax havens', amongst them all the Crown Dependencies. The OECD's decision to draw up a list of jurisdictions which permit harmful tax practices was a manifestation of the increasing international concern about offshore finance centres and worries about perceived tax leakage from onshore to offshore. The fact that the United Kingdom voted for such an initiative suggests that some, if not all, of these concerns are held by the United Kingdom government. Although it may be ironic that an organisation committed to global free trade is trying to limit the proliferation of offshore finance centres which, as already discussed, can be seen as an organic part of the very system they try to promote, the initiative nevertheless represents a serious threat to the island. The 35 listed tax havens were given one year to comply with OECD guidelines to prevent harmful tax competition or face economic sanctions. These sanctions include withholding taxes on certain transactions and the possible abrogation of existing treaties. Hence, the listing of Jersey as a tax haven by the OECD represents one of the most significant external economic threats faced by the island since the war, as the OECD's actions could cripple the island's finance industry.

Jersey's, as well as Guernsey's, response to the criticism from the OECD has been to adopt a more high risk strategy compared with that of the Isle of Man, which has drawn up a schedule of commitments to avoid being listed as an uncooperative tax haven by the OECD.[2] Jersey's response to being listed was to express disappointment at its classification and argue that the OECD process was flawed.[3] Moreover, the insular authorities felt that they had fully explained why Jersey did not meet OECD's criteria and, in return, the OECD should explain why it did not accept Jersey's explanations to enable Jersey to challenge these reasons as well. By the time this book is published, it will be evident whether it was wise to challenge the OECD in such a manner. Nevertheless, Jersey and Guernsey have chosen to adopt this confrontational approach, not only working together on preparing a response, but also persuading the meeting of the Commonwealth Finance Ministers in Malta to call for a more multilateral approach to the problem. In addition, the insular authorities are critical of the non-inclusion of Switzerland, Luxembourg and Hong Kong as tax havens. Again this might be evidence of unfairness, but the reality is that it is easier as a first step to persuade a small microstate to change a policy than these larger jurisdictions; hence Jersey's call for a level playing field may fall on deaf ears.

The British - Irish Council

The inclusion of the Bailiwick of Jersey, together with the other Crown Dependencies, in the British-Irish Council represents a radical departure from the Crown Dependencies' uncodified relationship with the United Kingdom. The Council was formed as a result of the 1998 'Good Friday Agreement' and institutes formal meetings of the leaders of each of the jurisdictions in the British Islands. As such, it is a small step towards both a more formalised relationship with the United Kingdom and a more federal relationship with the British Islands.

The establishment of the British-Irish Council was also a useful reminder that the United Kingdom's desire to avoid turbulence in its relationship with the Crown Dependencies can be overshadowed by other, more urgent considerations. The Bailiff, in his capacity as Deputy Governor, was informed of Jersey's inclusion in the Council shortly before the 'Good Friday Agreement' was signed. However, the States of Jersey were not informed until after the event, although the potential benefits which would result from peace in Northern Ireland led to the States accepting this turn of events.

The British-Irish Council is still in its early days. Although its future is currently uncertain, as its continued operation is dependent on the success of the "Good Friday agreement", its value to Jersey must be assessed on the basis of whether Jersey benefits more from this kind of formalised arrangement as opposed to the current uncodified relationship. The danger with a more formalised relationship is that it will leave Jersey vulnerable due to its size. The devolved Northern Ireland Assembly, the next smallest member of the Council, is almost twenty times larger. In terms of its contribution to the Council, Jersey lacks the scale to have the political clout of larger political units. In addition, Jersey delegations lack the administrative support available to other delegations. The British-Irish Council guarantees opt-outs for individual members and will normally operate by consensus. In blocking such a consensus, Jersey could be following a high-risk strategy, which would risk alienating its metropolitan power. To survive in such an unbalanced body, Jersey will have to develop very effective means to 'punch above its weight'. This is not to say that Jersey's position in such a council is unsustainable. A major argument in favour of accepting membership is that it is part of a far larger programme of reforms and Jersey, as a dependency, must either accommodate certain changes or become vulnerable to more widespread reforms initiated by the United Kingdom. Membership of the body may also strengthen Jersey's constitutional position by allowing more direct links with senior United Kingdom politicians. If the British-Irish Council is to work as far as Jersey is concerned, it must offer an opportunity for Jersey to successfully interact with the leaders of the rest of the British Islands.

Administration of the Relationship with the United Kingdom

The decision in June 2001 to change the civil service department which serves as the formal point of contact between the Jersey and United Kingdom authorities was an illustration of Jersey's low position on any United Kingdom government's agenda. Whilst this change may, on the face of it, appear radical, it is likely to have little impact on Jersey's relationship with the United Kingdom and does not change the fundamental parameters of the relationship. As with the Edwards Report, the Crown Dependencies were not consulted in advance on the decision and presented with *fait accompli*. Whilst this may look like a lack of respect for the conventions which govern the relationship, it is in fact more illustrative of a newly re-elected government's desire to be seen moving rapidly forward on its policy agenda. A major policy reform involved changing the nature of the Home Office from a ministry, which often seemed charged with all the activities that had no obvious home elsewhere, to a ministry focused on policing, prisons and immigration. This produced a more European-style Ministry of the Interior with the Lord Chancellor's Office taking responsibilities for human rights as well as the Crown Dependencies, thereby producing something akin to a Ministry of Justice. The new government's desire to effect this change resulted in the constitutional niceties of the relationship with the Crown Dependencies being forgotten or ignored. Thus the reform must not be seen as in any way driven by Jersey's needs or a change in perception of the Crown Dependencies by the United Kingdom government.

The Lord Chancellor's Department is smaller than the Home Office, which might be seen as an advantage as it will be easier to ensure that issues of concern to Jersey receive a higher priority. However, as already noted, such an achievement might be a double-edged sword and would certainly represent a radical change in United Kingdom policy. It should also be remembered that even in a smaller department, Jersey's issues will still not be the main items on the agenda. It is also perhaps ironic that the Crown Dependencies now come within the responsibilities of the Lord Chancellor whose post is most similar to that of Bailiff, and therefore also vulnerable to the outcome of the McGonnell case, discussed below.

The new minister with responsibility for Jersey does not sit in the Lords, but the Commons. This again is a departure from past practice, which is driven by the division of work between a smaller number of ministers, rather than any consideration of the position of the Crown Dependencies. It will have some significant effects in that statements and questions will now be handled by an elected Member of Parliament who is more vulnerable to pressure groups and pressure from parliamentary colleagues. Additionally, it may also focus any debate on the island to the Commons, where the insular authorities may have fewer supporters and more enemies than in the Lords.

Another threat to Jersey's relationship with its metropolitan power arose in 2000 when the possibility of a civilian Lieutenant Governor being appointed occurred as a result of the Home Office's decision to advertise the job in "the Times". The insular authorities repeated their strong preference for a Lieutenant Governor from a military background and one was appointed, once again illustrating that it is the insular authorities which desire the continuation of the post.[4]

Human Rights

The incorporation of the European Convention on Human Rights in the island was approved by the States in February 2000. Although a Bill of Rights was already under consideration in the island, this must be seen as an example of the insular authorities adopting a law to suit political imperatives in Westminster. This is inevitable given that guaranteeing the maintenance of human rights on the island forms part of the responsibilities of the United Kingdom authorities.

The new law will heighten the debate in Jersey on the role and influence of international law on the island and reduce Jersey's distinctiveness. However, by incorporating the Convention into Jersey law, the chance of cases going to the European Court of Human Rights, thereby embarrassing the United Kingdom, will be drastically reduced as these cases will be dealt with by the insular courts. Hence, the adoption of this law can be seen as increasing Jersey's autonomy by reducing the number of cases where appeals can be made to an international tribunal.

Clothier

In January 2001, the Report of the Review Panel on the Machinery of Government in Jersey (the Clothier Report) was published (for details of its recommendations - see Appendix 2). The fact that such a report was even commissioned represented an acknowledgement by the States of Jersey that the current system of government was failing to produce either effective or accountable government. Policy-making had become ponderous and large cost overruns on capital projects were becoming routine. Nor was the States functioning effectively enough to successfully host a major offshore finance centre in the 21st century, particularly considering that unless a dramatic reversal of policy occurs, the States will have to rely on the finance industry to ensure that Jersey continues to prosper economically. The recognition of an inefficient model of government was not brought about through pressure from the United Kingdom, although the pressure for effective government from the finance industry should be viewed as an external pressure. The potential for effecting change was increased by a generational change-over in some of the senior figures in the States and public administration.

The problems identified in the Clothier Report echoed those voiced in the earlier Peat Marwick Report and added several which could not appear in the earlier report due to the more restricted nature of Peat Marwick's remit. It will be interesting to see whether the intervening years and the perceived decline in the States' ability to deliver effective government result in more of the Clothier Report's recommendations being adopted compared to the Peat Marwick Report, where significant elements, such as the recommendation to significantly reduce the number of committees, went ignored.[5]

The Clothier Report addresses many of the concerns already raised regarding the structure of the island's government. The Report recommends several significant reforms of the electoral system. The most significant is the creation of a general election by holding elections for all States members on the same day. This would concentrate political debate and allow the public to make one clear decisive choice concerning in which direction of the States should head. The Report also reduces both rural bias and the size of the Chamber by removing the Constables' *ex-officio* right to sit in the States. This will allow the Chamber to better reflect the social structure of the island. A smaller States will make the Chamber less unwieldy and, furthermore, the adoption of a ministerial system with a cabinet and chief minister instead of the existing committee system will make it clear who is accountable for poor decisions or, just as importantly, difficult decisions not made. Critically, the development of a functioning opposition will lead to more effective scrutiny of policy and promotion of policy alternatives. The adoption of the ministerial system will be reflected in the civil service by the creation of fewer government departments with clearer and more logical remits. The Report also recommends that the Bailiff should cease to be president of the States, instead the States should elect their own Speaker. In addition, the Bailiff should cease to be the direct link to the United Kingdom authorities but remain 'Mr Jersey' as far as the order of precedence is concerned. On the whole, the Clothier panel's recommendations, I believe, represent a step forward towards a more efficient, accountable and responsible model of government. As an added bonus, the proposals for reforming the position of Bailiff will serve to pre-empt action in the European Court of Human Rights.

The Clothier Report is, however, not without its flaws. It is often excessively anglocentric in approach with throwaway comments, such as it being unclear whom Deputies deputise for. In addition, it proposes the title 'Member of the States of Jersey', which might be felt to be a cast-off English political title, whereas the existing term 'Deputy' is widely used and understood beyond the English speaking world.[6] The review panel also failed to appreciate the popular support for the post of Senator with its ability to offer alternative representation in a small, and therefore particularist, society.

If the Clothier Report's recommendations are largely accepted in Jersey, and the parallel Guernsey report's recommendations accepted in Guernsey, it confirms the conclusion expressed in Chapter 9 of this book, namely that Jersey and Guernsey are moving closer to the Manx political model as well as towards the more serious consideration of the issue of whether each jurisdiction should declare independence.[7]

Over the past two years, the issue of independence has been considered more seriously. I still maintain the argument, illustrated within the body of the book, that such a move would not only damage Jersey's economy, but paradoxically reduce its influence on the world. Moreover, I believe that such an act would be perceived, at best as a source of mild amusement, at worst as a petty act of petulance. Indeed, Jersey would find becoming independent a Pyrrhic victory.

The Bailiff

Since the thesis was written, the European Court of Human Rights has ruled in the case of McGonnell v. the United Kingdom (Application no. 28488/95). The ruling has provoked much interest and debate, not only about the role of the Bailiff, but about the analogous role of the Lord Chancellor in the United Kingdom.[8] This case represented the inevitable challenge to the merged powers inherent in the post of Bailiff. McGonnell brought a challenge under Article 6(1) of the European Convention on Human Rights against the Bailiff of Guernsey. The plaintiff contested that the Bailiff was not 'independent and impartial' when he ruled on an appeal against a planning decision as he had, as Deputy Bailiff, presided over the States when the relevant Detailed Development Plan was agreed. The Court found for the plaintiff, although it made clear that the application of Article 6 did not require compliance with any theoretical concepts, such as strict separation of powers.[9] Nevertheless, the test set for compliance is likely to make unworkable any system which does not have separation of powers given that the Court, in its ruling, stated that "Any direct involvement in the passage of legislation, or of executive rules, is likely to be sufficient to cast doubt on the judicial impartiality of a person subsequently called to determine a dispute over whether reasons exist to permit a variation from the wording of legislation or rules at issue."[10]

The problems caused by the lack of separation of powers was further illustrated by the fact that when the Clothier Report recommended a change to the role of Bailiff, the Bailiff felt he had to comment on the future of his role. In doing so, he took a position contrary to the senior committee in the States.[11] This would seem a further excellent example of the inherent contradictions in the role and illustrate the potential for constitutional conflict inherent in the role as currently structured.

Conclusion

Two years from the completion of the thesis, the islands remain prosperous, distinctive and autonomous. However, significant threats are emerging, which will require more, not less, management of external relations to counter. In this increasingly dynamic and changing environment, Jersey, as a microstate with a global economy and very little influence of its own, must adapt to ensure it manages its external relations in a sure-footed and successful way. Hence it must rely on its protecting power for representation and support in the international arena. The most effective way to preserve Jersey's status is not independence, and the illusion of freedom of action that would give, but the current relationship with the United Kingdom which offers the best of both worlds: the almost total freedom to amend any legislation to suit Jersey's needs, while enjoying the protection and support of a far larger nation. Recent developments, such as an improved regulatory structure and the Clothier Report, may yet form the basis of an effective response to any challenges facing Jersey going forward. More than ever, the successful management of external threats to the island's economy through positive management of dependency is essential to the survival of Jersey as we know it.

Luke Le Rendu
London, July 2001

References

[1] The Jersey Financial Services Commission website, section 3.3, 30/7/01.

[2] "Council of Ministers Proposes OECD Commitments", Press Release, Chief Minister's Office, Isle of Man, 30/11/00.

[3] The Jersey Financial Services Commission website, section 5.1.1., 30/7/01.

[4] Falle, P. "High flyer!", Jersey Evening Post, 1/9/00,

[5] op. cit., Peat Marwick, 52.

[6] Report of the Review Panel on the Machinery of Government in Jersey, Bridge & Company, London, 2000, 16.

[7] Report of the Panel to Review the Machinery of Government in Guernsey, Channel Print, Guernsey, 2000.

[8] For example Cornes, R. "McGonnell v. United Kingdom, the Lord Chancellor and the Law Lords", Public Law, Summer 2000, Sweet & Maxwell and Contributors, 166-177.

[9] McGonnell v. The United Kingdom, Application no. 28488/95, para 51.

[10] ibid., para 55.

[11] Falle, P. "Bailiff steps into reform debate", Jersey Evening Post, 16/2/01, 1.

Appendix 1
Protocol 3 to the United Kingdom Treaty of Accession to the European Economic Community

Protocol No.3 on the Channel Islands and the Isle of Man.

Article 1
1.The Community rules on customs matters and quantitative restrictions; in particular those of the Act of Accession, shall apply to the Channel Islands and the Isle of Man under the same conditions as they apply to the United Kingdom. In particular, customs duties and charges having equivalent effect between those territories and the community, as originally constituted and between those territories and the new Member States, shall be progressively reduced in accordance with the timetable laid down in Articles 32 and 36 of the Act of Accession. The Common Customs Tariff and the ECSC unified tariff shall be progressively applied in accordance with the timetable laid down in Articles 39 and 59 of the Act of Accession, and account being taken of Articles 109, 110 and 119 of that Act.

In respect of agricultural products and products processed therefrom which are the subject of a special trade regime, the levies and other import measures laid down in Community rules and applicable by the United Kingdom shall be applied to third countries.

Such provisions of Community rules, in particular those of the Act of Accession, as are necessary to allow free movement and observance of normal conditions of competition in trade in these products shall also be applicable.

The Council, acting by a qualified majority on a proposal from the Commission, shall determine the conditions under which the provisions referred to in the preceding subparagraphs shall be applicable to these territories.

Article 2
The rights enjoyed by Channel Islanders or Manxmen in the United Kingdom shall not be affected by the Act of Accession. However, such persons shall not benefit from Community provisions relating to the free movement of persons and services.

Article 3
The provision of the Euroatom Treaty applicable to persons or undertakings within the meaning of Article 196 of that Treaty shall apply to those persons or undertakings when they are established in the aforementioned territories.

Article 4
The authorities of these territories shall apply the same treatment to all natural and legal persons of the Community.

Article 5
If, during the application of the arrangements defined in this protocol, difficulties appear on either side in relations between the Community and these territories, the Commission shall without delay propose to the Council such safeguards measures as it believes necessary, specifying their terms and conditions of application.

The Council shall act by a qualified majority within one month.

Article 6
In this Protocol, Channel Islander or Manxman shall mean any citizen of the United Kingdom and Colonies who holds that citizenship by virtue of the fact that he, a parent or grandparent was born, adopted, naturalised, or registered in the island in question; but such a person shall not for this purpose be regarded as a Channel Islander or Manxman if he, a parent or grandparent was born, adopted or naturalised or registered in the United Kingdom. Nor shall he be so regarded if he has at any time been ordinarily resident in the United Kingdom for five years.

The administrative arrangements necessary to identify these persons will be notified to the Commission.

Appendix 2

Summary of Recommendations of the Report of the Review Panel on the Machinery of Government

1. A Chief Electoral Officer should be appointed

2. There should be a Central Register of Voters

3. Election expenses should be determined by the States

4. Polling Stations to remain open from early morning till late evening

5. On General election only for all Members of the States and for the 12 Parish Constables

6. Every candidate to produce a policy statement

7. The role of Senator should be abolished

8. Connétables should cease to be ex officio Members of the States

9. Comité des Connétables to be consulted whenever their Parish is particularly affected

10. An Electoral Commission to re-assign the vacant seats amongst the Parishes

11. All Members of the States to enjoy the same title, "Member of the States of Jersey" (MIS)

12. There should be an assembly of between 42 and 44 Members

13. There must be a majority of Members of the States not in executive office to provide scrutiny of those who are, by means of 3 or 4 Scrutiny Committees

14 Seven departments should be substituted for the 24 Committees

15. Each Department to have one Minister and two members

16. Ministers from each Department to form the Council of Members

17. There should be a Chairman of the Council who would be the Chief Minister of the Island

18. The Council of Ministers should have power to give directions to the Departments

19. Chief Minister to have the power to dismiss Ministers

20. The States to have the right to approve the appointment of Ministers and substitute Ministers nominated by the Chief Minister

21. External Relations to be in the province of the Chief Minister

22. The title "President" to be abandoned and replaced by "Minister"

23. The Council of Ministers to be subject to careful scrutiny by the balance of Members of the States

24. Proper facilities for communications and research should be provided for Members

25. The proceedings of the States to be taken down and printed

26. There should be a Treasury Department responsible for producing the annual budget and for personnel

27. A small number of Scrutiny Committees to be formed from among non-executive

Members of the States and elected by the States as a whole

28. The Chairmen of the Scrutiny Committees with one other Member of the States to form a Public Accounts Committee to examine and control expenditure

29. There should be created the post of "Auditor General" to assist the Public Accounts Committee

30. The first task of a new States of Jersey must be to elect its Speaker and then a Chief Minister

31. Provisions should be made for Written Answers to Members' Questions and for Adjournment Debates

32. The Chief Minister and Council of Ministers should have a Chief Secretary who would be Head of the Civil Service

33. There should be an Appointments Commission for senior appointments in the Civil Service

34. There must be an appellate mechanism for the challenge of quasi-judicial administrative decisions and a mechanism for dealing with planning problems of an exceptional kind.

35. There should be a more formal structure for the Parish Assembly

36. Special attention should be given to the Parish of St. Helier

37. The Bailiff should cease to act as president of the States or to take any political part in the Island's government and the States should elect their own Speaker

38. The Chief Minister should be the direct link to the Home Office in London

39. The office of Bailiff should continue to be the highest in the Island on all occasions when the order of precedence is observed

40. An Ombudsman should be appointed to hear and determine complaints of maladministration by Departments

41. There should be regular use of consultative or discussion papers

42. The proceedings of Scrutiny Committees should normally be in public

43. There should be regular opportunities for members to question the Chief Minister

44. The States should ensure that the fullest facilities are given to the writing and broadcasting media

Bibliography

N.B. Unless stated otherwise, positions of interviewees as stated in this thesis were those held at the time of the interview.

General and Microstate Texts

Baker, R., ed., Public Administration in Small and Island States, Kumarian Press, West Hartford, 1992.

Bogdanor, V., ed., Devolution in the United Kingdom, Oxford University Press, Oxford, 1999.

Bray, M., ed., Ministries of Education in Small States, Commonwealth Secretariat, London, 1991.

Brownlie, I., Principles of Public International Law, Clarendon, Oxford, 1996.

Burton, B., ed., Problems of Smaller Territories, Athlone Press, London, 1967.

Commonwealth Secretariat, A Future for Small States: Overcoming Vulnerability, Commonwealth Secretariat, London, 1997.

Commonwealth Secretariat, Vulnerability: Small States in Global Society, Commonwealth Secretariat, London, 1985.

Corbridge, S., Martin, R. & Thrift, N., Money, Power and Space, Blackwell, Oxford, 1994.

Dahl, R. & Tufte, E. R., Size and Democracy, Stanford University Press, Stanford, 1974.

Dommen, E. & Hein P., ed., States, Microstates and Islands, Croom Helm, Dover, 1985.

Drower, G., Britain's Dependent Territories, Dartmouth, Aldershot, 1992.

Duursma, J. C., Fragmentation and the International Relations of Micro-States, Cambridge University Press, Cambridge, 1996.

Geri, H. H. & Wright Mills, C., Max Weber: Essays in Sociology, Routledge & Kegan Paul Ltd., London, 1970.

Government of the Cayman Islands, Cayman Islands 1995: Annual Report, Government of the Cayman Islands, Cayman Islands, 1995.

Government of the Cayman Islands, Cayman Islands Yearbook, Government of the Cayman Islands, Cayman Islands, 1996.

Gray, J., False Dawn: The Delusions of Global Capitalism, Granta Books, London, 1998.

Hampton M. P., The Offshore Interface Tax Havens in the Global Economy, Macmillan Press Ltd, London, 1996.

Harden, S., ed., Small is Dangerous, Frances Pinter, London, 1985.

Hutton, W., The State We're In, Jonathan Cape, London, 1995.

Jalan, B., Problems and Polices in Small Economies, Croom Helm, London, 1982.

Kohr, L., The Overdeveloped Nation, Christopher Davis, Swansea, 1977.

Plischke, E., Studies in Foreign Policy. Microstates in World Affairs: Policy Problems and Options, American Enterprise Institute for Public Policy, Washington DC, 1977.

Powell, G. C., Economic Survey of Jersey, States Greffe, Jersey, 1971.

Rapaport, J., Muteba, E. & Therattil, E., Small States & Territories Status and Problems, Arno Press, New York, 1971.

Schumacher, E. F., Small is beautiful: A study of economics as if people mattered, Blond and Briggs, London, 1973.

St. John-Stevens, N., ed., The Collected Works of Walter Bagehot, The Economist, London, 1974.

206

Articles & Pamphlets

Aldrich, R. & Connell, J., "The Ends of Empire", The World Today, February 1998, 51-54.

Alesina, A. & Spolaore, E., "On the Number and Size of Nations", The Quarterly Journal of Economics, November 1997, 1027-1056.

Baldacchino, G., "Bursting the Bubble: The Pseudo-Development Strategies of Microstates", Development and Change, vol. 24, no. 4-5, 1993, 29-51.

Baldacchino, G., "Hitting the Limelight in Lilliput: A Critique of Expertise", International Association of Schools and Institutes of Administration Annual Conference, 1994.

Chenery, H. B. & Taylor, L., "Development patterns: among countries and over time." Review of Economics and Statistics, vol.1, no.4, 1968, 391-416.

Cornes, R., "McGonnell v. United Kingdom, the Lord Chancellor and the Law Lords", Public Law, Summer 2000, 166-177.

Cousins, J., Mitchell A., Sikka, P., and Willmott, H., "Auditors: Holding the Public to Ransom", Association for Accountancy and Business Affairs, Essex, 1998.

Elster, J., "The Impact of Constitutions on Economic Performance", Proceedings of the World Bank Annual Conference on Development Economics, 1994, 209-239.

Gillett, S., "Developing St. Helena", Public Administration and Development, vol. 3, 1983, 151-160.

Hampton, M. P., "Treasure Island or Fool's Gold: Can and Should Small Island Economies Copy Jersey?", World Development, vol.22 no. 2, 1994, 237-250.

Hope, K. R., "The administration of development in emergent nations. The problems in the Caribbean", Public Administration and Development, vol. 3, 1983, 49-59.

Kersell, J.E., "Government Administration in a small microstate: developing the Cayman Islands", Public Administration and Development, vol.7, 1987, 95-107.

"Little Countries: Small but Perfectly Formed", The Economist, 3/1/98, 63-65.

Murray, D. J., "Microstates: public administration for the small and beautiful", Public Administration and Development, vol.1, 1981, 245-256.

Report of the Study Group of the Commonwealth Parliamentary Association, The Security of Small States, Commonwealth Parliamentary Association, London, 1984.

Roberts, S. M., "Small Place, Big Money: The Cayman Islands and the International Financial System", Economic Geography, vol. 71, no. 3, 1995, 237-256.

Warrington, E., "A Capacity for Policy Management: Re-Appraising the Context in Micro-States", Asian Journal of Public Administration, vol. 16, no. 1, 1994, 109-131.

Warrington, E., "Lilliput Revisited", The Asian Journal of Public Administration, vol. 16, no. 1, 1994, 3-14.

Wettenhall, R., "Using All the Talents of a Legislature in Governing a Conversation with Ralph Vibert OBE", Australian Journal of Public Administration, vol. 53, No. 1, March 1994, 107-115.

European Union Papers

The European Community's Relations to French Overseas Departments, European Autonomous Regions, Overseas Countries and Territories and Independent Countries within EC Boundaries, Background Report issued by the Commission of the European Communities, London, 10/12/92.

French Reports

Assemblée Internationale des Parliamentaires de Langue Française, pamphlet issued by Secrétariat Général, Paris 1996.

Cartel, A., Basse Normandie Recommendation: Lower Normandy and the Channel Islands, Conseil

Economique et Social Régional, Caen, December 1994.

Cartel, A., Basse Normandie Report: Lower Normandy and the Channel Islands, Conseil Economique et Social Régional, Caen, December 1994.

International Agreements

The Convention between the United Kingdom of Great Britain and Northern Ireland and the King of the French for Defining and Regulating the Limits of the Exclusive Rights of the Oyster and Other Fisheries on the Coast of Great Britain and France of 1839, Paris, B.S.P. No 27/983, 1839.

The Special Agreement concluded between the Governments of the United Kingdom of Great Britain and Northern Ireland and the Government of the French Republic signed on 29th December 1950, ratified Paris 24th September 1951.

United Nations Resolution 1514(xv) adopted 14/12/60.

United Nations Resolution 14/12/70, "Programme of Action for the Full Implementation of the Declaration".

Ruling of International Courts

International Court of Justice Ruling of 17 XI 53.

Application to ECHR No.8873/80, Michael Dun v United Kingdom.

ECHR ruling in Gillow v UK, 5 EHRR, 581.

Application to ECHR No. 28488/95, Richard James Joseph McGonnell v the United Kingdom.

Tyrer v United Kingdom, (1978-80), MLR 13.

Case 32/79 Commission v United Kingdom [1980], E.C.R. 2403 at 2444, paragraphs 41 to 43.

United Kingdom

Government Papers

First Report of the Commissioners appointed to inquire into the state of the Criminal Law in the Channel Islands, London, 1847.

Hansard 1960-1998.

The Health Service Convention between the Governments of the United Kingdom of Great Britain and Northern Ireland and the Isle of Man and the States of Jersey, Guernsey, Alderney and the Chief Pleas of Sark, 1976, No. 6286.

Home Office Press Release, 20/1/98.

Home Office, Review of Financial Regulation in the Crown Dependencies, Cm 4109, The Stationery Office, 1998.

Report of the Committee of the Privy Council on Proposed Reforms in the Channel Islands, Cmd.7074, HMSO, London, 1947.

Report of the Committee of the Privy Council on the question of Contributions to Imperial Funds from the Islands of Jersey, Guernsey and Man, Cmd. 2586, HMSO, London, 1926.

Review of Financial Regulation in the Crown Dependencies, Cm. 4109, Stationary Office, London, 1998.

The Royal Commission on the Constitution, Cmnd 5460, HMSO, London, 1971.

Correspondence

Correspondence with R. Miles, Assistant Under Secretary of State, Home Office, 29/9/98.

Official Papers

PRO: HO 45/25272 - Minute dated 4/2/52.

PRO: HO284/3 - Letter from Sir Charles Cunningham to Sir Frank Newsham dated 24/9/57.

PRO: HO 284/3 - Letter to the Secretary of State from the Lieutenant Governor of Jersey, 20/1/58.

PRO: HO 284/3 - Memorandum of discussions in Jersey on Judicial Reform and the Office of Lieutenant Governor between Home Office and Insular Officials. The document is undated but refers to discussions in 1957-58.

PRO: HO 284/3 - Report of a discussion on Reform in Jersey, undated.

Speeches

Text of a Speech by the Hon. P. R. Caruana, Chief Minister of Gibraltar, to the European - Atlantic Group, 24/11/97.

Bermudas Perspective as a Dependent Territory, A Speech to the Dependent Territories Conference by Pamela Gordon, Premier, Bermuda, 4/2/98.

The Dependent Territories in the 21st Century, An Address to the Dependent Territories Conference by the Hon. P. R. Caruana, Chief Minister of Gibraltar, 4/2/98.

A New Partnership, A Speech to the Dependent Territories Association by Rt. Hon. Robin Cook, MP, London, 4/2/98.

Interviews

Interview with Mr P. Bentley, Barrister, Stanbrook and Hooper, 15/2/99.

Interview with Mr A. Mitchell, M. P., 19/10/98.

Interview with Mr R. M. Morris, Assistant Under Secretary, Home Office, 1991-96, 2/10/98.

Interview with Dr. R. Plender, Q.C., 11/12/98.

Interview with Mr T. Russell, Cayman Islands Representative in the United Kingdom and former Governor of the Cayman Islands, 21/4/97.

Crown Dependencies

Johns, R. A., & Le Marchant, C.M., British Isle Offshore Development since 1979, Frances Pinter, London, 1993.

Johns, R. A., & Le Marchant, C. M., Finance Centres: British Isle Offshore Development since 1979, Frances Pinter, London, 1979.

Articles & Pamphlets

Bentley, P., "Channel Islands and the UK: Their relationship: The Law: The Future?", paper presented at the IPC conference, November 1998.

Bentley, P., "Implications of recent EC Tax initiatives for the Channel Islands and the Isle of Man", EC Tax Journal, Vol. 3, Issue 2, 1998.

Grey, S., "The Blue Chip Islands", Accountancy: The Journal of The Institute of Chartered Accountants in England and Wales, vol. 114, no. 1213, September 1994, 34-38.

Horner, S. A., "The Isle of Man and the Channel Islands - A study of their status under Constitutional, International and European Law", European University Institute Working Paper No.98, European University Institute, Florence, 1984.

Plender, R., "The Channel Islands position in International Law", paper presented at the IPC conference, November 1998.

Robilliard, St. J. A., "The United Kingdom's Rights and Claims to Legislate for the Channel Islands", paper presented at the IPC conference, November 1998.

Jersey

Bois, F. de L., A Constitutional History of Jersey, States Greffe, Jersey, 1972.

Bunting, M., The Model Occupation: The Channel Islands under German Rule 1940-1945, Harper Collins Publishing, London, 1995.

Cruickshank, C., The German Occupation of the Channel Islands, The Guernsey Press Co. Limited, Guernsey, 1975.

Heyting, W. J., The Constitutional Relationship between Jersey and the United Kingdom, Jersey Constitutional Association, Guernsey, 1977.

Jameson, A. G., A People of the Sea: The Maritime History of the Channel Islanders, Methuen, London, 1986.

Kelleher, J. D., The Triumph of the Country: The Rural Community in Nineteenth Century Jersey, John Appleby Publishing, Jersey, 1994.

Le Feuvre, D., Jersey: Not Quite British, Seaflower, 1993.

Le Hérissier, R., The Development of the Government of Jersey, 1771-1972, States Greffe, Jersey, 1974.

Le Patourel, J., The Medieval Administration of the Channel Islands, Oxford University Press, London, 1937.

Pocock, H. R. S., The Memoirs of Lord Coutanche, Philimore, Chichester, 1975.

Powell, G. C., Economic Survey of Jersey, Corah & Bigwoods, Jersey, 1971.

Rodwell, W., Les Écréhous, Jersey, Société Jersiaise, Jersey, 1996.

Solly, M., Jersey: A Low-Tax Area, Tolley Publishing Limited, Croydon, 1982.

Syvret, M. & Stevens, J., Balleine's History of Jersey, Phillimore, Chichester, 1981.

Vibert, R., Memoirs of a Jerseyman, La Haule Books, Jersey, 1991.

Articles & Pamphlets

Société Jersiaise Annual Bulletin , vol. 1- 27 , 1875-1998.

Lord Bingham of Cornhill, "Incorporation of the European Convention on Human Rights: The Opportunity and the Challenge", Jersey Law Review, vol. 2, no. 3, 1998, 257-271.

Carnegie, R. A., "The 'Special Arrangements' made for the Channel Islands of the United Kingdom's accession to the European Community and their influence on Jersey's present relationship with the Community", unpublished M. Phil., University of Cambridge, 1993.

Christensen, J. E. & Hampton, M. P., "The Capture of the State in Jersey's Offshore Finance Centre", Discussion Papers, Department of Economics, Discussion Paper 119, University of Portsmouth, 1998.

Crill, P., "The ancient rôle of the Bailiffs of Guernsey and Jersey as 'Speakers'" in Société Jersiaise Annual Bulletin for 1997, vol. 27, pt. 1, 79-84.

"Democracy in the Channel Islands", Nos Iles: A symposium on the Channel Islands, C.I. Study Group, Middlesex, 1944.

Falle, R., A Brief History of the States of Jersey and the States Chamber", States Greffe, Jersey, 1986.

Hampton, M .P., "Creating Spaces. The Political Economy of Island Offshore Finance Centres: the case of Jersey", Geographische Zeitschrift, 84 vol. 2, 103-113.

Hampton, M. P., "'Treasure Island' Revisited. Jersey's Offshore Finance Centre Crisis: implications for other Small Island Economies", Department of Economics, University of Portsmouth, September 1997.

Hampton, M. P. & Christensen, J. E., "'Treasure Island' revisited. Jersey's offshore finance centre crisis: implications for other Small Island Economies", Environment and Planning, vol. 31, 1999, 1619-1637.

Hampton, M. P., Post-war tourism in small island economies: the case of Jersey, Department of Economics, University of Portsmouth, April 1995.

"Law and Justice", The Parliamentarian: Journal of the Parliaments of the Commonwealth, LXVII, No. 1, Jan. 1996, 55.

Le Brocq, N. S., Jersey looks forward, The Communist Party, London, 1946.

Le Brocq, N. S., "The State in Jersey", Marxism Today, vol.11, no.9, 1967, 273-276.

Le Hérissier, R., "Jersey: exercising power in a non-party system", Public Administration and Development, Vol. 18, 1998, 169-184.

Le Hérissier, R., "A Small State at the Cross Roads", Paper presented to IASIA Annual Conference, Durban, 1996.

Lemprière, R., "The Law of the Channel Islands", Solicitor Quarterly, October 1962, 289-302.

Le Quesne, G., "Jersey and Whitehall in the Mid-nineteenth Century", Third Joan Stevens Memorial Lecture, Société Jersiaise, Jersey, 1992.

Matthews, P., "Lé Rouai, Nouot' Duc" Jersey Law Review, vol. 3, June 1999, 177-204.

Mitchell, A. & Sikka, P., "Jersey: Auditors' Liabilities versus People's Rights", Political Quarterly, vol. 70, no.1, 1999, 3-15.

Omner, R. E., "'A peculiar and immediate dependence of the Crown': The basis of the Jersey Merchant Triangle", Business History XXV, 1983, 107-124.

Plender R., "The Rights of European Citizens in Jersey", Jersey Law Review, October vol. 2, no. 3, 1998, 220 - 242.

Potter, E. J. M., An Account of the Procedures of the States of Jersey, States Greffe, Jersey, 1989.

Powell, G. C., "Applicability of European Union Competition Regulations in Jersey", Jersey Law Review, vol. 7, 1997, 46-50.

Powell, G. C., "Jersey and EMU", Jersey Law Review, vol. 2, no. 1, 1998, 61-72.

Sikka, P., Limited Liability Partnerships (Insolvent Partnerships), (Jersey) Regulations 199, University of Essex, 14/4/98.

Southwell, R., "The Sources of Jersey Law", Jersey Law Review, vol.1, issue 3, 1997, 221-231.

Vibert, R., Parliament without Parties: The Committee System in The States of the Island of Jersey, States Greffe, Jersey, 1990.

Walker, J., "Limited Liability Partnerships: True Partnerships?", Jersey Law Review, vol. 2, issue 1, 1998, 1-13.

Wettenhall, R., "Using all the Talents of a Legislature in Governing", Australian Journal of Public Administration, Vol. 53, No. 1, March 1994, 107-115.

Government Papers

Actes des Etats, Rapport sur la question de Réformes, Bigwood, Jersey, 1946.

Code of Laws for the Island of Jersey, Bigwoods, Jersey, 1968.

Defence Contribution: Territorial Army Unit (P. 124/97) - Report, Defence Committee, States Greffe, 1998.

Deloitte and Touche, States of Jersey, Review of the Office of the Chief Adviser, Final Report and Recommendations, Deloitte and Touche, Jersey, 1997.

Economic Adviser, An Introduction to Jersey, Economic's Adviser's Office, Jersey, 1991.

Etat Civil Committee, Report on the Census for 1991, Etat Civil Committee, Jersey, 1991.

Etat Civil Committee, Report on the Census for 1996, Etat Civil Committee, Jersey, 1997.

Finance and Economics Committee, Statistical Review 1994-7, Office of the Chief Adviser, Jersey, 1994-1997.

Jersey Financial Services website.

Jersey Prison Board: Notes of Proposed Argument in Support of the Representation of the States of Jersey to the Queen's Most Excellent Majesty in Council in the matter of an Order in Council of the 23rd June, 1891, Le Lievre, Jersey, 1896.

KPMG Peat Marwick McLintock, States Of Jersey: A review of the machinery of government, States Greffe, Jersey, 1987.

Limited Liability Partnerships (Jersey) Law 199: Committee of Inquiry - Report, States Greffe, Jersey, 1997 R.C. 23/97.

Policy and Resources Committee, Human Rights Conventions: Reports for Jersey, R.C.14/94, States Greffe, Jersey, 1994.

Policy and Resources Committee, International Conventions and Agreements: Progress Report for the periods ending 30/9/94, 30/9/95, 31/3/96 and 30/9/96, States Greffe, Jersey, 1994-96.

Policy and Resources Committee, Report of the Review Panel on the Machinery of Government in Jersey, Bridge & Company, London, 2000.

Policy and Resources Committee, Strategic Policy Review and Action Plan 1994, States Greffe, Jersey, 1994.

Policy and Resources Committee, 2000 & Beyond: Strategic Policy Review 1995 Part 1& 2, States Greffe, Jersey, 1995.

Policy and Resources Committee, Strategic Policy Review & Action Plan 1996, States Greffe, Jersey, 1996.

Policy and Resources Committee, Strategic Policy Review & Action Plan 1997, States Greffe, Jersey, 1997.

Policy and Resources Committee, Treaties: Application to Crown Dependencies, R.C. 24/93, States Greffe, Jersey, 1993.

Powell, G. C., Annual Report to the Chief Adviser to the States, Office of the Chief Adviser, Jersey, November 1993.

Powell, G. C., Annual Report to the Chief Adviser to the States, Office of the Chief Adviser, Jersey, November 1994.

Powell, G. C., Jersey and the European Community An update 1992, Office of the Economic Adviser to the States, Jersey, 1992.

Report and Proposition of the Constitution and Common Market Committee relating to the arrangements proposed by the European Economic Community to meet the needs of Jersey, P.116/71, States Greffe, 1971.

Report and Recommendations of the Special Committee of the States of Jersey appointed to consult with Her Majesty's Government in the United Kingdom on all matters relating to the Government's application to join the European Economic Community, States Greffe, Jersey, 1967.

Report of the Common Market Committee on the Constitutional Question, States Greffe, Jersey, 1968.

Report of the Law Officers of the Crown for Jersey to the Common Market Committee on the Constitutional Issues Arising from the United Kingdom Government's Application to Join the European Community, States Greffe, Jersey, 1967.

Report of the Review Panel on the Machinery of Government in Jersey, Bridge & Company, London, 2000.

Speech to the States of Jersey by Geoffrey Rippon, QC, Chancellor of the Duchy of Lancaster, 19

November 1971. See States Minutes of this date.

States of Jersey, Budget Extract 1994-7, Jersey Evening Post, Jersey, 1994-97.

States of Jersey, Committees of the States: Reorganization, P. 107/96, States Greffe, Jersey, 1996.

States of Jersey, The International Finance Centre, Financial Services Department, Jersey.

States of Jersey Overseas Aid Committee, States Greffe, Jersey, 1994.

States Members Remuneration (P.31/96) Report, States Greffe, Jersey, 1996.

Correspondence

Correspondence with Mr. D. Breed, Ashburton (Jersey) Limited, Investment Managers, 5/12/95.

Laws

European Communities (Jersey) Law, 1973.

European Community Legislation (Implementation) (Jersey) Law, 1996.

Franchise (Jersey) Law, 1968.

The Sea Fisheries (Jersey) Law, 1962.

The Sea Fisheries (Jersey) Law, 1994.

States of Jersey Law, 1966.

Newspapers & Journals

Business Brief

Inside Jersey

The Islander Magazine

Jersey Evening Post

Jersey Now

Jersey Press

Jersey Weekly Post

Interviews

Interview with Sir Philip Bailhache, Bailiff of Jersey, 25/3/97.

Interview with Mr. P. Bastion, Chief Officer Agriculture and Fisheries Department, 4/4/97.

Interviews with Mr J. Christensen, Assistant Adviser (Economics), 30/8/96 & 5/1/98.

Interview with Mr G. Coppock, Greffier of the States, 1/4/97.

Interview with Sir Peter Crill, Bailiff of Jersey 1986-95, 10/4/97.

Interview with Deputy J. L. Dorey, President of the Agriculture and Fisheries Committee, 4/4/97.

Interview with Mr M. Furzer, Chief Officer, Immigration and Nationality Department, 1/4/97.

Interview with Jurat E. W. Herbert, 8/4/97.

Interviews with ex-Senator R. Jeune, C.B.E., President of Policy and Resources from its inception in 1989 to 1996, 26/3/97.

Interview with Deputy J. Johns, President of the Harbours and Airport Committee, 1/4/97.

Interview with Mr D. O. Moon, formerly Senior Partner, Mourant Du Feu & Jeune, 10/9/97.

Interview with Miss C. M. Newcombe, Deputy Greffier of the States, 19/3/96.

Interview with Mr R. Pallot, French Consul, 4/8/98.

Interview with Mr R. Pirouet, Managing Partner Ernst & Young (Jersey), 28/3/96.

Interview with Mr G. C. Powell, O.B.E., Chief Adviser to the States of Jersey, 25/3/96 & 16/9/97.

Interview with Senator N. L. Quérée, President of the Planning and Environment Committee, 11/4/97.

Interview with Senator J. S. Rothwell, President of the Tourism Committee, 6/8/98.

Interview with Senator R. J. Shenton, States Member from 1969 and longest serving member of the States at the time, 9/4/97.

Interview with Senator S. Syvret, 2/4/97.

Interview with ex-Senator R. Vibert, O.B.E., Member of the States 1957 - 87 and President of, amongst other Committees, the Constitution and Common Market Committee, 13/3/96.

Interview with Senator F. H. Walker, President of the Finance and Economics Committee, Vice President of the Policy and Resources Committee, 5/8/98.

Interview with His Excellency the Lieutenant Governor, Sir Michael Wilkes, K.C.B., C.B.E., 12/9/97.

Guernsey

Ingoldby, G., Out of Call or Cry The Island of Sark, Heinemann, London, 1990.

Marr, L. J., A History of the Bailiwick of Guernsey, Phillimore, Chicester, 1982.

Articles & Pamphlets

Beaumont, J. M., The Constitution and Administration of Sark, Guernsey Press, Guernsey, 1993.

Ehmann, D. & Le Pelley, P., A Guide to the Constitution of Guernsey (1994), Guernsey Press, Guernsey, 1994.

Loveridge, J., The Constitution and Law of Guernsey, La Societe Guernesiaise, Guernsey, 1975.

Government Papers

Guernsey Financial Services Commission, Annual Report 1995, Guernsey, 1995.

Ogier, J. P., Horticultural Profitability and Viability Report, Committee for Horticulture, Guernsey, 1996.

Population and Migration Committee, Guernsey Census 1996, Guernsey, 1997.

Report of the Panel to Review the Machinery of Government in Guernsey, Channel Print, Guernsey, 2000.

Report on the 1996 Guernsey Census, Population and Migration Committee, Guernsey, 1996.

States Advisory and Finance Committee, Guernsey, The European Economic Community and 1992, States of Guernsey, 1992.

States Advisory and Finance Committee, Guernsey Statistics 1996, States of Guernsey, Guernsey, 1996.

States Advisory and Finance Committee, Membership of the European Economic Community, Billet d'État, 15/12/71.

States Advisory and Finance Committee, 1996 Policy Planning, Economic and Financial Report, Billet d'État, 10/7/96.

States Advisory and Finance Committee, Policy Planning Economic & Financial Report 1996, States of Guernsey, 1996.

States of Guernsey, States Committees: Constitution and Operation Mandates Membership, 1/7/96.

Newspapers/Journals

Guernsey Evening Press and Star

Interviews

Interview with Mr J. Dickson, Head of Economics and Statistics, States of Guernsey, 13/8/96.

Interview with Mr S. Harlow, Managing Partner Ernst & Young (Guernsey), 13/8/96.

Interview with Mr. C. M. Le Marchant, Assistant Superintendent of Banks, Guernsey Financial Services Commission, 14/8/96.

Interview with Conseiller P. Morgan, President of Advisory and Finance, Constitution of the States Review Committee and Joint Guernsey Alderney Consultation Council, 14/8/96.

Interview with Mr A. Nicolle, External and Constitutional Affairs Officer, States of Guernsey, 15/8/96.

Interview with Deputy G. Norman, President of the Tourism Committee, 13/8/96.

Isle of Man

Kermode, D. G., Devolution at Work: A Case Study of the Isle of Man, Saxon House, Farnborough, 1979.

Kinvig, R. H., The Isle of Man: A Social Cultural and Political History, 3rd edition, Liverpool University Press, Liverpool, 1975.

Solly, M., Government and Law in the Isle of Man, Parallel Books, Isle of Man, 1994.

Articles & Pamphlets

Cain, T. W., "Constitutional Reform in the Twentieth Century", Proceedings of the Isle of Man Natural History and Antiquarian Society, Vol. 10, No. 3, April 1993-March 1995, 201-224.

Kermode, D. G., "Legislative-executive relationships in the Isle of Man", Political Studies, vol. XVI, no. 1, 1968, 18-42.

Richards, J., "Politics in Small Independent Communities: Conflict or Consensus?", Journal of Commonwealth and Comparative Politics, 1982, Vol 20 (2), 155-168.

Templeton, J. & Richards, J., "Elections in a small community: the case of the Isle of Man", Parliamentary Affairs, 1981, vol. 35, 322-34.

Government Papers

A Book of Precedents, Isle of Man Government, Isle of Man, 1992.

Council of Ministers, Second Interim Report on Future Constitutional Objectives, Isle of Man Government, Isle of Man, 1993.

Council of Ministers, The United Nations Convention on the Law of the Sea, Isle of Man Government, Isle of Man, 1995.

Isle of Man Government, Annual Review of Policies & Programmes, Isle of Man Government, Isle of Man, 1995.

Isle of Man Government, Budget Extract 1996, Nelson, Isle of Man, 1996.

Isle of Man Government, Industry Factfile, Isle of Man Government, Isle of Man, 1995.

Isle of Man Government, The Isle of Man, The European Community and 1992, Isle of Man Government, Isle of Man, 1992.

Isle of Man Press Releases, Council of Ministers Proposes OECD Commitments, Chief Minister's Office, Isle of Man, 2000.

Minute of the Court of Tynwald 11/4/90, T1469-T1472.

Minute of the Court of Tynwald 21/2/84, T703-T711.

The Official Isle of Man Yearbook 1996, Executive Publications, Isle of Man, 1996.

The Treaty on European Union and the European Economic Area Agreement , A Report by the Council of Ministers, Isle of Man, November 1993.

Speeches

Bates T. St. J. N., "Après le Déluge: Where should Man be Paddling?", Presentation to the Euroclub, Palace Hotel, 1/11/92.

Newspapers/Journals

Isle of Man Examiner

Interviews

Interview with Professor St. J. Bates, Clerk of Twywald, Secretary of the House of Keys and Counsel to the Speaker, 15/5/96.

Interview with Mr S. Carse, Economic Adviser to the Economic Affairs Division of the Isle of Man Treasury, 14/5/96.

Interview with Deemster T. W. Cain, 17/5/96.

Interview with Mr L. Kearns, Senior Partner, Ernst & Young (Isle of Man), 16/5/96.

Interview with Mr. J. Kissack, Chief Secretary to the Council of Ministers, Isle of Man Government, 14/5/96.

Interview with the Honourable M. Walker, Chief Minister, Isle of Man, 14/5/96.

Index

References to earlier forms of the organisation will be found under European Union.